PETERSON'S®

Master the™
Special Agent
Exam

13th Edition

About Peterson's®

Peterson's has been your trusted educational publisher for more than 50 years. It's a milestone we're quite proud of as we continue to offer the most accurate, dependable, high-quality educational content in the field, providing you with everything you need to succeed. No matter where you are on your academic or professional path, you can rely on Peterson's for its books, online information, expert test-prep tools, the most up-to-date education exploration data, and the highest quality career success resources—everything you need to achieve your education goals. For our complete line of products, visit **www.petersons.com**.

For more information or to give us feedback, contact Peterson's, 4380 S. Syracuse Dr., Denver, CO 80237; 800-338-3282 Ext. 54229; or visit us online at **www.petersons.com**.

ISBN-13: 978-0-7689-4574-4

Printed in the United States of America

10 9 8 7 6 5 4 3 2 1   23 22 21

Thirteenth Edition

Peterson's Updates and Corrections

Check out our website at **www.petersonsbooks.com/updates-and-corrections/** to see if there is any new information regarding the test and any revisions or corrections to the content of this book. We've made sure the information in this book is accurate and up to date; however, the test format or content may have changed since the time of publication.

Contents

PART II: DIAGNOSTIC TESTS

PART III: PREPARING FOR THE SPECIAL AGENT EXAM

PART IV: PRACTICE TESTS

PART V: APPENDIX

Before You Begin

OVERVIEW

- **How This Book Is Organized**
- **How to Use This Book**
- **Special Study Features**
- **Helpful Study Tips**
- **Tips for Test Takers**
- **Test Day Strategies**
- **Peterson's® Publications**
- **You're Well on Your Way to Success**

Peterson's® *Master the™ Special Agent Exam* has been carefully researched and written to help guide you through the extensive process of becoming a special agent. While the different federal agencies share common application, hire, and exam steps, individual agencies will additionally focus on specific tasks and responsibilities that pertain to fulfilling the roles and responsibilities of a special agent within the agency itself. The process from application through the hiring and interview stages, and then on to basic training is demanding and involves many steps that must be met in order to advance to the next phase of the qualifying process. This process can take 12–18 months to complete, and it hinges upon meeting or exceeding the qualifications set by each agency. Being a special agent is physically and mentally challenging, so it should come as no surprise that the process to becoming a special agent is challenging as well. The overarching goal is to make sure that the very best of the best candidates are hired.

HOW THIS BOOK IS ORGANIZED

Peterson's® *Master the™ Special Agent Exam* is organized into the following parts and chapters:

- **Part I: Introduction to Becoming a Special Agent**—Chapters 1–3 review the basics of federal job opportunities, including how to apply for a special agent position and what to expect from the hiring and interview processes.
- **Part II: Diagnostic Tests**—Chapter 4 provides three sample tests, one each for candidates interested in becoming a special agent with the Bureau of Alcohol, Tobacco, Firearms and Explosives (ATF), the US Immigration and Customs Enforcement (ICE), or the Federal Bureau of Investigation (FBI). Each agency-specific diagnostic test provides a sampling of the types of questions and topics covered on the actual exam.

- **Part III: Preparing for the Special Agent Exam**—Chapter 5 provides detailed coverage on the types of questions you will encounter on each of the special agent exams, including agency-specific question-types such as figural reasoning, investigative reasoning, and situational judgment. Chapter 6 reviews the basic mathematical concepts you will need to know in order to solve mathematical word problems.

- **Part IV: Practice Tests**—Practice Tests 1–3 are agency-specific sample tests. Each practice test contains examples of the question-types you will encounter on the actual ATF, ICE, or FBI exam.

- **Part V: Appendix**—Appendix A provides a brief overview of the Federal Law Enforcement Training Center (FLETC) in Glynco, Georgia.

HOW TO USE THIS BOOK

Peterson's® *Master the™ Special Agent Exam* will show you what to expect from three different federal agencies: ATF, ICE, and FBI. The intent is to familiarize you with what to expect in the application process and what you will encounter in the hiring phase, including examination elements such as question-types and topics.

Start by reviewing the information in **Part I**, paying careful attention to the hiring requirements. As mentioned, the application and hiring processes are extensive. There are many different steps that you must complete and numerous qualifications that must be met in order to advance to the next stage. Knowing what to expect at each stage of the process will help to eliminate uncertainty and better prepare you for what's to come.

Next, take one of the **Diagnostic Tests** in **Part II**. There are three to choose from, one each for ATF, ICE, and FBI. Pick the one that is tailored to the agency you plan to enter as a special agent. Not sure of your path yet? Take all three tests. The point of a diagnostic test is to expose you to the types of questions you will find on the actual exam itself. You'll learn what to expect as well as your strengths and weaknesses. Detailed answer explanations follow each diagnostic test. Review these explanations to see why an answer was correct and why the other answer choices were not.

Part III is the heart of the book. The narrative will cover, in-depth, the following types of questions:

- Logical/Verbal Reasoning
- Quantitative/Arithmetic Reasoning
- Investigative Reasoning
- Writing Skills
- Figural Reasoning
- Situational Judgment
- Preferences and Interests
- Personality Traits

There are common elements found in the ATF, ICE, and FBI special agent exams as well as distinct differences. Some of the test elements are scored, and some will assess personality traits and situational judgment. Chapter 5 breaks down, by question-type, what to expect on each exam. Pay careful attention to the examples and step-by-step instructions. A good part of the special agent exams focuses on logical, verbal, and investigative reasoning as mastering these skills is integral to becoming a special agent. Chapter 6 covers the mathematical concepts you will need to know to answer arithmetic and quantitative reasoning questions.

When you get to this part of the book, you should have a pretty good idea which agency you plan on working for as a special agent. To cement your learning, go to **Part IV** and complete the agency-specific **practice test** of your choice under timed conditions. When you have completed the practice test, compare your answers with the explanations found at the end of the test. If you find that you are struggling with a certain type of question, go back to Part III and review the applicable sections again.

In summary, if you know what to expect and then prepare yourself, you will have an easier time advancing through the process of becoming a special agent. The better prepared you are, the more confident you will feel about taking the specific special agent exam for the agency of your choice. If you feel confident, you are more likely to answer questions quickly and decisively, complete the exam, and advance to the next stage. Greater confidence will also help you enter the interview and physical portions of the hiring process without hesitation, so you will be better able to prove that you are fit to be a special agent.

SPECIAL STUDY FEATURES

Peterson's® *Master the™ Special Agent Exam* includes several features to maximize the effectiveness of your preparation.

Overview

Each chapter begins with a bulleted overview listing the topics covered in that chapter. This will allow you to quickly target the areas in which you are most interested.

Summing It Up

Each chapter ends with a point-by-point summary that reviews the most important items in the chapter. The summaries offer a convenient way to review key points.

Bonus Information

As you work your way through the book, look to the margins for bonus information and helpful advice. This information will come in one of the following forms:

 Notes highlight need-to-know information, whether it's details about the application process and scoring or the structure of certain test question types.

 Tips provide valuable strategies to help you answer the types of questions you will encounter on the various exams.

 Alerts identify test-specific items or topics to watch out for as you prepare.

Looking for Additional Practice? Check out www.Petersons.com!

Peterson's recognizes that the Special Agent testing process is primarily computer-based. To that end, we've included the tests you see in this book online. Go to **www.petersons.com/testprep/** and search our test prep career section for law enforcement to find Special Agent and other related exams. Enter the coupon code **%SPA21** at checkout to access the tests included in this book *plus* additional instructional materials and practice tests.

HELPFUL STUDY TIPS

The following are study tips to help you prepare for the special agent exam.

1. **Set up a study schedule.** Assign yourself a period each day devoted to preparing for your special agent exam. A regular schedule is best, but the important thing is to study daily, even if you can't do so at the same time every day.

2. **Study alone.** You will concentrate better if you work by yourself. Make a list of questions that you find puzzling and points of confusion. Later, discuss the items on the list with a friend who is preparing for the same exam. Exchange ideas and discuss more difficult questions at a joint review session shortly before the exam date.

3. **Eliminate distractions.** Choose a quiet, well-lit spot that is removed from distractions. Arrange your study area as best you can to not be interrupted.

4. **Start at the beginning and read carefully.** Underline points that you consider significant. Make marginal notes. Flag the pages you think are especially important.

5. **Concentrate on the information and instructional chapters.** Get yourself psyched to enter the world of a special agent. Learn how to handle logic-based questions and know your basic mathematical concepts.

6. **Take a practice test.** Focus on eliminating wrong answers; this is an important method for answering all multiple-choice questions, but it's especially vital for answering reasoning and judgment questions correctly. Take the practice test in one sitting and time yourself. While the practice tests in this book are shorter in length than the actual special agent exams, you can still learn to manage your time—and any test anxiety you may have—by simulating timed conditions.

TIPS FOR TEST TAKERS

Here's a list of general tips to help ensure that your score accurately reflects your understanding of the content on the exam, and your responses accurately reflect your personality and judgment.

- **Remain calm.** You know yourself best and which strategies or techniques will help you ease any test anxiety. A calm, clear mind will serve you better than a stressed out, fragmented mind.

- **Read the directions.** Multiple-choice questions on the special agent exam will only have one answer option that is correct. However, certain sections will remind you to base your answer solely on the information given, reminding you to not base your answer on what you *know* but on what you have *read*. Other questions will ask you to choose the statement that you agree/disagree with the most. Situational questions will ask you to choose the option that you would most likely do in a given situation. There are no correct answers to these questions, but they do provide key insights to your personality and character. Pay attention to the directions.

- **Focus on the questions you know.** Struggling with a question? Skip it and focus on answering the questions you *do* know. As time permits, you can go back to the questions you skipped.

- **Read the entire question and all answer choices before selecting your answer.** This is especially true for logical reasoning questions where you will be provided with information and asked to draw a conclusion or choose a statement that is true. At times, you will be asked to pick the option that *cannot* be validly concluded from the information given.

- **Eliminate answer options.** When you are unsure of the answer to a question, try eliminating the answers you know are incorrect. Then, guess from the remaining options.

- **Answer every question.** Remember, for the sections of the exam that are scored, your score will be based on the number of questions you answer correctly. Since there is no penalty for incorrect answers, take a guess! If you have eliminated the answers you know to be incorrect, your chances of choosing the correct answer have increased dramatically.

- **If time permits, go back and check your answers.** A word of caution. More often than not, your first answer will be the correct answer. But, if you feel like you need to review certain questions again, and you have the time, go for it.

- **Mark your answer sheet correctly.** This applies mainly to a paper-based test and not a computer-based test. However, it goes without saying that you should make sure you are marking the answer on the correct question on the answer sheet. This is especially true if you skip a question.

> **TIP**
> Do not memorize questions and answers. You might see questions on your exam that are very similar to the ones provided, but you will not see any of the exact questions you encounter in this book.

TEST DAY STRATEGIES

You may find it helpful to keep the following strategies in mind for the actual test day.

1. **Be prepared.** Research what you will need to bring with you on test day. The night before, make sure you have everything you need in one place. Decide on the outfit you will wear. Be comfortable but look professional.

2. **Eat smart.** Plan to eat before your Special Agent Exam. Avoid caffeine if it makes you jittery, and avoid sugary items that will cause a temporary spike to your energy level.

3. **Focus only on the test.** Don't plan any activities that day or squeeze the test in the middle of activities.

4. **Arrive rested, relaxed, and on time.** In fact, plan to arrive a little bit early. Leave plenty of time for traffic tie-ups or other complications that might upset you and interfere with your test performance.

5. **If the test is proctored, ask questions if there are any instructions you do not understand.** Make sure that you know exactly what to do. In the test room, the proctor will provide the instructions you must follow when taking the examination.

6. **Follow instructions exactly during the examination.** Do not begin until you are told to do so. Stop as soon as you are told to stop. Any infraction of the rules is considered cheating.

7. **Maintain a positive attitude.** This will help ease any test anxiety. A can-do attitude creates confidence.

PETERSON'S® PUBLICATIONS

Peterson's publishes a full line of books—career preparation, education exploration, test prep, and financial aid. Peterson's books are available for purchase online at **www.petersons.com**. Sign up for one of our online subscription plans and you'll have access to our entire test prep catalog of more than 150 exams *plus* instructional videos, flashcards, interactive quizzes, and more! Our subscription plans allow you to study as quickly as you can or as slowly as you'd like. For more information, go to **www.petersons.com/testprep/**. Peterson's publications can also be found at college libraries and career centers, and your local bookstore and library.

YOU'RE WELL ON YOUR WAY TO SUCCESS

Now it's time to make the most of this powerful preparation tool. Turn the page and find out everything you need to know about becoming a special agent. Remember to study hard *and* smart; we wish you the best of luck.

PART I
INTRODUCTION TO BECOMING A SPECIAL AGENT

Chapter 1

The Basics

OVERVIEW

- **The Structure of the Federal Government**
- **Compensation**
- **Benefits**
- **Work Schedules**
- **Advancement Opportunities**
- **Summing It Up**

THE STRUCTURE OF THE FEDERAL GOVERNMENT

The federal government is divided into three branches: Executive, Legislative, and Judiciary. The Executive branch is by far the largest, having the broadest scope and employing about 96 percent of all federal civilian employees. The Legislative branch is tasked with making laws. Congress is comprised of elected officials that serve in either the House of Representatives or the Senate. The Judicial branch is tasked with interpreting laws; it is composed of the Supreme Court and other federal lower courts. The following graphic illustrates the overall structure of the three branches.

Branches of US Government

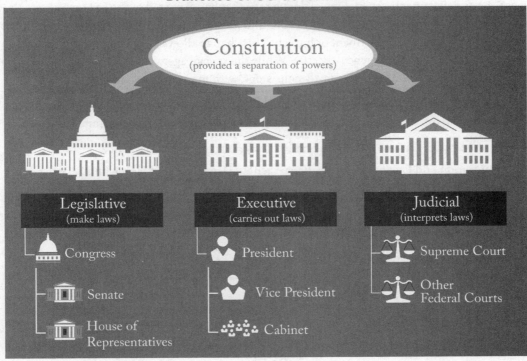

1

Most positions in national security, criminal investigation, and protective services fall within the Executive Branch. This branch is divided into fifteen executive departments and ninety independent agencies, including the US Postal Service and the Social Security Administration. The following table lists the names of the fifteen executive departments.

Executive Departments

Department of Agriculture	Department of Commerce	Department of Defense
Department of Education	Department of Energy	Department of Health and Human Services
Department of Homeland Security	Department of Housing and Urban Development	Department of the Interior
Department of Justice	Department of Labor	Department of State
Department of the Treasury	Department of Transportation	Department of Veterans Affairs

Three of the executive departments have missions that focus heavily on law enforcement, criminal investigation, and national security issues. These departments are the Department of Homeland Security, the Department of Justice, and the Department of the Treasury. Each of these departments is further divided into a series of federal agencies and bureaus that act as separate entities for filling job vacancies.

All directly funded government jobs are posted on the USAJOBS website (**www.usajobs.gov**). Positions with outside agencies and other related organizations that are not directly part of the executive branch of the government maintain their own hiring sites.

All federal agencies and departments follow standardized hiring processes and guidelines. However, the hiring processes and the guidelines that agencies follow to determine eligibility are subject to internal adjustments over time as departments see fit. One major change that has occurred in the last ten years is the phase out of the Treasury Enforcement Agent (TEA) exam and a compartmentalizing of special agent entrance exams back to their respective department or bureau. This change allows for greater flexibility to customize the testing experience to be more agency-specific. While the special agent exams may differ from agency to agency, the content of the exams remains fairly consistent, with many areas of overlap.

To assist you in your journey towards becoming a special agent in your chosen concentration, this book will focus on the following top three special agent departments and their respective entrance exams:

- Bureau of Alcohol, Tobacco, Firearms and Explosives (Department of Justice)
- US Immigration and Customs Enforcement Agency (Department of Homeland Security)
- Federal Bureau of Investigation (Department of Justice)

1

Several other agencies and bureaus require applicants for special agent and criminal investigator positions to take written exams similar to the ones covered in this book. These agencies are:

- Customs and Border Patrol (Department of Homeland Security)
- US Secret Service (Department of Homeland Security)
- Internal Revenue Service (Department of the Treasury)
- US Park Police (Department of the Interior)

COMPENSATION

Base Salary

Excellent pay and benefits are one outstanding aspect of federal employment. The average annual salary for all full-time federal employees now exceeds $80,000, and many employees earn beyond the standard wages of the basic pay system. Employees within the Special Agent delineation are paid according to a system known as the **General Schedule (GS)**. This pay schedule consists of a series of grade levels ranging from GS-1 to GS-15. There is a series of ten steps under each grade that an employee moves through, although at the GS-5, 7, 9, and 11 levels, employees often jump between grades rather than progress through the steps. While certain law enforcement positions are paid at a slightly higher rate (e.g., law enforcement officers), they are still considered to be GS positions.

Each position in the GS pay system falls into a structured occupational group and is assigned a particular job series classification. For example, GS groups include the Social Science, Psychology, and Welfare Group (GS-100 series) and the Inspection, Investigation, Enforcement, and Compliance Group (GS-1800 series). Within the larger groupings are a set of more specific job series. For example, under the Inspection, Investigation, Enforcement, and Compliance Group, there are the Investigative Analysis Series (GS-1805), the Import Compliance Series (GS-1889), and the Border Patrol Enforcement Series (GS-1896), among many others.

There are 343 different white-collar occupations that fall into this classification system. Some federal law enforcement job series that come under the GS Pay Schedule are the Criminal Investigator (Treasury Enforcement Agent) series (GS-1811) and the US Marshal series (GS-0082). A set of grade levels for each position is determined by the education and experience they require and by the duties, skills, responsibilities, and other factors they entail. Thus, when you apply for a particular position, HR specialists will determine whether you are qualified for the position and what pay level you qualify for by matching your credentials against a set of "qualification standards." These standards are written by the Office of Personnel Management (OPM) and are contained in the *General Schedule Qualification Standards*, which can be found online at **www.opm.gov/ policy-data-oversight/classification-qualifications/general-schedule-qualification-standards/**. Typically, new employees with bachelor's degrees and no experience in a career field start at the GS-5 level or the GS-7 level if a B average was maintained. A relevant master's degree will earn new hires a GS-9 position, and a doctorate qualifies hires for a GS-11 if the degree is related to the job to be filled.

1

The following tables show the general base salary annual rates by grade and step for 2021.

SALARY TABLE 2021-GS
Steps 1–5*

Grade	Step 1	Step 2	Step 3	Step 4	Step 5
1	$ 19,738	$ 20,400	$ 21,056	$ 21,709	$ 22,365
2	22,194	22,722	23,457	24,078	24,349
3	24,216	25,023	25,830	26,637	27,444
4	27,184	28,090	28,996	29,902	30,808
5	30,414	31,428	32,442	33,456	34,470
6	33,903	35,033	36,163	37,293	38,423
7	37,674	38,930	40,186	41,442	42,698
8	41,723	43,114	44,505	45,896	47,287
9	46,083	47,619	49,155	50,691	52,227
10	50,748	52,440	54,132	55,824	57,516
11	55,756	57,615	59,474	61,333	63,192
12	66,829	69,057	71,285	73,513	75,741
13	79,468	82,117	84,766	87,415	90,064
14	93,907	97,037	100,167	103,297	106,427
15	110,460	114,142	117,824	121,506	125,188

SALARY TABLE 2021-GS
Steps 6–10*

Grade	Step 6	Step 7	Step 8	Step 9	Step 10	Within Grade Amounts
1	$ 22,749	$ 23,398	$ 24,052	$ 24,078	$ 24,690	Varies
2	25,065	25,781	26,497	27,213	27,929	Varies
3	28,251	29,058	29,865	30,672	31,479	807
4	31,714	32,620	33,526	34,432	35,338	906
5	35,484	36,498	37,512	38,526	39,540	1,014
6	39,553	40,683	41,813	42,943	44,073	1,130
7	43,954	45,210	46,466	47,722	48,978	1,256
8	48,678	50,069	51,460	52,851	54,242	1,391
9	53,763	55,299	56,835	58,371	59,907	1,536
10	59,208	60,900	62,592	64,284	65,976	1,692
11	65,051	66,910	68,769	70,628	72,487	1,859
12	77,969	80,197	82,425	84,653	86,881	2,228
13	92,713	95,362	98,011	100,660	103,309	2,649
14	109,557	112,687	115,817	118,947	122,077	3,130
15	128,870	132,552	136,234	139,916	143,598	3,682

* Incorporates the 1% general schedule increase effective January 2021.
See www.opm.gov/policy-data-oversight/pay-leave/salaries-wages/2021/general-schedule/

Locality Pay

Although the Salary Table 2021-GS chart shows the broad range of pay, different locations will vary their entry level pay based on local cost of living and demand for workers. This is called **locality pay**, and it is listed on the job opening with a percentage. For example, the phrase "The locality pay for this position is 16.35%" equates to an adjusted base pay using the percentage provided.

Federal law enforcement officer employees can earn at least 15.95 percent more than the Salary Table 2021-GS chart's base salary figures, depending on the area. Higher locality rates are paid to employees in high-cost-of-living metropolitan areas such as Los Angeles, Boston, Chicago, Philadelphia, and New York. As of 2021, the highest locality rate was in the San Jose-San Francisco-Oakland area at 41.44 percent. Updated locality pay charts are located at **www.opm.gov/policy-data-oversight/pay-leave/salaries-wages/2021/law-enforcement-officer/**.

Law Enforcement Officer Pay

Federal employees who work in law enforcement receive special base rates, called Law Enforcement Officer (LEO) rates, for GS-3 through GS-10. The following tables detail the 2021 special rates.

SALARY TABLE 2021-GL (LEO)
Steps 1–5*

Grade	Step 1	Step 2	Step 3	Step 4	Step 5
3	$ 29,058	$ 29,865	$ 30,672	$ 31,479	$ 32,286
4	32,620	33,526	34,432	35,338	36,244
5	37,512	38,526	39,540	40,554	41,568
6	39,553	40,683	41,813	42,943	44,073
7	42,698	43,954	45,210	46,466	47,722
8	44,505	45,896	47,287	48,678	50,069
9	47,619	49,155	50,691	52,227	53,763
10	52,440	54,132	55,824	57,516	59,208

SALARY TABLE 2021-GL (LEO)
Steps 6–10*

Grade	Step 6	Step 7	Step 8	Step 9	Step 10	Within Grade Amounts
3	$ 33,093	$ 33,900	$ 34,707	$ 35,514	$ 36,321	$ 807
4	37,150	38,056	38,962	39,868	40,774	906
5	42,582	43,596	44,610	45,624	46,638	1,014
6	45,203	46,333	47,463	48,593	49,723	1,130
7	48,978	50,234	51,490	52,746	54,002	1,256
8	51,460	52,851	54,242	55,633	57,024	1,391
9	55,299	56,835	58,371	59,907	61,443	1,536
10	60,900	62,592	64,284	65,976	67,668	1,692

* Incorporates the 1% general schedule increase effective January 2021.
See www.opm.gov/policy-data-oversight/pay-leave/salaries-wages/2021/law-enforcement-officer/

1

Law Enforcement Availability Pay

Law Enforcement Availability Pay (LEAP) provides a 25 percent increase in base salary added to any locality pay received. This program is designed to provide a simplified means of compensating law enforcement personnel for the long hours associated with enforcement activities. Agents eligible for LEAP receive higher basic pay, more take-home pay, increased earnings for retirement contributions, and a simpler overtime system.

Foreign Language Award Program

This program authorizes cash awards for employees of certain agencies who possess and make substantial use of one or more foreign language(s) in the performance of their official duties. The Secret Service participates heavily in this program given the proximity of their position to foreign nationals. In addition, Immigration and Customs Enforcement (ICE) also utilizes this program for agents located in certain regions with higher populations where English is not the primary spoken language.

Cost of Living Adjustments

The federal government grants its employees cost of living adjustments each year. While these cost of living increases vary from year to year, recent adjustments have been about 1.4 percent, with 2020 being a particularly large jump to 2.6 percent. Therefore, each year of federal employment promises two salary increases—the step or grade increase and the cost of living increase.

BENEFITS

One of the advantages of federal employment is the comprehensive benefits that are offered to eligible employees. This section provides a brief overview.

Holidays, Vacation Leave, and Sick Leave

All full-time federal employees receive 10 paid holidays per calendar year. Eligible full-time employees accrue 13 days of vacation for the first three years of service, 20 days of vacation for 3–15 years of service, and 26 days after 15 years of service. Maximum accrual limits may apply in a "use it or lose it" system. Additionally, full-time employees accrue 13 days of sick leave annually regardless of time of service. Sick leave is not subject to a maximum limit and can be carried over from year to year.

Insurance

Eligible employees can choose from a variety of health, vision, and dental insurance plans regardless of any pre-existing conditions. Life insurance plans include both traditional life insurance and the Employee Benevolent fund for catastrophic events requiring immediate assistance.

Retirement

The Federal Employees Retirement System (FERS) guarantees each employee a specific monthly payment based on the employee's age, length of creditable service, and "high three" average salary. FERS employees also pay Social Security taxes and may participate in the Thrift Savings Plan (TSP), which is similar to a traditional 401(k) plan with matching options.

Transportation Subsidies

Monthly transportation subsidies help to offset the cost of transportation to and from work. Employee designated parking and discounted parking passes may also be offered.

1

Enhanced Benefits

Certain federal law enforcement employees are eligible to earn enhanced benefits, including low-cost life insurance and a special LEO Retirement Program. See **www.opm.gov** for more information.

WORK SCHEDULES

At the discretion of agency management, several schedule options are offered. These include full-time, part-time, flexible, and compressed schedules. Flexible work schedules, commonly called **flextime**, allow workers to vary their arrival and departure times. Compressed schedules allow employees to complete the basic work requirement of 80 hours in a two-week pay period in fewer than ten working days. The federal government is actively working towards secure, home-based employment options as well.

ADVANCEMENT OPPORTUNITIES

When entering federal service, a new employee's grade level and base pay (salary) are determined by his or her education level and amount of work experience. As noted in the base salary section, entry-level professional positions are normally filled at the GS-5 or GS-7 levels. New employees usually come in at the Step 1 rate for a given grade. However, people seeking positions in areas where there are shortages (engineers, physicists, chemists, metallurgists, and other scientific occupations) may be allowed to come in at a higher level. Progression in many professional positions occurs according to what is known as a **career ladder**.

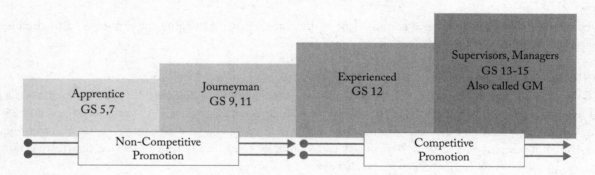

In a typical career ladder, an individual would be promoted accordingly. For example, a new hire's initial base rate might be GS-5, and promotions would progress to GS-7, GS-9, GS-11, GS-12, and so on. GS-5 and GS-7 amount to an apprenticeship for gaining experience in a particular position. GS-9 and GS-11 are journeyman positions in which the employee is more experienced but still not completely capable of performing all the functions required for that position. At the GS-12 level, the employee is considered "full-performance"—that is, experienced in all aspects of the job. Promotions along the career ladder come relatively quickly (about one promotion every year or two, assuming good performance). These promotions occur automatically and are normally noncompetitive in that the employee is not competing against anyone else.

Promotions above a GS-12 are usually competitive. In other words, all interested candidates have to formally apply for the position, and a slot at that level must exist. Supervisors and managers in grades 13 through 15 are under a pay-for-performance system. These positions are easily identifiable because they will have a GM rather than a GS designation on the vacancy announcement.

SUMMING IT UP

- The federal government is structured into three major branches: **Executive**, **Legislative**, and **Judicial**.

  - The Executive branch is by far the largest, having the broadest scope and employing about 96 percent of all federal civilian employees.

  - The Legislative branch is tasked with making laws. Congress is comprised of elected officials that serve in either the House of Representatives or the Senate.

  - The Judicial branch is tasked with interpreting laws; it is composed of the Supreme Court and other federal lower courts.

- Most positions in national security, criminal investigation, and protective services fall within the Executive branch, which is further divided into fifteen executive departments and ninety independent agencies.

- The primary focus of the Department of Homeland Security, the Department of Justice, and the Department of the Treasury is law enforcement, criminal investigation, and national security issues.

- The exam landscape for special agents has shifted dramatically in the past 10 years.

  - The Treasury Enforcement Agent (TEA) exam is no longer in use for general special agent applications.

  - Individual bureaus and agencies have now compartmentalized their tests.

- This study guide focuses on exams for the following agencies/bureaus:

  - Bureau of Alcohol, Tobacco, Firearms and Explosives (ATF)

  - Immigration and Customs Enforcement (ICE)

  - Federal Bureau of Investigation (FBI)

- The following agencies/bureaus require applicants to take and pass exams that are similar in format and focus to the ones discussed in depth within this guide:

  - US Secret Service (Department of Homeland Security)

  - Internal Revenue Service (Department of the Treasury)

  - Customs and Border Patrol (Department of Homeland Security)

  - US Park Police (Department of the Interior)

- Employees within the Special Agent delineation are paid according to the **General Schedule (GS)**. This pay schedule consists of a series of grade levels ranging from GS-1 to GS-15. There is a series of ten steps under each grade that an employee moves through.

- The pay scale for federal employment can be mitigated by locality pay, cost of living adjustments, special law enforcement rates, availability pay, and cash award programs.

- The federal government offers an ample benefits package for all employees that includes the following:

  - Vacation, sick leave, and holidays

  - Insurance

  - Retirement

  - Transportation subsidies

Chapter 2

How to Apply

OVERVIEW

- **The USAJobs Website**
- **FBI Application Process**
- **The Online Resume**
- **Military Applicants**
- **Summing It Up**

THE USAJOBS WEBSITE

Since all special agent positions are part of the federal government, **job opening announcements (JOAs)** and application submissions are started through the online federal government application portal at **www.USAJobs.gov**. ICE and ATF applications are completed entirely through this portal. FBI positions are posted on this portal, but the site will redirect you to an FBI-specific application portal for the application process. However, the process once there is identical to the USAJobs portal.

This section will provide an overview of how to navigate the USAJobs website and the tools embedded within it that can help streamline the application process. The application process is composed of five main steps, as shown in the following graphic.

Application Process

The first three steps are completed online at **www.USAJobs.gov**. This chapter provides a breakdown of Steps 1–3 and includes helpful tips to maximize your online application experience. Be prepared, however, as even though the process has been simplified, entering all necessary information requires time and accuracy.

2

Step 1: Create a Profile/Account

Every applicant must create a USAJobs account. Select *Sign In* and follow the steps to "Create an account." This account will be used for every job you apply for within the federal government. You will need a working email address to register.

When you set up your profile, you will be asked to complete some common demographic questions. There are icons and descriptions for possible groups that you may belong to. These identifying factors are used to narrow your job search—determining the positions for which you may or may not be eligible and subsequently establishing your hiring path. Be sure to select all groups to which you belong.

You will identify yourself as a US Citizen or foreign national. Additionally, you will select if you legally identify as any of the following:

- Veteran
- Federal employee
- National Guard & Reserves member
- Military spouse
- Recent graduate
- Student
- Individual with disabilities
- Senior executive
- Native American
- Family of overseas employees
- Land & base management
- Peace Corps & AmeriCorps VISTA member

After you work through the Hiring Path section, the site will guide you through a basic work history, experience, and education section. You will have the opportunity to add further information after your initial submission.

You will then have access to four separate USAJobs features: Home, Profile, Documents, and Preferences. These areas house all of the information required for applying for any job within the federal government. The following descriptions provide more details on the purpose of each tab.

TIP

Do not rush through the application process! It is more important to be thorough than quick. Incomplete or missing information may disqualify you from the pool of eligible candidates.

2

- **HOME:** This is your headquarters for job searches. As you work through searching and applying for jobs, everything automatically populates in this section.

- **PROFILE:** This provides a snapshot of your profile based on demographics. This is the page that will have your current contact information. Each federal agency will use this information to reach you if you are selected for the testing component of the application process.

- **DOCUMENTS:** This section contains documents related to your work experience, education, and references, including your resume. Currently, the site provides access to the online Resume Builder. You may also upload your own resume. For many agencies, the Resume Builder option is required. As such, you may need to re-enter information from your existing resume into the Resume Builder.

- **PREFERENCES:** This section is specifically aimed at helping you focus your job search. The prompts here ask about possible locations, type of employment (full time, part time, temporary, etc.) work shifts, and more. Make sure that your preferences accurately reflect your employment interests.

Step 2: Search JOAs

Once you have created your account, you may search for JOAs that fit your preferences and immediately apply to those jobs. You can search by job titles, agency names, and keywords among other options. After entering your keywords, you can apply various filters to your search, save your search, and sort the results. Options to customize include the following:

1. **Filters:** Select from a variety of filters to limit your search results, and filter by work schedule, appointment type, security clearance, hiring path, salary, and more. You can also select department and agency filters to refine your results.

2. **Save Search:** In addition to being able to save specific job postings, you can also save an entire search. You can find saved items in your HOME tab. By saving a search to your account, you will be notified via email when new jobs that fit your criteria open.

3. **Sort By:** To help you sort your JOAs, a *Sort By* feature allows you to choose how you want to view the matching jobs. By default, the site sorts jobs by relevance to your query. However, by interacting with the menu, you can sort by closing date (to see the positions that are closing soon), salary, and more.

TIP
Using the key phrase "Special Agent" in your search will help to narrow your search even more.

Step 3: Applying for Jobs

To apply for an ATF or ICE special agent position, you can use the *Resume Builder* option or simply upload your resume. Resume Builder is designed to walk you through all employment, education, references, and other common resume components using an intuitive system. Simply complete the provided fields (or select a previously built resume if that option appears for you) and follow the steps. As part of the Resume Builder, you will see verification of the position that you're applying to and progress for the application itself. If you decide to upload your resume, follow the *Federal Resume Guidelines* as outlined later in this chapter.

Applications consist of the following five parts:

1. **Select Resume:** Select, upload, or create a resume using the Resume Builder.

2. **Select Documents:** Select or upload required documents; a checklist should be provided.

3. **Review Package:** Review the documents you selected for submission; verify that you selected the correct resume and required documents.

4. **Include Personal Info:** Offer personal details (on a voluntary basis).

5. **Position Specific Questions:** Answer specific questions related to the special agent position and division to which you are applying.

While every effort has been made to centralize the initial application process through USAJobs, each agency and, subsequently, each job position within an agency will have unique requirements. The JOAs are set up in such a way that you will be able to see these requirements. However, you alone are responsible for the information you include and the attachments you provide with your submission.

FBI APPLICATION PROCESS

Candidates can search for FBI Special Agent job announcements on both the USAJobs.gov and FBIJobs.gov websites. However, if your search begins on the USAJobs platform, you'll find a link in the *How to Apply* section of the posting that will direct you to the FBI application portal housed on the agency site. It is on the FBI portal where you will complete the necessary application requirements for the special agent position you are interested in. After creating your FBI account, you will be directed to follow the steps listed in the interface of the site. The following graphic illustrates what you can expect:

TIP

Set aside a good chunk of time to update your resume *before* you officially start the application process. Your resume is the primary way for you to communicate how qualified you are. This way, you can easily add keywords used in the JOA to your resume and increase your chances of making it to the next step in the process.

FBI Initial Application & Screening Process

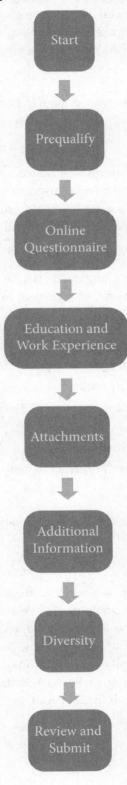

Start

Prequalify

Online Questionnaire

Education and Work Experience

Attachments

Additional Information

Diversity

Review and Submit

2

Start and Prequalification

In order to proceed with the application process, you must first agree to terms and conditions and acknowledge prequalification notices. You'll answer a series of simple questions meant to screen out people that do not meet the basic qualifications for any federal government position.

Online Questionnaire

The online questionnaire contains a series of yes-or-no questions that apply to your qualifications for an FBI special agent position.

Education and Work Experience

In this part of the application, you'll insert information related to your education and work experience. This includes details related to your degree, major, college/university, minor, grade point average, and graduation date. When adding education information, use the "lookup" feature and enter your terms in the *Description* field. The *Content Item ID* field is for internal FBI codes and will yield errors if words are entered.

Attachments

Here you will attach the required documents indicated in the job announcement posting. Regardless of the exact special agent position you are applying for, you will need to submit the following documents:

- Resume
- Official or unofficial college transcript(s)
- SF-50 *Notification of Personnel Action* (current & former federal employees)
- Statement of Service Letter (active-duty military personnel)
- DD-214 *Certificate of Release or Discharge from Active Duty* (military veterans: member 4 or service 2 copy)
- VA letter dated within one year (for disabled veterans)
- SF-15 *Application for 10-Point Veterans' Preference* (optional for disabled veterans)

Additional Information

In this section, you will be asked to provide additional information related to demographics, government background, and military background.

Diversity

Providing diversity information (e.g., gender, race, religion, etc.) is *optional* and *voluntary*. Your answers will not count against you as the bureau remains committed to selecting the best applicants in a nondiscriminatory manner. However, keep in mind that, as a special agent, you will be interacting with many different types of people from a vast array of cultures and backgrounds. Your diversity could be a valuable asset. The FBI recognizes this and has created a Diversity Agent Recruitment (DAR) Program in an effort to build a diverse and inclusive workforce. The DAR program hosts by-invitation recruitment events to help introduce potential applicants from diverse backgrounds to the special agent career path.

Review and Submit

In this last step, you'll have a chance to review the contents of your submission package before you officially submit. Take time to ensure that all the information entered is accurate and complete. It is especially important for you to double check that all attachments are accounted for; missing documents will disqualify your application. When you are ready, follow the steps to officially submit your application.

2

THE ONLINE RESUME

Your resume is the primary means of communicating how well-qualified you are for a special agent position. In an effort to help applicants present all pertinent information using government formatting and thereby simplifying the application process across governmental agencies, the FBI designed a federal resume template and published a *Federal Resume Guide* to help applicants get started. A PDF of the *Federal Resume Guide* can be found at **www.archives.gov/files/careers/jobs/forms/resume-guide.pdf**. We recommend reading this guide *before* you complete the online application submission process.

The *Federal Resume Guide* includes samples for the following types of resumes:

- **Chronological:** Lists information in reverse chronological order, with the most recent job being placed first and the oldest job placed last.
- **Functional (Competency-Based):** Places a primary focus on skills, abilities, accomplishments, job traits, and personal characteristics (competencies) rather than job titles.
- **Combination:** Includes elements of both the chronological and functional styles of resumes by identifying relevant skills and accomplishments and then detailing employment and education in chronological order.
- **Targeted:** This type of resume is tailored for a specific company or position. It can be a combination of any of the three styles listed and is typically used when you know positions exist at a particular company but are not applying to an advertised vacancy.

There is no "one-size-fits-all" approach to creating your resume style. What you bring to the table in terms of skill set, work history, education, and more is uniquely yours. So how do you provide the information your resume needs, in a government format, while highlighting what makes you the best candidate for the job opportunity?

The first step is to gather and document all the information you want reflected on your resume. At a minimum, your resume should include the following:

- Personal information (e.g., name, address, phone number, etc.)
- Objective/Summary statement
- Education
- Work experience
- Other relevant qualifications

2

The following pages provide an outline of common information found on a resume. Use this as a guideline. Even if you don't know what style of resume you will use, you will at least have the necessary information handy.

SUMMARY STATEMENT

- Provide three to five brief statements highlighting your most important and relevant skills. This serves as a roadmap for the rest of your resume.

PROFESSIONAL SKILLS

- List skills related to your education, those acquired throughout your career, and any personal skills that you want to highlight.
- Include, if applicable, the following:
  - Foreign language skills and proficiency (novice, intermediate, or advanced) in speaking, reading, and/or writing
  - Technology skills

PROFESSIONAL WORK EXPERIENCE

- List your full-time, professional work history.
- List experience in reverse chronological order.
- The following **MUST** be included:
  - Position & title
  - Name of organization and location (city/state)
  - Start & end date (month/year)
  - Salary (per hour/month/year)
  - Hours per week (full time or part time)
  - Supervisor name (or HR rep who can verify employment) and phone number
  - Brief description of duties, major roles, responsibilities, and accomplishments

OTHER WORK EXPERIENCE

- List any other work experience, including part-time jobs, internships, seasonal positions, and/or temporary employment.
- List other work experience in reverse chronological order.
- The following **MUST** be included:
  - Position & title
  - Name of organization and location (city/state)
  - Start & end date (month/year)
  - Salary (per hour/month/year)
  - Part-time / internship / seasonal / temporary
  - Supervisor name (or HR rep who can verify employment) and phone number
  - Brief description of duties, major roles, responsibilities, and accomplishments

EDUCATION

- Start with your highest-level degree and work backward.
- The following **MUST** be included:

  ○ Type of degree and major
  ○ College or university and city/state
  ○ Minor and/or dual major (if applicable)
  ○ Date of graduation (month/year)
  ○ Grade point average (GPA)
  ○ Honors or awards (if applicable)

CERTIFICATIONS/ACHIEVEMENTS

- List any certification or licenses you currently hold.
- The following **MUST** be included:

  ○ Name of the certification
  ○ Organization that granted it and location (city/state)
  ○ Date(s) the certification is in effect (month/year)

TRAINING

- List any formal training, including accreditations.
- The following **MUST** be included:

  ○ Name of the training and location (city/state)
  ○ The sponsoring organization
  ○ Start & end date (month/year)
  ○ Number of hours completed

VOLUNTEER EXPERIENCE/COMMUNITY SERVICE

- List any volunteer work and/or community service that may showcase additional skills that you have acquired apart from your professional career.
- List experience in reverse chronological order.
- The following **MUST** be included:

  ○ Name of organization and location (city/state)
  ○ Start & end date (month/year)
  ○ Brief description of duties, major roles, responsibilities, and accomplishments

Once you have compiled all the information you want reflected on your resume, choose the resume style that best fits the job opportunity and your qualifications. You have the option of using the Resume Builder tool on the USAJobs website to build your resume from scratch, or you can import the data from your current resume into the Resume Builder tool. A third option is to build your resume in a separate word processing program and attach the final product to your application. However, this option may not be made available to you through the official JOA. If this third option is available, you MUST make sure that your resume is formatted according to government specifications and submitted in an approved format.

MILITARY APPLICANTS

Applicants with a current or former military background are awarded preference points on certain job postings. The JOA will state if the veterans' preference applies. The types of preference and available points awarded are detailed in the following table.

Veterans' Preference

Type of Preference	Description
None	Employee has no veterans' preference.
5-point	Employee has a 5-point veterans' preference.
10-point/disability	Employee has a 10-point veterans' preference due to compensable disability or is a recipient of the Purple Heart.
10-point/compensable	Employee is entitled to a 10-point preference due to a compensable, service-connected disability of less than 30%.
10-point other	Persons entitled to a 10-point preference in this category: (1) Both the spouse and mother of veterans occupationally disabled because of a service-connected disability, and (2) the widow/widower and mother of a deceased wartime veteran.
10-point/compensable/30%	Veteran is entitled to 10-point preference due to a compensable, service-connected disability of 30% or more.
No Points/Sole Survivorship Preference (SSP)	Veteran is not entitled to preference.

List your military service on your resume and include the following information:

- Rank/Grade/Job Title
- Start and end date, or date of expected separation (month/year)
- Branch of military (Active or Reserve)
- Unit address
- Salary (base salary with locality, minus allowances)
- Full-time or part-time (if you were a reservist)
- Supervisor/First Line Leader (name, title, and phone number)
- Veterans' Preference
- Brief description of your primary duties, responsibilities, and accomplishments

SUMMING IT UP

- **USAJobs.gov** is the online federal government application portal. All **job opening announcements (JOAs)** are posted on this site, including special agent positions with ATF, ICE, and FBI.

- Applicants must sign up and create their own **USAJobs profile**. Once this step is completed, users can search JOAs, build a resume with the Resume Builder tool, submit applications, and keep track of the progress of existing applications.

- Users can customize their search experience by applying a variety of filters to narrow the results, sort based on specified preferences, and save specific jobs or searches to return to later.

- ICE and ATF applicants complete their entire initial application via the USAJobs website.

- FBI applicants are able to use USAJobs to locate JOAs for the agency and are able to see all of the necessary information, including who can and cannot apply.

  - Application for a FBI special agent position occurs on the FBI internal application site, which is easily accessed from USAJobs under the JOA for each position.

  - Applicants must register for an account on the FBI application site and then complete a multi-step process to apply to an agency position.

- The **federal resume** was designed by the FBI in an effort to help applicants present all pertinent information using government formatting and simplify the application process across governmental agencies. For more information, including detailed explanations of the what and how of creating a federal resume, see **www.archives.gov/files/careers/jobs/forms/resume-guide.pdf**.

- The federal government places a high preference on **veterans** for special agent positions and has an entire section for veterans to help them apply and utilize their active-duty experience towards a career within the agency.

Chapter 3

The Hiring Process

OVERVIEW

- **Common Federal Hiring Requirements**
- **ATF-Specific Hiring Requirements for a Special Agent**
- **ICE-Specific Hiring Requirements for a Criminal Investigator**
- **FBI-Specific Hiring Requirements for a Special Agent**
- **Summing It Up**

Making it through the online application process and into the assessment and interview process is an exciting accomplishment—but not a guarantee. You may be among many applicants who are competing for one position, and the final selection will be based on several series of tests and interviews. Eligible candidates are advanced through the hiring process on an as-needed basis, not on any conventional schedule. Delays, such as medical clearance, hiring freezes, etc., can arise anytime during the process. Therefore, it is important to understand that, although the timeline for each phase of the hiring process can vary, the process can take 12–18 months from the submission of your application to placement.

COMMON FEDERAL HIRING REQUIREMENTS

Although each agency has a unique role in the federal government, the ATF, ICE, and FBI agencies share the same set of basic pre-hire requirements. Each candidate must meet the following prerequisite requirements to be eligible for hire:

- Be a US citizen
- Male candidates born after December 31, 1959, must certify at the time of selection that they have registered with the Selective Service System or are exempt from having to do so under Selective Service law. Possess a current and valid automobile operator's license
- Meet the Law Enforcement Age Requirement
- Qualify and maintain firearms proficiency (i.e., must not have been convicted of felonies and certain misdemeanors, including a misdemeanor crime of domestic violence)

If the basic pre-hire requirements are met, eligible candidates will then be expected to complete the common federal hiring requirements shown in the following table as part of the stepped hiring process.

Common Federal Hiring Requirements

Step	Requirement
1	Meet specific age qualifications
2	Meet education and/or work experience qualifications
3	Take a series of written and oral assessments
4	Meet the physical fitness standards
5	Participate in a series of interviews
6	Take and pass a standard medical examination by an authorized government physician and meet medical requirements. Medical requirements include: • Ability to perform physically strenuous activity • Visual and hearing standards • Weight in proportion to height • Physical, emotional, and mental requirements for the position • Current vaccination records
7	Take and pass a drug test
8	Successfully complete a background investigation for a top-secret security clearance. This will include (1) employment verifications, (2) criminal and credit history checks, and (3) fingerprinting.
9	Take and successfully complete a polygraph examination
10	Carry a firearm and be willing to use deadly force, if necessary

It is important to note that, although each agency shares common hiring requirements, the specific requisites for each agency may vary. It is equally as important to understand and comply with each of the respective agencies' conditions. The rest of this chapter details the agency-specific requisites for Steps 1–5 for ATF, ICE, and FBI respectively.

3

ALERT

It is very important to thoroughly review all job requirements to ensure you are prepared for what is to come during the hiring process. Once the basic prerequisites are met, eligible candidates will receive notification of acceptance into the next phase. Every candidate will then be expected to complete the common requirements as part of the stepped hiring process.

ATF-SPECIFIC HIRING REQUIREMENTS FOR A SPECIAL AGENT

The Bureau of Alcohol, Tobacco, Firearms and Explosives performs criminal investigations, regulates the firearms and explosives industries, and supports other law enforcement agencies. In line with the Constitution and laws of the United States of America, the ATF assists with the prevention of terrorism, safeguards the public, and helps to minimize violent crimes.

Within the US Department of Justice, the ATF is a distinctive law enforcement agency that counteracts, identifies, and responds to acts of terrorism and violent crimes. The agency also investigates and prosecutes terrorist acts and violent crimes that involve the following:

- Firearms, explosives, and arson
- Felonious gangs
- Repeat and violent criminals
- Illicit use and smuggling of firearms and explosives
- Illegal diversion of alcohol and tobacco products

ATF also unites with communities, industries, and other law enforcement and public safety agencies to protect the population they serve through intelligence sharing, instruction, research, and technology.

The ATF strives to hire a distinct class of determined men and women who seek a challenge in their career and embrace a high level of integrity, trustworthiness, dignity, and honesty. Therefore, it makes sense that the process towards becoming an ATF special agent is filled with many steps from application to hire. The following are more specific details within each requirement and important factors to consider when moving through the hiring process.

Step 1: Meet Specific Age Qualifications

Applicants must be at least 21 years of age and not older than 36 at the time of appointment. In accordance with Public Law 100-238, this position is covered under law enforcement retirement provisions. Candidates must be appointed before reaching their 37th birthday. Exception may be granted for a preference eligible veteran, or an individual who is presently serving or have previously served in a federal civilian law enforcement retirement-covered position. In cases of prior federal service worked in a primary law enforcement position, applicants must be less than 37 years of age after subtracting years/months of prior federal service. The maximum entry age limit was established under the age discrimination prohibitions contained in Section 15 of the Age Discrimination and Employment Act. This means that if a candidate is 45 years old but has been a police officer for the last 15 years, the candidate can subtract these 15 years from their current age (45) and be considered a "30-year-old candidate" at the time of application for a Special Agent position.

Step 2: Meet Education and/or Work Experience Qualifications

It is important to note that, while a degree is not required to become an ATF special agent, a degree, experience in a related field, or a combination of the two is essential for the position and will establish an agent's pay grade.

For additional information on the education and/or experience required, download the *Special Agent Informational Packet* at **https://www.atf.gov/resource-center/docs/atfp23104sainfopacket2014pdf/download**.

Step 3: Take a Series of Written and Oral Assessments

All applicants must take and pass the ATF Special Agent Examination and the ATF Special Agent Applicant Assessment. The test session is approximately four hours for both tests. The Office of Personnel Management (OPM) administers and scores both tests.

The **ATF Special Agent Examination** is a basic aptitude test to make certain candidates have the skills and mental ability essential for the job. It is divided into the following sections:

- **Part A—Verbal Reasoning:** This part tests a candidate's verbal reasoning skills by asking the candidate to read various paragraphs and then answer multiple-choice questions based on the given information.

- **Part B—Quantitative Reasoning:** This part evaluates quantitative reasoning skills by requiring candidates to show basic arithmetic skills.

- **Part C—Investigative Reasoning:** In this part, candidates are provided information about a case and tasked to employ investigative skills by demonstrating the ability to infer information from the facts provided.

Candidates will also participate in the **ATF Special Agent Application Assessment Test**, a psychological assessment that measures personality and preference. The purpose of the evaluation is to help determine a candidate's aptness for a career as an ATF agent.

Step 4: Meet the Physical Fitness Standards

ATF agents are required to perform a physically demanding role by executing tasks such as defensive tactics, arrest procedures, and competent use of firearms under dangerous conditions. Upon taking and passing the written exam and assessment tests, you will be required to demonstrate your physical condition in the Pre-Employment Physical Task Test (PTT). This test is administered to measure a candidate's physical abilities in the following areas:

- Sit-ups (the maximum number performed in one minute without stopping)

- Push-ups (the maximum number performed in one minute without stopping)

- One and one-half mile run (the minimum completion time for a 1.5-mile run)

To pass, you must meet or exceed certain age and gender-based minimum benchmarks. See **https://www.atf.gov/careers/pre-employment-physical-task-test** for more information regarding the specific benchmarks. A candidate's inability to meet the minimum declared PTT benchmarks for any *one* of the examined areas will result in *elimination* from the hiring process. *There is no remediation.*

Candidates are required to travel to and from the selected PTT location at their own cost. Before taking part in the PTT, you will need to complete and execute the Physical Waiver and Score Sheet. The special agent in charge will appoint the location of the PTT at the

---

3

NOTE

There is a comprehensive sample ATF test found in Part IV of this study guide. The ATF website also provides sample questions that are similar in complexity and type to the ones you find on the actual exam. See **www.atf.gov/careers/preparing-atf-special-agent-exam**.

NOTE

The physical tasks are completed as one set in the order presented: sit-ups first, then push-ups, and finally the 1.5-mile run.

designated ATF Field Division office where the test will be executed. After successful completion of the PTT, you will continue with the hiring process. Again, if you do not meet the minimum benchmarks for your age for *all* of the physical test elements, you will become ineligible and removed from the pool of candidates for the position you applied for.

Step 5: Field Panel Interview

After you have passed all three tests, you will be asked to appear for a field panel interview. This phase places you in front of an oral interview panel that will assess your communication skills. Questions vary, but it is important to be focused, handle stress, project confidence, and have a general ability to connect past experience with the current job opening to be able to get through the interview.

Questions you may come across are mostly situational or are typical of interview questions like the following:

- How do you typically handle conflict? Give me an example.
- Describe a time when you foresaw possible challenges and established preventive processes.
- Give me an instance when you took initiative and accepted the lead.
- Give me an example of a time when you influenced others.
- Give me an example of a situation when you used your investigative skills to resolve an issue.
- Tell me about a difficult decision you have made in the last year.
- Give me an instance when you attempted to accomplish something and were unsuccessful.
- Tell me about a time when you were required to make an unpopular choice.
- Tell me about a time when you delegated a project effectively.
- Tell me about a time when you missed an obvious solution to a problem.

After the field panel interview, you will be required to submit a writing sample. It is important to make sure your English skills are up to par.

Subsequent Common Career Requirements

After accomplishing steps 1–5, successful completion of steps 6–10 of the Common Federal Hiring Requirements will advance you through the hiring process. If you are ultimately chosen for the position you applied and qualified for, your pay grade will be dependent upon your education and experience. Your next step will be to travel to the Federal Law Enforcement Training Center (FLETC) in Glynco, Georgia.

Currently, all newly hired agents will be required to attend a 12-week Criminal Investigators Training Program (CITP) at FLETC. Upon completion of CITP, special agent trainees will be required to participate in the ATF-specific Special Agent Basic Training. This physically and mentally challenging 15-week intensive program is designed to prepare new agents with the knowledge and abilities they will need to carry out the objectives of the ATF agency.

ICE-SPECIFIC HIRING REQUIREMENTS FOR A CRIMINAL INVESTIGATOR

Immigration and Customs Enforcement, Homeland Security Investigations (ICE-HSI) is a critical investigative arm of the Department of Homeland Security (DHS). Its mission is to safeguard the United States of America from the transnational crime and illegal immigration that jeopardizes the national security and public safety of the country and its citizens. This mission is accomplished through the execution of the more than 400 federal statutes and concentrates on smart immigration application, averting terrorism, and reducing the illegal traffic of people and goods.

ICE-HSI seeks to employ extremely driven and committed men and women who have the ability, resourcefulness, and bravery to carry out the duties that enable them to meet the mission of the agency. The process to becoming a criminal investigator is grueling, and, although security vetting takes three months to complete, it may take up to a year or more to advance to the end of the hiring process. As with the ATF, the starting point is meeting the minimum pre-hire requirements listed at the beginning of this chapter. If you are determined to be a qualified candidate, you will proceed through the steps of the common federal hiring requirements. Although all agencies take part in the stepped eligible candidate hiring requirements, there are specific differences in some of these requirements for ICE-HSI that will be detailed in the following sections.

Step 1: Meet Specific Age Requirements

Applicants must be at least 21 years of age. The day immediately preceding an individual's 37th birthday will be the last day to be referred for selection consideration. However, the age restriction may not apply if you are a preference-eligible veteran, or if you are currently serving or have previously served in a federal civilian law enforcement position covered by Title 5, U.S.C., section 2108, item (3). For additional information, go to the FEDSHIREVETS website at **https://www.fedshirevets.gov/job-seekers/veterans-preference/**.

Step 2: Meet Education and/or Work Experience Qualifications

Entry-level ICE agents should attain, at a minimum, a bachelor's degree. If you received Superior Academic Achievement (SAA) during your undergraduate degree, you would not have to attain the one year of graduate study typically required. To be worthy under this requirement, SSA must have been completed in a curriculum that qualifies you for the position to be filled. SAA is based on *one* of the following:

- Class standing
- Grade point average
- Honor society membership

NOTE

ICE-HSI Special Agents are also known as Criminal Investigators.

For the GL-9 level, possession of a master's degree can waive the required experience necessary. However, the education requirement can be waived by those with sufficient experience and by US veterans. For specific guidelines on waiving certain requirements, click on the career progression tab at **https://www.ice.gov/careers/criminal-investigator**.

Step 3: Take and Pass a Series of Written and Oral Assessments

This step is divided into two stages. In Stage I, you will need to complete the following:

- **Occupational Questionnaire:** Education, experience, and training will be assessed using an online occupational questionnaire. A score between 70 and 100 will be determined based on your answers. If you receive the minimum score requirements for the position, you will proceed to the writing assessment.

- **Writing Assessment:** The writing assessment is a part of Phase I of the ICE Special Agent Test Battery. This test assesses your overall writing ability and includes, but is not limited to, grammar, punctuation, organization, presentation of ideas, vocabulary, and spelling.

- **Candidate Experience Record:** Also a part of the Phase I Special Agent Test Battery, this test assesses your professional and academic experiences related to special agents.

Upon successful completion of Stage I, candidates will proceed to Stage II to complete the following:

- **Special Agent Test Battery Phase II:** This proctored section of the test is administered at more than 500 US testing centers. International testing centers are not available. The Phase II test will assess the following:

    - *Logical reasoning*—tests candidate's ability to understand complex written material and to draw correct conclusions from the information given.

    - *Arithmetic reasoning*—tests candidate's ability to calculate, solve, and express mathematic word problems using different mathematical operations.

    - *Writing abilities*—assesses the candidate's knowledge of standard written English in a coherent and organized manner.

- **Supporting documentation:** Candidates who meet the basic score requirements for the proctored Special Agent Test Battery will also have their resume and necessary supporting documentation checked to confirm that they have met the minimally required criteria for advancement to the next phase.

Chapter 5 of this book details the types of questions you will find on the proctored part of the Special Agent Test Battery. Chapter 6 reviews the basic arithmetic concepts you will need to know to complete the arithmetic reasoning section. Part IV provides a sample practice test to help you cement your learning.

> **NOTE**
> The Writing Assessment and Candidate Experience Record are the first in a series of tests known as the Special Agent Test Battery. These Phase I initial assessments are not proctored, do not need to be facilitated by a testing center, and can be completed from any computer with an internet connection.

Step 4: Participate in a Series of Interviews

If you have made it this far, then you are ready for the structured and personal interviews. These are a series of interviews that will assess your mental and emotional abilities.

Structured Interview

There will be a panel of three senior-level criminal investigators in this interview who will ask situational questions that do not require you to possess technical knowledge to answer. These questions are designed to measure and evaluate your diligence, emotional development, regard for the needs of others, judgment, and decision-making skills. A "pass" must be received to move on to the next interview.

Personal Interview

Two senior-level ICE-HSI management administrators will conduct this interview to review your background and work history. Take note of the following structure of the interview:

- Candidates will first be given information on:
    - ICE-HSI mission
    - ICE-HSI criminal investigator responsibilities
    - Academy and training obligations
    - Work/life adjustments

- Candidates are then asked questions regarding the responsibilities of a criminal investigator. For example:
    - How are you able to handle the duties of working long days, being on-call 24 hours a day seven days a week, available on holidays, and being away for long periods of time?
    - How do you support the agency's needs for candidates to work anywhere and at any time, including remote areas around the United States?

Step 5: Meet the Physical Fitness Standards

Upon successful completion of the series of interviews, candidates will have to participate in and pass the Pre-Employment Physical Fitness Test (PFT-P). The PFT-P is conducted at a local HSI office and will require the following:

- 32 sit-ups in 1 minute or less
- 220-yard sprint in 47.73 seconds or less
- 22 push-ups in 1 minute or less
- 1.5 miles run in 14 minutes 25 seconds or less

These four tests will need to be completed in that order, using proper form, in the time allotted, and with no more than 5 minutes of rest between assessments. After successful completion of the PFT-P, the candidate will continue with the hiring process.

ALERT

If a candidate is offered a criminal investigator position, that candidate is expected to participate in a vigorous physical fitness regimen and then required to pass the Physical Fitness Test (PFT) 3 times.

Subsequent Common Career Requirements

After accomplishing steps 1–5, successful completion of steps 6–10 of the Common Federal Hiring Requirements will advance you through the hiring process. If you are chosen for the criminal investigator position you applied and qualified for, your pay grade is dependent upon education and experience. Your next step will be to travel to FLETC in Glynco, Georgia.

At this time, new special agents must go to the basic Criminal Investigator and Special Agent Training at the FLETC. The courses include the 12-week FLETC Criminal Investigator Training Program (CITP) and the 15-week HSI Special Agent Training (HSISAT). The HSISAT program provides extensive training in agency-specific criminal and immigration law, surveillance and undercover operations, firearms training, court case development, and physical fitness. For additional information about these programs see **https://www.ice.gov/news/releases/ice-hsi-academy-trains-special-agent-candidates**.

FBI-SPECIFIC HIRING REQUIREMENTS FOR A SPECIAL AGENT

The FBI seeks to hire individuals who can bring a unique set of skills that prioritize the core values of the agency and adhere to the mission of the organization—to protect the American people and uphold the Constitution of the United States. The FBI has a series of steps through their Special Agent Selection System (SASS) that allows the organization to assist candidates through the hiring process. It is a psychologically and physically challenging process constructed to recognize the most qualified candidates. The SASS typically takes one year to complete, often longer. As with the ATF and the ICE-HSI agencies, meeting the minimum pre-hire eligibility requirements may pre-qualify you for a position. Although all agencies also take part in common career requirements, there are specific differences in some of these conditions that require further clarification for candidates to the FBI Special Agent position.

Step 1: Meet Specific Age Requirements

Candidates must be between 23 and 36 years of age. Since special agents have a mandated retirement age at 57 years old, they must become a special agent by their 37th birthday. Therefore, candidates must apply for the Special Agent position prior to their 36th birthday to allow sufficient time to complete the SASS. If it is determined that a candidate would reach 37 years of age before selection to the Special Agent position, the FBI may choose to disqualify that individual.

NOTE
Have additional questions about FLETC training? See Appendix A or go to the FAQ section at this link: **https://www.fletc.gov/student-faqs.**

Step 2: Meet Education and/or Work Experience Qualifications

FBI Special Agent candidates must meet the following education and/or work experience qualifications:

- Have a minimum of a bachelor's degree from a US accredited college or university
- Have at least 2 years of full-time professional work experience; or one year if you have earned an advanced degree (master's or higher)
- Professional work experience may come in different capacities and can be identified as:
  - any position requiring a bachelor's degree that includes managerial, supervisory, or leadership responsibilities.
  - beginning a law enforcement career and getting experience on a local or state police force or in a sheriff's department.
  - any high-level management position in professional athletics organizations, including a full-time career with Major League Sports (NFL, NBA, MLB, NHL, etc.) or International Competitions such as the Olympics.
  - full-time volunteer work (Peace Corps), fellowships, and paid graduate work programs. These may be deemed professional work experience and can be verified on a case-by-case basis.
- Internships, seasonal jobs, temporary employment, summer work, and/or volunteer work are NOT typically deemed professional work experience.

After submitting the application and all required documentation, candidates who pass this portion of the screening will be asked to participate in the next phase.

Step 3: Take and Pass a Series of Written and Oral Assessments

Phase I is a computerized and proctored three-hour exam that is comprised of the following five assessments:

1. Logic-Based Reasoning
2. Figural Reasoning
3. Personality Assessment
4. Preferences and Interests
5. Situational Judgment

Phase I must be scheduled within 21 days of invitation. Candidates will receive a pass or fail within one hour of completion.

Upon successful completion of the Phase I testing, candidates will be notified via email to access and complete the Required Information sections of the application. This consists of the following segments:

- Special Agent Physical Fitness Test (SA PFT) self-evaluation
- Critical Skills
- Self-Reported Language

ALERT

To move forward in the process, you must complete and submit the Required Information sections of the application.

Upon successful completion of the Required Information, candidates will be scheduled to appear at the Processing Field Office (PFO) for a Meet and Greet/Review Process opportunity. At this session, evaluators will perform an in-person interview of your application and certify the information you have submitted. Your information will be competitively assessed for Phase II using the Core Competency Evaluation. This category rating system assesses candidates independently on the following competencies:

Core Competency Evaluation

Core Competency	Question Raised
Collaboration	How did you Resolve and Manage Conflict, Demonstrate Political Savvy, Work with Others, and/or Liaise with an employee, coworker, team, or organization?
Communication	How did you Persuade, Listen, and Interpret and/or Share Information with an employee, coworker, team, or organization?
Flexibility/Adaptability	How did you Adapt and Manage Change by yourself, with an employee, coworker, team, or organization?
Initiative	How were you Proactive, how did you Develop Yourself and/or how did you Serve the Public by yourself, with an employee, coworker, team, or organization?
Interpersonal Ability	How did you Establish Rapport with others, Show Sensitivity to Differences, Resolve and Manage Conflict and/or Work with Others to achieve common goals?
Leadership	How did you Mentor, Direct, Inspire and/or Set Strategic Direction for an employee, coworker, team, or organization?
Organizing and Planning	How did you Plan, Prioritize, and Follow Through by yourself, with an employee, coworker, team, or organization?
Problem Solving and Judgment	How did you Identify Problems and Opportunities, Make Decisions, Manage RISKS, and/or Evaluate and Analyze Problems/Situations by yourself, with an employee, coworker, team, or organization?

Upon successful completion of the Meet and Greet/Review Process, a candidate will move into Phase II. This phase has two components: (1) a writing assessment and (2) a structured interview.

Before a candidate is asked to participate in the Structured Interview, the Phase II Writing Assessment must be done first and within 14 days of receiving an invitation from the successful completion of the Meet and Greet. The Phase II Writing Assessment is held in a

NOTE
It takes a candidate an average of 23 weeks to move from Phase I to Phase II.

trained, proctored environment at the local Personal Security Interview (PSI) center. The PSI center allows the candidate to choose a date and time convenient to their schedule.

The writing assessment is 2.5 hours long. The assessment tests your ability to analyze information and assesses your ability to compile two well-written, thorough reports. You should be able to demonstrate your ability to effectively use standard written English. This includes, but is not limited to, grammar, punctuation, organization, presentation of ideas, vocabulary, and spelling (without the use of "spell check" software features). Detailed instructions and writing materials will be provided to candidates so a report can be written based on a fictional scenario. For more information and writing samples, see **https://www.fbijobs.gov/sites/default/files/Testing-Overview.pdf.**

Step 4: Participate in a Series of Interviews

After the successful completion of the Phase II Writing Assessment, the candidate will receive an email invitation to a one-hour long Structured Interview that is performed by a panel of three special agents at one of the nine regional sites. All travel and booking procedures will be given prior to testing and candidates will be compensated for their travel expenses upon conclusion of their travel and the timely submission of travel expense receipts.

At this session, the presentation follows a typical performance-based interview, and the panel uses standardized recording benchmarks to assess the skills that are critical for the Special Agent position. There are no trick questions, and the interview guidelines are straightforward. Keep in mind the following helpful tips:

- Be yourself!
- The panel members do not know anything about you other than your name.
- The panel assessors will take notes during the interview to help them document the findings—do not let this divert your attention.
- Give detailed information when responding to interview questions.
- Give the best illustrations of your abilities and skills, gleaning from ALL your life experiences—not just the most current ones.

Candidates receive their Phase II outcomes within two weeks of completing the tests. If you fail Phase II, you are eligible for retesting at least one year from the interview date. However, not all candidates are asked to retest. Those who meet the FBI's current needs can be invited back for a retest. For those candidates who fail twice, they will be deactivated and deemed ineligible for future opportunities as a Special Agent. Additional retesting information can be found at **https://www.fbijobs.gov/sites/default/files/Testing-Overview.pdf.**

Step 5: Meet the Physical Fitness Standards

After successfully passing Phase II and barring any inclement weather, candidates will need to take part in and pass the Physical Fitness Test (PFT) at least two times during the application period and/or at the FBI Academy. The location and timing of the official PFT can occur:

- At the processing field office shortly after passing Phase II
- No more than 60 days prior to reporting to the Basic Field Training at the FBI Academy
- At least once while at the FBI Academy during the first week of Basic Field Training

The basic PFT entails four main trials, with a fifth trial maintained for those candidates going into the Tactical Recruitment Program (TRP). These trials are used because they accurately measure the candidate's general fitness level in relation to the critical duties presented by the FBI Special Agents. The four main trials are managed in the following order with no more than five minutes of rest between each trial:

- Maximum number of continuous sit-ups in one minute
- Maximum number of continuous pushups (untimed)
- Timed 300-meter sprint
- Timed 1.5-mile run

The Protocol and Scoring Guide can be found at **https://www.fbijobs.gov/sites/default/files/how-to-apply.pdf**.

NOTE

Candidates can request a different BFTC date only once, with sufficient cause, after an initial BFTC date is provided.

Subsequent Common Career Requirements

Upon successful completion of the Phase II and PFT requirements, a Conditional Appointment Offer (CAO) is made. A candidate has five days to accept or turn down the CAO while the remaining common career requirements are completed. The successful completion of this year-long (in many cases longer) SASS will allow the candidates to progress to the FBI Academy if the PFT is not more than 60 days old. Candidates are then allowed to be scheduled for the Basic Field Training Course (BFTC) at the FBI Academy in Quantico, VA. Agent trainees are assigned based on the demands of the FBI and, although paid, they must successfully complete all segments of the BFTC to be completely hired as FBI Special Agents.

SUMMING IT UP

3

- The **application process** is the beginning of an extensive hiring process by the ATF, ICE-HSI, and FBI agencies. The specific **mission** of each agency differs but similarly requires that candidates possess the unique qualities and skill sets that strive to serve the American people and uphold the Constitution of the United States.

- While processes may vary with each of the agencies, a candidate can expect the **hiring process** to take 12–18 months to accomplish. Every step through the hiring process aims to ensure that the best candidates are chosen for the grueling but rewarding job of Special Agent or Criminal Investigator.

- Along with the detailed application, all agencies require candidates to meet the following common **basic prerequisites**:

  - Be a US citizen

  - Possess a current and valid automobile operator's license

  - Meet the Law Enforcement Age Requirement

  - Qualify and maintain firearms proficiency (i.e., must not have been convicted of felonies and certain misdemeanors, including a misdemeanor crime of domestic violence)

- To be eligible for federal employment, male candidates born after December 31, 1959, must certify, at the time of selection, that they have registered with the Selective Service System or are exempt from having to do so under Selective Service law.

- Upon meeting basic prerequisites, each agency requires a list of **common career requirements** designed to meet the specific needs of each of the agencies.

- Candidates must meet specific **age qualifications**.

  - ATF applicants must be at least 21 years of age and not older than 36 at the time of appointment.

  - ICE-HSI applicants must be at least 21 years of age. The day immediately preceding an individual's 37th birthday will be the last day to be referred for selection consideration.

  - FBI candidates must be between 23 and 36 years of age for consideration.

- Candidates must meet **education** and/or **work experience** qualifications.

  - A degree is not required to become an ATF special agent, but a degree, experience in a related field, or a combination of the two is essential for the position.

  - Entry-level ICE agents should attain, at a minimum, a bachelor's degree.

  - FBI candidates need to have a minimum of a bachelor's degree from a US accredited college or university, have at least two years of full-time professional work experience, or have one year of full-time professional work experience if the candidate has earned an advanced degree (master's or higher).

- Candidates must take the applicable series of **written and oral assessments**.

  - ATF Special Agent exams measure a candidate's verbal, quantitative, and investigative reasonings while the ATF Special Agent Applicant Assessment Test measures a candidate's personality and preference.

  - The ICE-HSI Special Agent battery of tests are administered in two stages.

    - Stage I consists of three parts: the Occupational Questionnaire, the Writing Assessment, and the Candidate Experience Record

    - Stage II also consists of three parts: Logical Reasoning, Arithmetic Reasoning, and Writing Abilities

  - FBI Phase I tests are divided into five assessments: Logic-Based Reasoning, Figural Reasoning, Personality Assessment, Preferences and Interests, and Situational Judgment. Upon passing, the FBI administers the Required Information test, consisting of the Special Agent Physical Fitness Test (SA PFT) self-evaluation, Critical Skills, and Self-Reported Language.

- Each agency has a series of **Physical Fitness Tests** that candidates must take (and pass) to measure their abilities to meet the physical demands of every special agent position within their respective roles.

- Every agency administers its own set of **panel and personal interviews** to assess a candidate's abilities to handle possible situations with respect to the job requirements. These interviews address communication skills, ability to handle stress, basic knowledge of roles, and other important skill sets necessary to meet the demands of these roles.

- Each agency also has similar common career requirements that each candidate, within their respective agency, must meet and pass in order to advance in the hiring process. These include the following conditions:

  - Take and pass a drug test.

  - Successfully complete a background investigation for a top-secret security clearance. This will include employment verifications, criminal and credit history checks, and fingerprinting.

  - Take and successfully complete a polygraph examination.

  - Carry a firearm and be willing to use deadly force, if necessary.

- Once candidates have met and passed ALL the preceding requirements, they are offered a Special Agent or Criminal Investigator position. Each candidate is then required to fulfill a series of on-the-job training programs at their respective agency's academy facilities.

PART II
DIAGNOSTIC TESTS

Chapter 4

ATF, ICE, and FBI Diagnostic Tests

OVERVIEW

INTRODUCTION TO THE DIAGNOSTIC TEST

The purpose of a diagnostic test is twofold: (1) to introduce you to the type of questions you will find on the actual test and (2) to highlight your strengths and weaknesses. The following pages present three different diagnostic tests, one for each of the special agent disciplines. The structure of each of the tests mimics what you will encounter on the actual test. While the types of questions you will encounter on the diagnostic test are reflective of the types of questions you will find on the actual test, the number of questions on the diagnostic test only constitutes a small sampling of the number of questions that will be presented on the actual test.

At the beginning of each diagnostic test, you will find a recommended time allotment. Use this maximum time limit to gauge your test-taking performance under time constraints.

When you are finished, check your answers against the answer key, and read the detailed answer explanations. Where applicable, step-by-step breakdowns of mathematical solutions are provided.

An Assessment Grid is provided at the end of each test. This grid breaks down, by question number, the types of questions on the test. Use this grid to assess your strengths and pinpoint the areas where you need improvement.

ATF DIAGNOSTIC TEST ANSWER SHEET

1. Ⓐ Ⓑ Ⓒ Ⓓ Ⓔ   6. Ⓐ Ⓑ Ⓒ Ⓓ Ⓔ   11. Ⓐ Ⓑ   16. Ⓐ Ⓑ Ⓒ Ⓓ Ⓔ

2. Ⓐ Ⓑ Ⓒ Ⓓ Ⓔ   7. Ⓐ Ⓑ Ⓒ Ⓓ Ⓔ   12. Ⓐ Ⓑ   17. Ⓐ Ⓑ Ⓒ Ⓓ Ⓔ

3. Ⓐ Ⓑ Ⓒ Ⓓ Ⓔ   8. Ⓐ Ⓑ Ⓒ Ⓓ Ⓔ   13. Ⓐ Ⓑ   18. Ⓐ Ⓑ Ⓒ Ⓓ Ⓔ

4. Ⓐ Ⓑ Ⓒ Ⓓ Ⓔ   9. Ⓐ Ⓑ Ⓒ Ⓓ Ⓔ   14. Ⓐ Ⓑ Ⓒ Ⓓ Ⓔ   19. Ⓐ Ⓑ Ⓒ Ⓓ Ⓔ

5. Ⓐ Ⓑ Ⓒ Ⓓ Ⓔ   10. Ⓐ Ⓑ Ⓒ Ⓓ Ⓔ   15. Ⓐ Ⓑ Ⓒ Ⓓ Ⓔ   20. Ⓐ Ⓑ Ⓒ Ⓓ Ⓔ

ATF DIAGNOSTIC TEST

30 Minutes—20 Questions

DIRECTIONS: For Questions 1–6, you will be given a paragraph that contains all the information necessary to infer the correct answer. Use **only** the information provided in the paragraph. Do not make any assumptions or consider information beyond what is presented. Also, assume that all information given in the paragraph is true, even if it conflicts with some fact known to you. Only one correct answer is possible based on the information in the paragraph.

1. Special agents suspect there is an illegal narcotics ring in a home in an affluent neighborhood. The agents legally obtain evidence by observing people leaving and arriving to the house, many of whom do not seem to be part of the same family. The agents also legally obtain tips from neighbors and take photos of suspicious activities at all times of the day and night. Agents believe they have probable cause to request a search warrant. Probable cause exists when facts and circumstances known to the agents would lead a reasonable person to believe a crime has been committed.

   From the information provided above, it can be validly concluded that:

   A. The request for a search warrant will be granted because the agents have provided enough information for probable cause.

   B. The request for a search warrant will be granted because the agents have violated the reasonable right to privacy.

   C. The request for a search warrant will be granted because the agents used credible witnesses.

   D. The request for a search warrant will be denied because all the evidence was obtained illegally.

   E. The request for a search warrant will be denied because the evidence was obtained before the warrant was issued.

2. While at a gas station, an agent sees Mr. Smith selling individual jars of liquid from the back of his truck to the gas station customers. The agent suspects he is selling moonshine illegally and calls into his office to request backup from fellow agents. The agent decides to get closer to the truck and smells a strong alcohol odor. He portrays himself as a customer and purchases two jars of the liquid. Right after the purchase, Mr. Smith is arrested and read his rights, and all contents of his truck are secured. At his trial for possession of a controlled substance, Mr. Smith's attorney makes a motion to suppress the evidence found in his client's vehicle. The presiding ATF counsel counters by stating that evidence in a trial is deemed admissible if it is relevant to the case and if it is obtained by a reliable source.

   From the information provided above, it can be validly concluded that:

   A. The two jars purchased by the agent will be admitted, while the contents found in the truck will be suppressed.

   B. The contents in the truck will be admitted, while the two jars purchased by the agent will be suppressed.

   C. All the evidence is admissible.

   D. None of the evidence is admissible.

   E. Mr. Smith's rights were not read, and therefore, the evidence is not admissible.

3. Flint's Auto Shop has been operating for 20 years providing car care services. During that time, patrons have suspected illegal arms activity has been taking place at Flint's, but, with fear permeating the community, they have never reported their suspicions. Throughout the years, special agents have been given necessary information but not enough to indict the owners of Flint's Auto Shop for arms dealing. The agents are patiently waiting for timely, reliable, and reasonable evidence to establish probable cause for a search. On February 8, 2018, an established and reliable informant, Tom, told the special agents that he saw a major arms deal negotiated between the owners of the auto shop and the locally known drug dealers that took place on May 10, 2017. The senior agent on the case applies for a search warrant for guns solely based on this information.

From the information provided above, it can be validly concluded that:

A. The request for the search warrant will be denied because the officer did not verify the information provided by Tom.

B. The request for the search warrant will be denied because the information provided by Tom is insufficient to establish probable cause.

C. The request for the search warrant will be granted because the agent has demonstrated probable cause.

D. The request for the search warrant will be granted because Tom meets the standards of the Aguilar Spinelli test.

E. The request for the search warrant will be granted because the senior agent meets the standard of the Aguilar Spinelli test.

4. The Simoni crime family owns several nightclubs in Grantham County and has been known to serve alcohol to underage patrons. After the nightclubs failed three mandated compliance checks of underage alcohol sales, Agent Jeff was assigned as the lead investigator in a six-month-long sting operation. A second agent was assigned to the case to pose as an underage customer. Four months into the operation, an associate of the Simoni family threatened the safety of the undercover agent and, in the process, compromised the agent's identity. In a last-minute attempt to keep the case from dissolving and to keep the undercover agent safe, Agent Jeff sought an emergency arrest warrant of key Simoni family members. Agent Jeff considered the circumstances of the case to be exigent, meaning that making these arrests would keep the undercover agent safe and allow the investigation to continue. Agent Jeff also took into consideration that the Simoni family was a potential flight risk since they own homes in other countries.

From the information provided above, it can be validly concluded that:

A. The emergency arrest warrant was denied because the Simoni crime family is not a flight risk.

B. The emergency arrest warrant was denied because, under exigent circumstances, the consequences of the law enforcement have not been compromised.

C. The emergency arrest warrant was denied because the attempt to keep the case open is irrelevant while the safety of the undercover agent is of the utmost importance.

D. The emergency arrest warrant was granted because the agents have insufficient evidence to believe that the key members of the Simoni family will bring harm to the undercover agent and destroy evidence.

E. The emergency arrest warrant was granted because, under exigent circumstances, it is necessary to prevent physical harm to the undercover agent and to remove any factors that could improperly frustrate legitimate law enforcement efforts.

5. While entering the courthouse for a misdemeanor traffic violation hearing, Cathy was required to place all her belongings through a magnetometer as a standard measure of practice for all government facilities. During the routine inspection of her briefcase for explosives, it was discovered that the briefcase had a suspicious small package. The security officer escorted Cathy to a private area and asked her if he could search the contents of her briefcase. She expressed that she was running late to her hearing and did not have time to go through this process. The officer explained to her that no one is allowed into the courthouse without inspection of personal belongings and that searches in a federal courthouse comply with the Fourth Amendment's reasonable right to privacy. After a short debate, Cathy relented and allowed the security officer to open her briefcase. Upon inspection of the briefcase, it was discovered that it contained two small bags of a white powdery substance. A drug-detection dog was brought in to smell the contents of the bags, and it was determined that the substance was cocaine.

   From the information provided above, it can be validly concluded that:

   A. Cathy's Fourth Amendment rights were violated because the inspection infringed on her right to reasonable privacy.

   B. Cathy's Fourth Amendment rights were violated because she did not give her permission to search her briefcase.

   C. Cathy's Fourth Amendment rights were violated because the security officer had no probable cause that there were explosives in her briefcase.

   D. Cathy's Fourth Amendment rights were not violated because the search was in compliance with the Fourth Amendment.

   E. Cathy's Fourth Amendment rights were not violated because there was probable cause to search her briefcase for cocaine.

6. Explosives are defined as substances or devices capable of producing a volume of rapidly expanding gases that exert a sudden pressure on their surroundings. Although there are mechanical and nuclear explosives, the most common explosives are chemical. All mechanical explosive devices produce a physical reaction, such as that caused by overloading a container with compressed air. While nuclear explosives are by far the most powerful, they have all been limited to military weapon use.

   From the information provided above, it can be validly concluded that:

   A. All explosives that have been limited to military weapons use are nuclear explosives.

   B. All mechanical explosives are produced by overloading a container with compressed air.

   C. Some nuclear explosives have not been restricted to military weapon use.

   D. No chemical explosives have been restricted to military weapon use.

   E. Some devices in which a physical reaction is produced, such as that caused by overloading a container with compressed air, are mechanical explosives.

7. A telephone conversation with a new witness is taking longer than expected. The allocated time for the conversation was 62 minutes, but the actual conversation lasted 2.25 hours. How many extra minutes did the conversation last?

    A. 60 min.

    B. 66 min.

    C. 73 min.

    D. 135 min.

    E. 197 min.

8. Each afternoon, Agent Brunswick takes a stroll during his break. If his stride is 2.5 feet and his goal is one mile, how many strides will he have to take to reach his goal?

    A. 912

    B. 1,312

    C. 1,712

    D. 2,112

    E. 2,512

9. At the weekly staff meeting, there are always breakfast-to-go bags that include either a breakfast biscuit sandwich, vegetarian breakfast burrito, or a bagel. Today there are 9 breakfast biscuit bags, 8 breakfast burrito bags, and 6 bagel bags. If the unmarked bags are set on a table, what is the probability of selecting a bagel breakfast-to-go bag?

    A. $\frac{5}{23}$

    B. $\frac{6}{23}$

    C. $\frac{1}{3}$

    D. $\frac{1}{2}$

    E. $\frac{17}{23}$

10. To gather background information on a new case, Agent Stelly must read 156 pages from a classified file. She reads at a rate of 13 pages per minute and allows herself a 5-minute break after every 52 pages. Based on this information, how long will it take her to read the entire file?

    A. 12 minutes

    B. 13 minutes

    C. 17 minutes

    D. 22 minutes

    E. 27 minutes

> **DIRECTIONS:** For Questions 11–13, read the scenario carefully and then evaluate each conclusion using the following options:
>
> • True, which means that you can infer the conclusion from the facts presented.
>
> • False, which means that the conclusion cannot be true given the facts presented.

The Federal Communications Commission (FCC) is a government regulations commission created under the Communications Act of 1934. The role of the FCC is to serve as a regulator of public airwaves and broadcasting media, requiring all radio and television stations to apply for licensing as long as they agree to follow FCC rules and regulations. The FCC is also responsible for media ownership limits that prevent monopolies of coverage and information and for censorship of materials deemed inappropriate for mass broadcasting.

In order to maintain their licenses, broadcasting stations must be cognizant of the equal time rule, which requires all noncable and radio stations to grant equal opportunities for airtime and advertising to registered candidates running for public office. The rates must be equal; candidates may advertise beginning forty-five days before a primary election and sixty-days before a general election. A request for equal opportunity under this rule must be submitted within one week of the day an opportunity is initially given to the first candidate. For instance, if a television show were to grant 12 minutes and 5 seconds to Candidate A in the general election, then that same time must be granted to Candidate B as long as Candidate B submits the request within one week of the day that Candidate A appears on air.

However, the FCC waives the equal time rule in cases of newscasting. If a newscaster or guest on a news channel were to speak solely on the actions of a candidate, cover a political rally, or secure a short/spontaneous interview with a candidate, the equal time rule would not apply. Another loophole to the equal time rule arises in the form of supporters. As long as the candidate does not appear in the material, a station may give airtime to the supporters of one candidate without giving equal time to the supporters of the other candidate.

11. If ZBZ News were to broadcast 5 minutes and 26 seconds of station anchor Bobbi Dryden on the scene of a Republican presidential candidate's political rally, it is obligated, under FCC regulations and the equal-time rule, to broadcast 5 minutes and 26 seconds of a Democratic presidential candidate's political rally.

    A. True

    B. False

12. Radio station WRAL reserves the right to give advertising time to supporters of a particular candidate and not another because it is a radio station and not a television station.

    A. True

    B. False

13. If TV station WBS were to charge a political candidate $200,000 for a 30-second spot of advertising on their network 30 days before a primary election, it must give the same price and time to the opposing political candidate 28 days before the primary election.

    A. True

    B. False

DIRECTIONS: For Questions 14–20, you will be presented with a paragraph and several related statements. Read them carefully, then answer the questions that follow the investigative situation. You may refer to the paragraph and statements as often as needed.

Jahmal Washington, age 67, wrote a letter to the Social Security Administration requesting a determination of the monthly retirement benefit that he would be eligible to receive at age 68. The letter that he received from Social Security informed Mr. Washington that his retirement benefits would be minimal. Although he had been a regular contributor to the Social Security system for 28 years, his level of contributions at that time had been very low, and he had made no contributions at all over the last 15 years. Because Mr. Washington's contributions had been made before the big inflationary jump in salaries and in most people's contributions, his benefits were to be calculated on a very low base. Mr. Washington strongly contested the Social Security determination on the grounds that he had not interrupted his contribution history.

During the course of the investigation, the following statements were made:

1. *Jahmal Washington stated that for the past 15 years he had been employed as supervisor of the distribution center at Erwin Cotton Mills, Inc.*

2. *Alejandro Torres, operating manager and chief stockholder of Erwin Cotton Mills, said that Jahmal Washington had indeed been employed at the mill for the past 15 years.*

3. *Jahmal Washington stated that he had had his FICA contribution withheld from every paycheck throughout his working life.*

4. *Tom Feroni, bookkeeper, said that Erwin Cotton Mills was an extremely profitable business.*

5. *Frank Razo, company treasurer, said that Erwin Cotton Mills always made timely payments to the IRS to cover employment taxes for all its employees.*

6. *Denise Jones, IRS spokesperson, said that Erwin Cotton Mills filed and paid employment taxes for a very short payroll.*

7. *Social Security spokesperson Katherine Rogowski said that, in the past 15 years, Erwin Cotton Mills had never filed a W-2 for Jahmal Washington.*

8. *Linwood Ryan, president of Bennett Cotton and Textiles, said that Jahmal Washington had been a fine employee and that he had hated to lose him to Erwin Cotton Mills 15 years ago when he couldn't match their salary offer.*

9. *Tom McRogers, auditor, said that Erwin Cotton Mills' books appeared to be in perfect order.*

10. *John Schmitz, a former Erwin Cotton Mills employee, said that he had left the company because he felt that there was something illegitimate about the operation.*

14. Which two statements together indicate that Jahmal Washington is justified in his protest of the Social Security determination?

   A. Statements 1 and 3
   B. Statements 1 and 8
   C. Statements 2 and 6
   D. Statements 4 and 10
   E. Statements 6 and 7

15. Which statement might be classified as a character reference?

   A. Statement 2
   B. Statement 5
   C. Statement 6
   D. Statement 8
   E. Statement 10

16. Which statement seems to lend some legitimacy to Statement 10?

   A. Statement 2
   B. Statement 4
   C. Statement 5
   D. Statement 7
   E. Statement 9

17. Which statement casts suspicion on Frank Razo?

   A. Statement 4
   B. Statement 6
   C. Statement 7
   D. Statement 9
   E. Statement 10

18. Which statement, along with Statement 7, would likely trigger an investigation on suspicion of fraud?

   A. Statement 2
   B. Statement 4
   C. Statement 6
   D. Statement 9
   E. Statement 10

19. Which two statements seem directly contradictory?

   A. Statements 1 and 2
   B. Statements 3 and 7
   C. Statements 4 and 6
   D. Statements 4 and 8
   E. Statements 4 and 9

20. Which statement could indicate either a clever cover-up or collusion?

   A. Statement 3
   B. Statement 4
   C. Statement 6
   D. Statement 8
   E. Statement 9

ANSWER KEY AND EXPLANATIONS

1. A	6. E	11. B	16. D
2. C	7. C	12. B	17. C
3. B	8. D	13. A	18. A
4. E	9. B	14. A	19. B
5. D	10. D	15. D	20. E

1. **The correct answer is A.** The paragraph indicates that the agents legally observed numerous unrelated people come and go from the home. They were also able to legally photo document "suspicious activity" as well as obtain tips from neighbors. Based on the definition of probable cause given in the last sentence, it is reasonable to conclude that the request for a search warrant will be granted because the agents have provided enough information for probable cause. Choice B is incorrect because the agents have not violated the reasonable right to privacy. The credibility of the witnesses cannot be inferred from the information given, so choice C can be eliminated. None of the evidence mentioned was illegally obtained, thereby eliminating choice D as well. Choice E doesn't make sense. Judges issue warrants if they agree, based on totality of the circumstances, that adequate cause exists.

2. **The correct answer is C.** Based on the information given, the agent observed the activities, called in for backup, obtained evidence, made the arrest, read the suspect his rights, and the evidence was secured. Therefore, it is reasonable to assume that protocol was followed, and it can be inferred that all the evidence obtained is admissible, thus eliminating choices A, B, and D as valid conclusions. The fifth sentence states that Mr. Smith was read his rights, so choice E cannot be correct.

3. **The correct answer is B.** The fourth sentence indicates that the agents are waiting for timely, reliable, and reasonable evidence to establish probable cause. Tom revealed what he had witnessed nearly nine months after the fact, which calls into question the timeliness and reliability of his recollection of the events he witnessed. Therefore, it can be validly concluded that the request for the search warrant will be denied based on a lack of probable cause. This eliminates choice C. Because the information is insufficient, its verification (choice A) is not a factor. Choices D and E are incorrect because the paragraph does not provide information regarding the standards of the Aguilar Spinelli test.

4. **The correct answer is E.** Based on the information given, the identity of the undercover agent was compromised by an associate of the Simoni family. It is reasonable then to believe the undercover agent's life was in imminent danger and that any evidence collected through the agent during the sting operation would have been compromised. Therefore, there is sufficient evidence presented to conclude that exigent circumstances exist, and the emergency arrest warrant was granted. Choice A is incorrect because it would be unreasonable to conclude that the Simoni family was not a flight risk since they have homes in other countries. Choices B, C, and D misapply the concept of exigent circumstances.

5. **The correct answer is D.** The paragraph states that it is standard practice for individuals entering the courthouse to be subject to having belongings run through a magnetometer. This is standard for all government facilities. When the security offer saw something suspicious, he was lawfully required to investigate further. This is not an infringement on Cathy's rights. Administrative inspections, though warrantless, are permissible under the Fourth Amendment. Therefore, searches in a federal courthouse comply with the Fourth Amendment. This eliminates choices A, B, and C. There is no indication of probable cause to support sufficient suspicion that Cathy had any drug paraphernalia in her possession, so choice E is not a valid conclusion.

6. **The correct answer is E.** The third sentence states the overlap between all mechanical explosives and devices in which a physical reaction is produced, such as that caused by overloading a container with compressed air. From this, we can safely conclude that some devices in which a physical reaction is produced, such as that caused by overloading a container with compressed air, are mechanical explosives. Choice A is incorrect because the paragraph does not provide sufficient information to validly conclude that all explosives that have been restricted to military weapons are nuclear weapons. It may be that some types of explosives other than nuclear weapons also have been restricted to military weapons. Choice B takes the relationship between mechanical explosives and the example of the container of compressed air to an extreme. The conclusion in choice C contradicts the last sentence. While the paragraph does state that chemical explosives are the most common, the conclusion provided in choice D cannot be reached since there is a lack of reference to military restriction and ease of access.

7. **The correct answer is C.** Start by multiplying the number of hours the conversation lasted by 60 (the number of minutes in an hour). Then subtract 62 (the allocated time) from the resulting number to solve.

$$2.25 \times 60 = 135 \text{ min.}$$
$$135 - 62 = 73 \text{ min.}$$

8. **The correct answer is D.** There are 5,280 feet in a mile. Divide this number by 2.5 feet:

$$\frac{5,280}{2.5} = 2,112 \text{ strides}$$

9. **The correct answer is B.** The probability of selecting a bagel breakfast to-go bag is the number of bagel breakfast to-go bags divided by the total number of breakfast to-go bags.

$$\frac{6}{(9 + 8 + 6)} = \frac{6}{23}$$

10. **The correct answer is D.** Divide the number of pages read by 13 to find the number of minutes Agent Stelly spent reading:

$$\frac{156 \text{ pages}}{13 \text{ pages per min.}} = 12 \text{ min.}$$

Then divide the number of pages read by 52 to find the number of breaks that she took:

$$\frac{156 \text{ pages}}{52 \text{ pages per break}} = 3 \text{ breaks}$$

Since the third break would technically occur after Agent Stelly finished reading the entire file, we factor only 2 of the breaks into the total minutes. Multiply the 2 breaks by the time spent per break:

$$2 \text{ breaks} \times 5 \text{ min.} = 10 \text{ min.}$$

Finally, add the times to solve:

$$12 \text{ min.} + 10 \text{ min.} = 22 \text{ min.}$$

11. **The correct answer is B.** The statement is FALSE; the equal time rule does not extend to newscasters and political rallies.

12. **The correct answer is B.** The statement is FALSE; the station reserves the right to give advertising to supporters of a particular candidate, *not* because it is a radio station, but because the equal time rule does not extend to supporters.

13. **The correct answer is A.** The statement is TRUE; the equal opportunity rule states that a request for equal opportunity must be submitted within a week of its prior use ("use" in this case meaning the first broadcast).

14. **The correct answer is A.** The fact that he had been working in a supervisory position, presumably at a fairly high salary, for fifteen years (Statement 1) and the fact that his FICA contribution had regularly been withheld (Statement 3) most certainly justified Jahmal Washington's challenge to the Social Security Administration's determination of benefits.

15. **The correct answer is D.** Basically, Linwood Ryan's statement (Statement 8) is nothing more than a character reference for Mr. Washington; however, it does serve to corroborate the fact that Mr. Washington began work for Erwin Cotton Mills 15 years ago and that he received a good salary in his position there.

16. **The correct answer is D.** In Statement 10, John Schmitz presents no evidence; his statement is strictly one of opinion. However, Statement 7 gives us pause that there may be some truth to what John Schmitz says. The fact that Erwin Cotton Mills never filed W-2 forms and presumably never paid taxes related to Jahmal Washington's employment and salary lends credence to Schmitz's hunch that not all aspects of the business were strictly in accordance with law.

17. **The correct answer is C.** Frank Razo, the company treasurer, who certainly should have been well-informed as to the financial operations of the company, claimed that employment taxes were paid covering all employees of the company. However, the Social Security spokesperson stated in Statement 7 that Jahmal Washington had not been issued a W-2 in the past 15 years.

18. **The correct answer is A.** The fact that a person had worked in one place for 15 years in itself would raise no eyebrows, nor would the fact that no W-2s were filed for any one individual. However, the assertion by the manager of the company that Jahmal Washington was employed by his company (Statement 2) combined with the statement by the Social Security Administration that the company had made no filings on behalf of that individual should raise suspicions about the company's practices and should immediately trigger an investigation and audit.

19. **The correct answer is B.** Jahmal Washington saw the regular deductions being taken from his paycheck and, presumably, saw the total each year on the W-2 copies that he received, yet the Social Security Administration claimed that the original W-2s had never been filed and that it was unaware of his employment over the last 15 years.

20. **The correct answer is E.** In Statement 9, the auditor, Tom McRogers, stated that the company's books appeared to be in perfect order. Either the fraud was so cleverly executed as to escape detection by the auditor, or the auditor was in some way party to the scheme.

ASSESSMENT GRID

The following table breaks down the questions on this ATF Diagnostic Test by question-type. Find the question numbers and question-types that gave you trouble and those you may need to spend more focused study-time on. Then read through Chapters 5 and 6 of this book, paying extra attention to the areas where you feel you need to improve.

Question Type	Question Number
Verbal Reasoning	1-6
Quantitative Reasoning, Section 1	7-10
Quantitative Reasoning, Section 2	11-13
Investigative Reasoning	14-20

ICE DIAGNOSTIC TEST ANSWER SHEET

1. (A) (B) (C) (D) (E)   6. (A) (B) (C) (D) (E)   11. (A) (B) (C) (D) (E)   16. (A) (B) (C) (D) (E)

2. (A) (B) (C) (D) (E)   7. (A) (B) (C) (D) (E)   12. (A) (B) (C) (D)   17. (A) (B) (C) (D) (E)

3. (A) (B) (C) (D) (E)   8. (A) (B) (C) (D) (E)   13. (A) (B) (C) (D)   18. (A) (B) (C) (D) (E)

4. (A) (B) (C) (D) (E)   9. (A) (B) (C) (D) (E)   14. (A) (B) (C) (D)   19. (A) (B) (C) (D) (E)

5. (A) (B) (C) (D) (E)   10. (A) (B) (C) (D) (E)   15. (A) (B) (C) (D)   20. (A) (B) (C) (D) (E)

ICE DIAGNOSTIC TEST

30 Minutes—20 Questions

DIRECTIONS: For Questions 1–4, select the only answer that *can* be validly concluded or the only answer that *cannot* be validly concluded from the related paragraph. Using only the information provided in the paragraph, make a logical conclusion based on what is presented. Assume all the information in the paragraph is true, even if it conflicts with some fact known to you.

---

1. The Federal Communications Commission (FCC) is a government regulations commission responsible for regulating all public airwaves and broadcasting media in the United States. If the FCC wishes to change or adopt a new rule, then they must first release a Notice of Proposed Rule-making (NPRM) and ask for public comment. After receiving public comment, the FCC can adopt some or all proposed rules, adopt a modified version of some or all proposed rules, ask for public comment on additional issues, or end the rulemaking without adopting or changing any rules at all.

   From the information given above, it can be validly concluded that

   A. after receiving public comment, the FCC always adopts either some or all of the proposed rules.

   B. when considering changing or adopting a new rule, the FCC can either release an NPRM or ask for public comment.

   C. if the FCC does not wish to change or adopt a new rule, then they must not release an NPRM and ask for public comment.

   D. the FCC must always change or adopt a new rule if they release an NPRM.

   E. some public airwaves and broadcasting media in the United States are not regulated by the FCC.

2. When undergoing arrest or interrogation for illegal immigration, both officers and detainees must be aware of their rights. All persons being detained have the right to remain silent and to refuse to discuss their citizenship status with the arresting officer. Agents do not have the right to search any person or their personal belongings without probable cause. However, if a detainee is a legal immigrant over the age of 18, then they must show their immigration papers to the arresting officer upon request.

   From the information given above, it can be validly concluded that

   A. if a detainee is under the age of 18, then they must not show their immigration papers to the arresting officer upon request.

   B. if a person is not a detainee that is a legal immigrant over the age of 18, then they must not show their immigration papers to an arresting officer upon request.

   C. no persons being detained are not illegal immigrants.

   D. some persons being detained are illegal immigrants and do not have the right to remain silent and to refuse to discuss their citizenship status with the arresting officer.

   E. if a person who is an illegal immigrant is being detained, then they do not have the right to remain silent and to refuse to discuss their citizenship status with the arresting officer.

3. When entering the country through border security, all persons must undergo customs processing. If a person is a lawful permanent resident (LPR) who has maintained their status as an LPR, then that person is only required to answer questions pertaining to their identity and permanent residency. No person who is an LPR can be denied entry into the country for failure to answer other questions. If a person is a noncitizen visa holder, then they may be denied entry into the country for failing to answer other questions.

From the information given above, it can be validly concluded that

A. if a person is not an LPR, then they can be denied entry into the country for failure to answer other questions.

B. if a person fails to answer other questions not pertaining to identity or permanent residency, then they must not be an LPR.

C. if a person is an LPR, then they are not required to answer any questions posed to them.

D. no person who is a noncitizen visa holder can be denied entry into the country.

E. all persons who are denied entry into the country are noncitizen visa holders.

4. The Legal Immigration and Family Equity (LIFE) Act of 2000 provided relief for some members of the "late legalization" class-action lawsuits. Only individuals who were wrongly denied amnesty under the Immigration Reform and Control Act (IRCA) of 1986 or individuals who were members of three class-action lawsuits against the government were given relief under this provision. This relief allowed all qualifying individuals to file for new adjustment applications. Eva was not a member of one of the three class-action lawsuits against the government, but she was wrongly denied amnesty under the 1986 IRCA law.

From the information given above, it can be validly concluded that

A. Eva is not a qualifying individual for relief under any provision of LIFE.

B. Eva is a qualifying individual and is due the right to file for new adjustment applications.

C. all members of the "late legalization" class-action lawsuits are due relief under LIFE.

D. some individuals who were denied amnesty under the 1986 IRCA law do not qualify for relief.

E. all qualifying individuals were wrongly denied amnesty under the 1986 IRCA law.

DIRECTIONS: In Questions 5–10, mathematical questions are presented in the form of word problems. You must extrapolate the data and compute the correct answer based on the information provided. If the exact answer is not given as one of the response choices, select *E. none of these.*

5. Agent Maurice bought 10 new notepads at $6.00 each and 5 pens at $2.00 each. How much did he pay in total?

   A. $30.00

   B. $50.00

   C. $60.00

   D. $70.00

   E. none of these

6. The customs office has a total area of 450 square feet. If the front side of the office is 40 feet wide, how long is the left side of the office?

   A. 11.25 ft.

   B. 15.25 ft.

   C. 22.25 ft.

   D. 490 ft.

   E. none of these

7. The sum of two consecutive even integers is 26. What are the two numbers?

   A. 12 and 14

   B. 13 and 13

   C. 13 and 14

   D. 14 and 16

   E. none of these

8. Bethany has six times as many dimes as quarters in her desk drawer. She has a total of 21 coins totaling $2.55. How many dimes does she have?

   A. 21

   B. 18

   C. 12

   D. 6

   E. none of these

9. Senior Agent Pulaski's son, Salvatore, is 4 years older than his brother, Jude Thaddeus. Jude Thaddeus is 13 years old. What age will Salvatore be when Jude Thaddeus is twice as old as he is now?

   A. 30

   B. 24

   C. 22

   D. 20

   E. none of these

10. The cost of fuel rises by 2 cents a gallon. Last week, ICE Agent Jules bought 20 gallons at the old price. This week, he bought 10 gallons at the new price. Altogether, the fuel costs $60.20. What's the new price for 1 gallon?

   A. $3.00

   B. $2.50

   C. $2.00

   D. $1.85

   E. none of these

DIRECTIONS: For Question 11, select the one option that represents a change that should be made to correct the sentence. If no change is needed, choose *E. No correction is necessary.*

---

11. After completing an investigation, each agent that worked on the case is required to submit a individual summary report.

   A. Change <u>a individual</u> to <u>an individual</u>
   B. Change <u>submit</u> to <u>submits</u>
   C. Change <u>individual</u> to <u>individually</u>
   D. Change <u>report</u> to <u>reports</u>
   E. No correction is necessary

DIRECTIONS: For Questions 12 and 13, select the one option that is correctly punctuated.

---

12. A. Its important to keep your shoes and brass polished at all times so that you will be ready whenever the call to perform comes.

   B. It's important to keep your shoes, and brass polished at all times so that you will be ready whenever the call to perform comes.

   C. Its important to keep your shoes, and brass polished at all times so that you will be ready whenever the call to perform comes.

   D. It's important to keep your shoes and brass polished at all times so that you will be ready whenever the call to perform comes.

13. A. When preparing for an investigation, read all supporting documents, and research any area that is new to you.

   B. When preparing for an investigation read all supporting, documents, and research any area that is new to you.

   C. When, preparing for an investigation, read all supporting documents and research any area that is new to you.

   D. When preparing for an investigation read all supporting documents and research any area that is new to you

---

DIRECTIONS: For Questions 14 and 15, select the one sentence that uses the correct capitalization.

---

14. **A.** The US Immigration and Customs Enforcement (ICE) has announced that Special Agent Brown will head their Guam office.

   B. The US Immigration and Customs Enforcement (ice) has announced that Special Agent Brown will head their Guam office.

   C. The US Immigration and Customs Enforcement (ICE) has announced that special agent Brown will head their Guam office.

   D. The US Immigration and Customs Enforcement (ICE) has announced that special Agent Brown will head their guam Office.

15. **A.** On May 16, 1987, Shadow wolf Officers, based on the Native American Tohono O'odham Nation in southern Arizona, arrested six men and women attempting to smuggle drugs across the border.

   B. On may 16, 1987, shadow wolf officers, based on the Native American Tohono O'odham Nation in southern Arizona, arrested six men and women attempting to smuggle drugs across the border.

   C. On May 16, 1987, Shadow Wolf officers, based on the native american tohono O'odham nation in southern Arizona, arrested six men and women attempting to smuggle drugs across the border.

   D. On May 16, 1987, Shadow Wolf officers, based on the Native American Tohono O'odham Nation in southern Arizona, arrested six men and women attempting to smuggle drugs across the border.

DIRECTIONS: For Questions 16–18, select the one option that correctly spells the missing word in the sentence.

---

16. For any _____ from a training day, excused or not, a cadet must submit a report to the team leader.

   A. absence

   B. abcense

   C. absance

   D. absentes

   E. absented

17. It is important to _____ the contributions of all agencies involved in the capture of the criminals.

  A. acknowlege

  B. aknowledge

  C. acknowledge

  D. adknowlege

  E. acnowledge

18. Each person's name must begin with a _____ letter.

  A. capitol

  B. capital

  C. Captail

  D. captoil

  E. chapital

DIRECTIONS: For Question 19, select the correct sentence order to form a clear, concise, and coherent paragraph. If no correction is necessary, choose *E. no correction is necessary.*

19.

  1. US Immigration and Customs Enforcement (ICE) has oversight of 400 programs designed to protect the security and public safety of the citizens of the United States.

  2. Some of the programs that are under ICE oversight are the Criminal Alien Program (CAP), the Cultural Property, Art and Antiquities (CPAA) Program, and the Victim Assistance Program.

  3. With so many programs to oversee, ICE relies on partnerships with local law enforcement agencies to help combat transnational crime.

  4. As a result of these partnerships, ICE is able to complete the mission of public safety.

  A. 4–1–2–3

  B. 3–1–2–4

  C. 1–4–3–2

  D. 2–1–3–4

  E. no correction is necessary

DIRECTIONS: For Question 20, select the correct paragraph order to form a clear, concise, and coherent document. If no change to the paragraph order is necessary, choose *E. no correction is necessary.*

20.

1. Did you know that you can get a full body workout by gathering your bowls, spoons, mixers, and ingredients? Think about it. You are transporting bags of sugar and flour and the other necessary ingredients from their storage place to the area where you plan to mix them. Combining the dry ingredients in a separate bowl, creaming the sugar and butter, and then adding the dry ingredients to your mixture will get your muscles warmed up in no time. For the best workout, hand mix the ingredients rather than use an electric mixer.

2. Baking a cake can be therapeutic in several ways. The act of following directions and making decisions can have a calming effect. The physical aspect of baking provides an outlet to release negative energy. The aroma that emanates from the oven can release happy endorphins.

3. Once you have mixed all your ingredients, you'll need to pour your batter into the baking pans and bake. Now you can sit back and enjoy the wonderful aromatic results of your efforts. Taking in deep, long breaths then slowly exhaling will release serotonin and increase your well-being and happiness. So, next time you are feeling stressed, try baking a cake!

4. The act of baking challenges you to examine small details and make decisions. First, you'll need to choose a recipe based upon the ingredients you have on hand. Then you'll need to decide if you should increase or decrease quantities based upon how many people you plan to bake the cake for. Once you have decided what to bake, you'll need to gather the proper baking essentials.

A. 3–4–2–1

B. 4–2–1–3

C. 2–4–1–3

D. 1–4–3–2

E. no correction is necessary

ANSWER KEY AND EXPLANATIONS

1. C	**6.** A	**11.** A	**16.** A
2. B	**7.** A	**12.** D	**17.** C
3. A	**8.** B	**13.** A	**18.** B
4. B	**9.** A	**14.** A	**19.** E
5. D	**10.** E	**15.** D	**20.** C

1. **The correct answer is C.** Given the information provided by the passage, it must be true that if the FCC wishes to change or adopt a new rule, then they must first release an NPRM. Therefore, if the FCC does not wish to change or adopt a new rule, then it is not necessary for them to release an NPRM or ask for public comment.

2. **The correct answer is B.** Based on the information given, it must be true that if a detainee is a legal immigrant over the age of 18, then they must show their immigration papers to the arresting officer upon request. If these preconditions are true, it must also be true that a person who is not a detainee and who is a legal immigrant over the age of 18 must not show their immigration papers to an arresting officer.

3. **The correct answer is A.** Based on the information given, it must be true that no person who is an LPR can be denied entry into the country for failure to answer questions not pertaining to identity or permanent residency. In other words, if an LPR were to refuse to answer such questions, they could not be denied entry into the country. So then, if a person is not an LPR, then they can be denied entry into the country for failure to answer other questions.

4. **The correct answer is B.** Based on the information provided in the passage, it must be true that qualifying individuals are people who fit into one of two categories: members of the three class-action lawsuits filed against the government or those individuals wrongly denied amnesty under the 1986 IRCA law. Eva was wrongly denied amnesty under the 1986 IRCA law, so she fits into one of the two categories. She is a qualifying individual and is due relief. Relief means the ability to file for new adjustment applications.

5. **The correct answer is D.** First, multiply the number of notepads bought by the price:

$$\$10.00 \times 6 = \$60.00$$

Next, multiply the number of pens bought by the price:

$$\$2.00 \times 5 = \$10.00$$

To solve, add the two numbers:

$$\$60.00 + \$10.00 = \$70.00$$

6. **The correct answer is A.** Set up an equation using the area formula. Substitute the numerical values for the area and the width, then solve as follows to find the length:

$$l \times w = A$$
$$40l = 450$$
$$l = \frac{450}{40}$$
$$l = 11.25 \text{ ft.}$$

7. **The correct answer is A.** Of the answer options given, only the integers 12 & 14 and 13 & 13 add up to 26. Since the question is asking for the two consecutive *even* numbers, choice B is eliminated.

8. **The correct answer is B.** Start by converting the given information into equation form. Let x equal the number of dimes and y equal the number of quarters. In equation form, we have:

$$x = 6y$$

The total amount of coins is 21, so it also holds true that:

$$x + y = 21$$

Based on this information, we can solve for y as follows:

$$x + y = 21$$
$$6y + y = 21$$
$$7y = 21$$
$$y = \frac{21}{7}$$
$$y = 3 \text{ quarters}$$

Now solve for x:

$$x = 6y$$
$$x = 6(3)$$
$$x = 18 \text{ dimes}$$

We now know that Bethany has 18 dimes. Check the solution to see if the calculations are correct:

$$18 \times \$0.10 = \$1.80$$
$$3 \times \$0.25 = \$0.75$$
$$\$1.80 + \$0.75 = \$2.55$$

9. **The correct answer is A.** If Jude Thaddeus is 13 years old now, twice his age is 26 years old. If Salvatore is 4 years older, he is 17 years old today but will be $26 + 4 = 30$ years old when Jude Thaddeus is 26.

10. **The correct answer is E.** Let x be the old price of gas, and let y be the new price. In equation form, we have the following two formulas:

$$y = x + 0.02$$

$$20x + 10y = \$60.00$$

First, solve for x by substituting $x + 0.02$ in the place of y:

$$20x + 10(x + 0.02) = \$60.20$$
$$20x + 10x + 0.20 = \$60.20$$
$$30x + 0.20 = \$60.20$$
$$30x = \$60.20 - 0.20$$
$$30x = \$60.00$$
$$x = \frac{\$60.00}{30}$$
$$x = \$2.00$$

The old price of gas is \$2.00/gallon. Now solve for y to calculate the new price:

$$y = x + 0.02$$
$$y = \$2.00 + 0.02$$
$$y = \$2.02$$

11. **The correct answer is A.** When a noun begins with a vowel sound, the article adjective must be *an* instead of *a*.

12. **The correct answer is D.** An apostrophe is needed after the *t* for the contraction *It's*, meaning "it is." *Its* is a possessive pronoun, which eliminates choices A and C as correct. Choice B is incorrect because there is no need for the comma after the word *shoes*. Commas are used to separate a series or to join two independent clauses.

13. **The correct answer is A.** A comma is needed after the dependent clause "When preparing for an investigation." This eliminates choices B and C as correct. Choice D is missing a period at the end of the sentence.

14. **The correct answer is A.** Proper nouns, including organizations, professional titles, and countries, must be capitalized.

15. **The correct answer is D.** Months of the year are always capitalized. Proper nouns—including countries, professional titles, and states—must be capitalized. Directional words (such as southern) are not capitalized unless they are a part of a proper noun.

16. **The correct answer is A.** The correct spelling is *absence*.

17. **The correct answer is C.** The correct spelling is *acknowledge*.

18. **The correct answer is B.** The correct spelling is *capital*.

19. **The correct answer is E.** No correction is necessary as the sentences are presented in the correct order. Sentence 1 is the topic sentence. Sentence 2 provides supporting information. Sentence 3 provides additional supporting information. Sentence 4 draws a concluding statement as indicated by the phrase "As a result."

20. **The correct answer is C.** Paragraph 2 gives the thesis statement: "Baking a cake can be therapeutic in several ways." Paragraph 4 details the first way that baking is therapeutic as well as the first step in baking a cake. Paragraph 1 goes into detail regarding the physical, therapeutic effects of baking a cake. Paragraph 3 concludes with sitting back and enjoying the aromatic results.

ASSESSMENT GRID

The following table breaks down the questions on this ICE Diagnostic Test by question-type. Find the question numbers and question-types that gave you trouble and those you may need to spend more focused study-time on. Then read through Chapters 5 and 6 of this book, paying extra attention to the areas where you feel you need to improve.

Question Type	Question Number
Logical Reasoning	1–4
Arithmetic Reasoning	5–10
Writing Skills Assessment	11–20

FBI DIAGNOSTIC TEST ANSWER SHEET

1. Ⓐ Ⓑ Ⓒ Ⓓ Ⓔ   6. Ⓐ Ⓑ Ⓒ Ⓓ Ⓔ   11. Ⓐ Ⓑ Ⓒ Ⓓ   16. Ⓐ Ⓑ Ⓒ Ⓓ

2. Ⓐ Ⓑ Ⓒ Ⓓ Ⓔ   7. Ⓐ Ⓑ Ⓒ Ⓓ Ⓔ   12. Ⓐ Ⓑ Ⓒ Ⓓ   17. Ⓐ Ⓑ Ⓒ Ⓓ

3. Ⓐ Ⓑ Ⓒ Ⓓ Ⓔ   8. Ⓐ Ⓑ Ⓒ Ⓓ Ⓔ   13. Ⓐ Ⓑ Ⓒ Ⓓ   18. Ⓐ Ⓑ Ⓒ Ⓓ

4. Ⓐ Ⓑ Ⓒ Ⓓ Ⓔ   9. Ⓐ Ⓑ Ⓒ Ⓓ   14. Ⓐ Ⓑ Ⓒ Ⓓ   19. Ⓐ Ⓑ Ⓒ Ⓓ

5. Ⓐ Ⓑ Ⓒ Ⓓ Ⓔ   10. Ⓐ Ⓑ Ⓒ Ⓓ   15. Ⓐ Ⓑ Ⓒ Ⓓ   20. Ⓐ Ⓑ Ⓒ Ⓓ

FBI DIAGNOSTIC TEST

30 Minutes—20 Questions

DIRECTIONS: For Questions 1–4, using *only* the information given, choose the response option that best answers the question.

---

1. A flower shop arranges flowers into bouquets. All roses are paired with one other kind of flower. There is one type of flower that is used in every bouquet the shop makes. Peonies and hydrangeas are always arranged together. The shop recently sold a bouquet made from peonies, hydrangeas, and baby's breath.

   Based on the information above, which of these statements MUST be true?

   A. Only the baby's breath can be paired with roses.

   B. Peonies, hydrangeas, and baby's breath are always sold together.

   C. No roses are ever sold with another flower.

   D. Baby's breath is always sold with peonies.

   E. Roses can only be sold with peonies.

2. A car dealership only sells three types of cars, and two of them are limited editions. No blue cars are sold for over $24,000. All cars sold for over $24,000 are limited editions. Some red cars are sold for over $24,000.

   Based on the information above, what MUST be true?

   A. All red cars are limited editions.

   B. Some blue cars are limited editions.

   C. No limited edition cars are red cars.

   D. No blue cars are limited editions.

   E. Some red cars are limited editions.

3. Two candidates are running for public office. Only Candidate A is campaigning for a centralized national healthcare system. Both Candidate A and Candidate B are campaigning for higher education funding. No candidate is campaigning for stricter gun control legislation.

   What MUST be true?

   A. Candidate B is only campaigning for higher education funding.

   B. Candidate A is campaigning for both a centralized national healthcare system and stricter gun control legislation.

   C. Both candidates are campaigning for more lenient gun control legislation.

   D. Candidate A is only campaigning for a centralized national healthcare system.

   E. Candidate B is not campaigning for a centralized national healthcare system.

4. Only field agents are assigned to Team 1. Some persons assigned to Team 1 are not licensed to carry a firearm. Not all persons assigned to Team 2 are licensed to carry a firearm. All persons assigned to Team 2 are not field agents.

What MUST be true?

A. All field agents are licensed to carry a firearm.

B. No persons on Team 2 are licensed to carry a firearm.

C. Some field agents are not licensed to carry a firearm.

D. Not all field agents are assigned to Team 1.

E. Some people on Team 2 are licensed to carry a firearm.

DIRECTIONS: For Questions 5–8, review the sequenced images and patterns. Focus on the arrangement and how each sequence connects to each other. Select the logical missing piece in the last sequence using the information provided in the overall nine-part sequence.

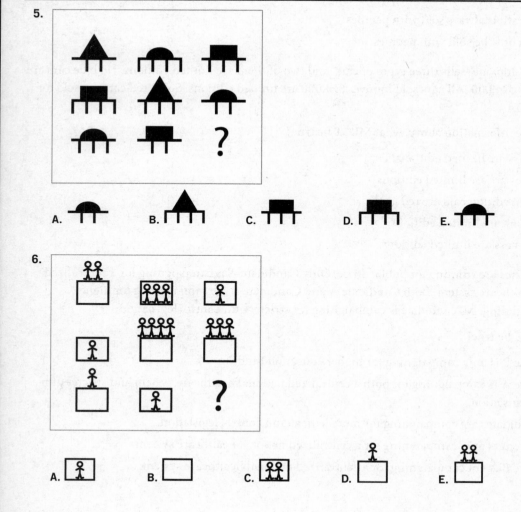

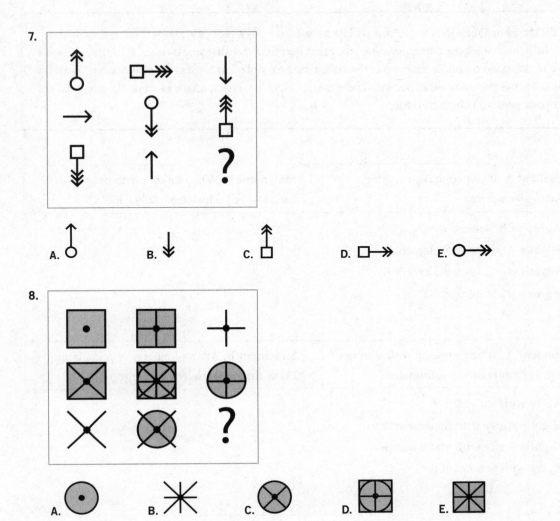

7.

A. ○
B. ↓↓
C. □↑↑
D. □→→
E. ○→→

8.

A. ●
B. ✳
C. ⊗
D. ⊞
E. ▦

DIRECTIONS: For Questions 9–12, you will be presented with a pair of statements. Read each statement carefully, and mark the corresponding letter that best fits your answer. At times, it may be difficult to choose which one you relate to more as the statements may present topics that you connect with on both sides. This is normal and expected. There are no right or wrong answers since the answers are based on your personal characteristics.

9.

Statement A: If someone is struggling, I like to give advice.	**Statement B:** When talking with people, I tend to be inclusive of others' ideas.

A. I Agree with Statement A.
B. I Slightly Agree with Statement A.
C. I Slightly Agree with Statement B.
D. I Agree with Statement B.

10.

Statement A: When working with a group, I uplift and motivate my teammates.	**Statement B:** After a long day of socializing, I take time to myself to recharge.

A. I Agree with Statement A.
B. I Slightly Agree with Statement A.
C. I Slightly Agree with Statement B.
D. I Agree with Statement B.

11.

Statement A: After an argument, I assess where I went wrong.	**Statement B:** I am good at listening to others and following instructions.

A. I Agree with Statement A.
B. I Slightly Agree with Statement A.
C. I Slightly Agree with Statement B.
D. I Agree with Statement B.

12.

Statement A: When in a disagreement, I endeavor to fully understand my opponent's viewpoints.	**Statement B:** I like to process my thoughts before discussing a difficult topic.

A. I Agree with Statement A.
B. I Slightly Agree with Statement A.
C. I Slightly Agree with Statement B.
D. I Agree with Statement B.

DIRECTIONS: For Questions 13–16, read each statement carefully. Respond with how strongly you agree or disagree with the statement provided. Try not to dwell too long on each question, and do not attempt to "read into" the statement. There are no right or wrong answers since the answers are based on your personal characteristics.

---

13. When working on a team, I am likely to take charge of assuming a position of leadership.

    A. Strongly Agree

    B. Agree

    C. Neither Agree nor Disagree

    D. Disagree

    E. Strongly Disagree

14. When working on a major project, I prefer to work in short, efficient bursts of time rather than longer, dedicated periods of time.

    A. Strongly Agree

    B. Agree

    C. Neither Agree nor Disagree

    D. Disagree

    E. Strongly Disagree

15. It is preferable to work in smaller group settings as opposed to within a large network of people.

    A. Strongly Agree

    B. Agree

    C. Neither Agree nor Disagree

    D. Disagree

    E. Strongly Disagree

16. It is more important to do a job well and thoroughly than it is to do a job quickly and efficiently.

    A. Strongly Agree

    B. Agree

    C. Neither Agree nor Disagree

    D. Disagree

    E. Strongly Disagree

DIRECTIONS: For Questions 17–20, you will be presented with various scenarios, each of which will have five response options to choose from. The scenarios describe situations and problems that you are likely to encounter in a typical work environment. Each response option will propose a different way of responding to the scenario. Choose the response option that is most consistent with how you would actually respond. Try not to dwell too long on each question, and do not attempt to "read into" the response. There are no right or wrong choices, just what is best for you.

17. You have worked for the FBI since 2017. You have shown great aptitude for investigations and are interested in moving into a more challenging leadership role. Agent Young was hired six months ago but has also demonstrated strong leadership skills. A promotion opportunity arises to which you and Agent Young both apply. Agent Young receives the promotion even though she has significantly less experience with the FBI. What would you MOST likely do?

    A. Say nothing and try harder during the next round of promotions.

    B. Meet with HR to investigate the proper procedure for promotional advancement to ensure the procedures are being followed.

    C. Meet with your direct supervisor to discuss what you could do better next time to increase your chances of promotion.

    D. Ask around to see if other employees know why Agent Young got the promotion and you didn't.

    E. Create a clear plan to increase your leadership skills so you are better prepared for the next round of promotions.

18. During a routine drug bust, you and Agent Tully are bagging up evidence. The total haul equates to four full evidence bags of cocaine. After loading everything up and heading back to the office, Agent Tully informs you that he needs to leave early because of a family emergency. You proceed to transfer the evidence bags inside the building but discover there are only three bags present in the vehicle. What would you MOST likely do?

    A. Not say anything and log in the bags as usual since there is no proof that Agent Tully did anything wrong.

    B. Immediately call Agent Tully's supervisor and report the missing evidence bag but say nothing about Agent Tully leaving early.

    C. Immediately call Agent Tully's supervisor and explain that he left early and now an evidence bag of cocaine is missing.

    D. Call 911 to report the evidence bag as stolen.

    E. Immediately call Agent Tully's supervisor to report the discrepancy and wait for instruction on how to proceed.

19. The breakroom at FBI headquarters is frequented by a variety of employees on a daily basis. Agents, supervisors, HR employees, and several other departments use the facilities present, but all are asked to maintain it with pride. Agent Kristoff routinely makes a sandwich and leaves the ingredients out on the counter for someone else to deal with, but no one ever confronts him. What would you MOST likely do?

   A. Create an anonymous typed memo addressing the problem and leave it on Agent Kristoff's desk.

   B. Create a typed memo outlining the problem, get as many signatures from fellow employees as possible, and leave it on Agent Kristoff's desk.

   C. Approach Agent Kristoff directly as he is about to, yet again, abandon his lunchroom mess.

   D. Try to casually run into him during lunch preparations and discuss the topic without specifically calling him out.

   E. Meet with him privately in his office and discuss the problem directly but in a nonconfrontational way.

20. You're working closely with your supervisor on a presentation regarding proper evidence labeling, as there have been some inconsistencies lately. You are excited because you were personally asked to help on this presentation, and it may increase your chances for promotion. On the day of the presentation, your supervisor informs you that she does not need your assistance at the meeting. She proceeds to do the presentation without any mention of your assistance. What would you MOST likely do?

   A. Say nothing at the meeting but ask your supervisor in private why she excluded you from the presentation.

   B. Request a meeting with your supervisor's boss to inform them of the lack of integrity of your supervisor.

   C. Request a meeting with your supervisor and inform her that you do not appreciate her excluding you from the presentation after the two of you worked together leading up to the meeting.

   D. Demand that your supervisor issues a public apology and identifies you as the co-author of the presentation.

   E. Go to HR to report the discrepancy and request a formal investigation into your supervisor's ethical behavior.

ANSWER KEY AND EXPLANATIONS

1. A	**3.** E	**5.** B	**7.** E
2. E	**4.** C	**6.** B	**8.** A

1. **The correct answer is A.** Based on the information given, roses can only be paired with one other kind of flower, and there is one kind of flower that is sold in every bouquet. Peonies and hydrangeas are always sold together, but they were also paired with baby's breath. Therefore, the baby's breath must be included in every bouquet, and the only other flower that can be sold with a rose is the baby's breath.

2. **The correct answer is E.** The paragraph states that some red cars are sold for over $24,000, and all cars sold for over $24,000 are limited editions. If this is true, then some red cars must be limited editions.

3. **The correct answer is E.** Given that all the information in the passage is true, it must be true that only Candidate A is campaigning for a centralized national healthcare system. In that case, Candidate B must not be campaigning for a centralized national healthcare system.

4. **The correct answer is C.** Based on the information given in the first two statements, only field agents are assigned to Team 1, or in other words, all persons assigned to Team 1 are field agents. Some of those persons assigned to Team 1 are not licensed to carry a firearm, and thus some field agents must not be licensed to carry a firearm.

5. **The correct answer is B.**

There are two parts to this sequence: (1) shapes and (2) a set of tick lines.

In every sequence of three, there must be the following:

- 1 triangle shape, 1 rectangle shape, and 1 half-moon shape
- A set of 2 tick lines, a set of 3 tick lines, and a set of 4 tick lines

Based on this information, the third sequence is missing a triangle and a set of 4 tick lines. The image shown in choice B has the missing elements.

6. **The correct answer is B.**

There are two parts to this pattern.

- The first part mirrors a simple subtraction formula. The top sequence is three people minus one person equals two people. The second sequence is $4 - 1 = 3$.
- The second part of the pattern follows the orientation of the figures on top of the box or inside the box, in each row, from top to bottom. The first column has figures on top of the box, alternating to inside the box in the second row, then alternating back on top in the third row. The second column has figures inside the first box, outside on the top in the second box, and a figure inside the third box.

Based on the information given, the bottom sequence is $1 - 1 = 0$. Since the subtraction answer is 0, there is no figure displayed.

7. **The correct answer is E.**

There are three parts to this sequence: (1) arrow direction, (2) number of arrow tips, and (3) shape of the nock. In every sequence, there must be the following:

- 1 arrow pointing upward, 1 arrow pointing downward, and 1 arrow pointing to the right
- 1 arrow tip, 2 arrow tips, and 3 arrow tips
- A square-shaped nock, a circle-shaped nock, and no nock

Based on the sequence information, the third row is missing an arrow pointing to the right, 2 arrow tips, and a circular-shaped nock. The image shown in choice E contains all the missing elements to complete the sequence.

8. **The correct answer is A.**

There are three parts to this pattern: (1) a series of small circles, (2) a subtraction problem, and (3) a series of shape combinations. The first part shows that the center small circles remain in place for every image. The second and third parts include a subtraction problem by elimination of a shape and/or combination of shapes.

Based on this information, the top sequence shows the second image (square/cross combination) minus the first image (square alone) equals the third image (cross). The second sequence follows the same pattern—second image (square/cross/circle/letter X combination) minus the first image (square/letter X combination) equals the third image (circle/cross). Therefore, it follows that the bottom sequence is circle/letter X combination minus the letter X equals circle. The image shown in choice A correctly completes the third row sequence.

ASSESSMENT GRID

The following table breaks down the questions on this FBI Diagnostic Test by question-type. Find the question numbers and question-types that gave you trouble and those you may need to spend more focused study-time on. Then read through Chapters 5 and 6, paying extra attention to the areas where you feel you need to improve.

Question Type	Question Number
Logic-Based Reasoning	1–4
Figural Reasoning	5–8
Personality Assessment	9–12
Preferences and Interests	13–16
Situational Judgment	17–20

PART III
PREPARING FOR THE SPECIAL AGENT EXAM

Chapter 5

Special Agent Exam Review

OVERVIEW

- **Special Agent Exam Components**
- **Logical/Verbal Reasoning (All 3 Exams)**
- **Quantitative Reasoning (ATF) and Arithmetic Reasoning (ICE)**
- **Investigative Reasoning (ATF only)**
- **Writing Skills Assessment (ICE only)**
- **Figural Reasoning (FBI only)**
- **Character and Personality Assessments (FBI Only)**
- **Summing It Up**

SPECIAL AGENT EXAM COMPONENTS

ATF, ICE, and FBI each have their own separate exams as of the publication date of this book. However, there is some overlap with regards to areas of testing. The following table illustrates the common and unique components of each exam.

Special Agent Exam Components by Agency

Question Type	ATF	ICE	FBI
Logical/Verbal Reasoning			
Quantitative/Arithmetic Reasoning			N/A
Investigative Reasoning		N/A	N/A
Writing Skills Assessment	N/A		N/A
Figural Reasoning	N/A	N/A	
Personality Assessment	N/A	N/A	
Preferences and Interests	N/A	N/A	
Situational Judgment	N/A	N/A	

There are a total of eight question-types that can be found in various parts/subtests between the three special agent exams. Two of these question-types overlap while the remaining six are dependent on the agency. However, even though a type of question may be excluded on the actual exam, this does not mean the topic will not be covered in some capacity later during the interview process (refer to Chapter 3 for extensive information regarding this). It is in your best interest to review every question-type and remain ready to test on the topics if and when they are presented later during your interview process.

LOGICAL/VERBAL REASONING (ALL 3 EXAMS)

The ATF, ICE, and FBI agencies would state that reasoning is an essential skill for success in the special agent role. Without adequate reasoning ability, an agent cannot practice strong decision-making or problem solving. Similarly, special agents must be able to read laws, legal commentary, and regulations. To do so requires strong reading comprehension, critical thinking, and the ability to discern what is relevant and what is not to arrive at what is true.

As such, the logical reasoning section of each special agent exam assesses your capability in handling the information you will receive at FLETC. These test sections also assess your ability to practice the independent reasoning that is so vital in the day-to-day tasks of a special agent.

What is Logical Reasoning?

Each special agent exam assesses your ability to draw valid conclusions based upon the facts of a situation. You will encounter statements that will indicate relationships between different groups or categories. Often, those statements will be qualified by others. Always, the specific wording of statements will affect your ability to draw one conclusion or another. As the test taker, you then must consider how the different premises of a situation affect and restrict what can be known with certainty.

To grasp the purpose of these questions, imagine logic as a method for detecting and validating relationships. In our daily conversations and tasks, we're inclined to believe conclusions based on how an idea or fact is stated or what we know or believe about a situation. When we interrogate the structure of statements and think in terms of truth and falsehood, however, only certain types of relationships are logically valid. In law and investigation, those relationships play key roles. Whether interviewing a suspect or reviewing good-faith search-and-seizure exemptions, understanding how the facts of a situation relate logically is invaluable. Relationships may exist between different categories (groups or classes) or propositions (something that can be true or false) and thus may lead to valid or invalid inferences. In logical reasoning, you can categorize to determine where groups overlap and where they do not to understand whether a relationship exists (or does not) or is true (or false).

In logical reasoning, many relationships can be deduced from the presence of certain words and phrases. These **indicator words** have specific purposes in the statement of facts in

NOTE

Words such as *all* or *every* imply that what is true of one group is true of another. However, not everything that is true for the second group is true of the first group.

5

logical discourse. To reason validly, special attention must be paid to the use of words, their order, and their relationships with other statements.

Let's learn more about the kinds of indicator words (quantifiers and phrases) you will encounter in the ATF, FBI, and ICE exams.

"All" Statements

Statements that include words such as *all* or *every* suggest that what is true of one group or category is true of another. However, these statements are not commutative; not every-thing that is true for the second group is true of the first group. To help illustrate, let's look at an example.

> **Example statement:** All whales are mammals.

Represented graphically, we see the group mammals containing a small group called whales.

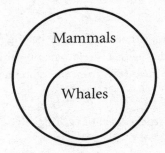

Now, it's easier to see that every whale belongs to the group mammals. But what if we reverse the statement? Is it still valid?

> **Invalid inference:** All mammals are whales.

This inference is invalid as it states that the group of all mammals is contained by the category whales. We know that is not sound as it contradicts what we know from reality (humans are not whales). But more importantly, we know that it is not a valid interpretation of our initial statement.

> **Valid inference:** Some things that are mammals are whales.

"All" statements indicate that the subject of the statement is nested entirely within a larger category. Because of that hierarchy (mammals represent a larger group than whales), we can only validly infer that "some" mammals are whales (i.e., at least one mammal is a whale). If provided a statement about the existence of another group of mammals, say primates, we could validly conclude that not all mammals are whales. But, for the purposes of the special agent exams, we have to work *only* with the information given.

NOTE

No is absolute. If one thing is true for one group, it is *never* true of the other. If one thing is true of the second group, then it is also *never* true of the first.

5

"No" Statements

Statements that use *no* and *none* function as absolutes. A statement that uses the word *no* implies that there is no overlap between the two groups or categories indicated. This means that if one thing is true for one group, it is never true of the other; if one thing is true of the second group, then it is also never true of the first.

> **Example statement:** No penguins can fly.

Represented graphically, we see both groups, but there is no overlap between them.

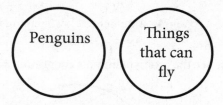

While penguins and things that can fly may belong in reality to a larger group (birds, for instance), we are provided with no relationship other than their mutual exclusion here. What inferences can we then draw from this statement?

> **Invalid inference:** Some things that can fly are penguins.

Because of the "no" statement, we know that there is no overlap between these two groups. Not one member of the first group belongs to the second and vice versa. Any inferences must adhere to the relationships created by the indicator words.

> **Valid inference:** No things that can fly are penguins.

Unlike "all" statements, "no" and "none" statements are commutative. They can be reversed and still uphold the initial relationship.

"Some" and "Not All" Statements

NOTE

A "not all" statement can also be worded as a "some do not" statement.

When assessing statements that use phrases such as *some* or *not all*, you should recognize that these statements acknowledge the existence, or lack thereof, of a connection between the two groups but nothing as totalizing as "all" or "none." "Some" statements imply that a connection does exist, but they do not imply that some connection does not. "Not all" statements (also worded as "some do not") imply that parts of one group do not apply to the second group. However, these statements alone cannot be used to draw valid conclusions as they are not concrete premises. They must be paired with either an "all" or "none" statement.

> **Example statement:** Some men are not bachelors.
> All bachelors are unmarried men.

These two statements form the foundation of a **syllogism**, a classical unit of logical reasoning that offers two premises (a major and a minor premise) and then leads to a conclusion. To accept the premises then requires that we also accept the conclusion if the syllogism is valid in its construction. The overlapping or middle term *bachelors* allows us to connect the two premises together. But recall how "some" and "some are not" function.

> **Invalid inference:** Some men are unmarried men.

In everyday usage, *some* is used to mean "part of a group" and may be used to infer that if some members belong to one group then others must belong to a different group. However, in logical reasoning, the word *some* translates to "at least one," which means that at least one member of the group, perhaps all members, is present in an indicated category. For the invalid inference shown, we do not know the number of members of a group with "some." We do not know if other categories could be available or unavailable for the excluded members of the set, and we do not know that unmarried men exist in the situation, let alone that some men belong to that group. We only know that if unmarried men exist, they are called bachelors and that some men are not bachelors, not that some men are. In the case above, there might not be any bachelors, only married men, those who are separated, or widowers, etc. If that's the case, what can we validly conclude then?

> **Valid inference:** Some men are not unmarried men.

In everyday conversation, the conclusion of this syllogism sounds redundant. Unmarried men and bachelors are synonymous. But it is still valid. When we consider the facts, we only have enough information to determine that there are some members of the group men that do not belong to the group unmarried men, not that some do.

"If–Then" Statements

There are statements that use **sentential logic**—logical statements that use "If–then." This form of logic asserts that if one thing is true, then another thing must be true. Assuming that all statements given in the test are true, then all such statements are valid. However, it is invalid reasoning to state that if the second statement is true then the first must also be true. Consider the following example:

> **Example statement:** If I flip the light switch down, then the lights turn off.

If you were given this statement and then told that the switch was flipped down, you would be able to infer that the lights were then turned off. That's referred to as *modus ponens*. But what if the condition and the consequence are reversed? Is that logically valid?

> **Invalid inference:** If the lights turn off, then I flipped the light switch down.

This inference is a formal fallacy called **affirming the consequent**. This error arises from failing to consider that there may be alternate conditions (electrical outage, malfunction) that can lead to the same result. Those conditions are not stated; nevertheless, this is still an invalid form of reasoning as no restriction was placed on the reason for why the lights turn off, only that flipping the light switch will do so.

> **Valid inference:** If the lights did not turn off, then the light switch was not flipped down.

This last statement is referred to as the **contrapositive** of the initial statement. It is a form of *modus tollens*. While there may be other causes behind lights turning off, we can know that if the lights do not turn off then the antecedent, flipping the light switch, did not occur.

"Only" Statements

The indicator word *only* is similar to *all* in the sense that it implies a concrete connection. If only members of the first group belong to the second group, then that must mean that all things belonging to the second group are within the first group. However, this does not mean that all things belonging to the first group are the second group. This is also true of "None but" statements.

> **Example statement:** Only persons that are good die young.

Here, it is clear that no person other than those that are good die young. The first condition of the statement is required to fulfill the second. We could abstract this statement to say "Only members of A do B." What can be logically concluded from this?

> **Invalid inference:** All persons that are good die young.

Though "only" and "all" statements may share some similarity, they are not interchangeable. "Only" statements provide a condition for membership in a group while "all" statements label every member. If we abstract the invalid inference and compare it to the abstraction in the previous paragraph, we see "All members of A do B as only members of A do B." While all members of group A are capable of doing B, they are not guaranteed to do so. While the possibility exists, it is not a logical certainty.

> **Valid inference:** Every person who dies young is good.

NOTE

Only provides a condition for membership in a group while *all* labels every member.

NOTE

If and only if is reversible and absolute. One thing is true if and only if another condition is true.

"If and Only If" Statements

The final indicator phrase that might appear is *if and only if*. As opposed to the "If-then" construction from earlier, "if and only if" statements allow us to infer that if one condition is true then the other must be as well. The statement is reversible and absolute.

> **Example statement:** A person is employed by the company if and only if that person is on the payroll.
>
> **Invalid inference:** Some persons employed by the company are not on the payroll.
>
> **Valid inference:** A person is on the payroll if and only if that person is employed by the company.

5

Keep in mind that these example statements have been closer to classical syllogisms than more common logical structures. The questions for the ATF, ICE, and FBI tests will provide more premises. However, to accept the premises as true (required by the tests) is still then to narrow the conclusion to only one possible answer.

Let's learn more about how the tests present these statements and then look at a few examples that simulate the rigor and complexity of the task ahead.

Question Structure and Dissection

Each logical reasoning question will have a short passage that provides the facts of a situation. All passages will be accompanied by five answer choices, only one of which is the correct answer. No passages or questions will require any outside information. While you may have prior knowledge related to the subject of a passage, it likely will not be helpful (perhaps an obstacle) in answering the given question. Focus on the facts in front of you and let them dictate the correct answer. Some answers are designed to be technically true but cannot be validly concluded from the information given.

Let's return to a question from the FBI diagnostic test and dissect its structure and reasoning.

> A flower shop arranges flowers into bouquets. All roses are paired with one other kind of flower. There is one type of flower that is used in every bouquet the shop makes. Peonies and hydrangeas are always arranged together. The shop recently sold a bouquet made from peonies, hydrangeas, and baby's breath.
>
> Based on the information above, which of these statements MUST be true?
>
> **A.** Only the baby's breath can be paired with roses.
>
> **B.** Peonies, hydrangeas, and baby's breath are always sold together.
>
> **C.** No roses are ever sold with another flower.
>
> **D.** Baby's breath is always sold with peonies.
>
> **E.** Roses can only be sold with peonies.

The goal is to establish what conclusions are definitive based upon this information (and only this information). These statements provide you with a combination of universal and specific facts. The overlap between these statements can allow us to come to some valid conclusions, but only one will be present among the answer choices.

First, let's delineate the universal statements. We will even arrange them in order of more universal to more particular:

1. One type of flower is included in every bouquet.
2. All roses are paired with one other kind of flower.
3. Peonies and hydrangeas are always arranged together.

From this information and rearrangement, we can draw a variety of inferences. First, we know that since one type of flower is included in every bouquet, every bouquet will have at least two types of flowers, excluding a bouquet that contains only the type of flower included in every bouquet. Second, we know that roses are arranged with another flower, but we don't know yet if that other flower is the universal flower or if roses are.

The third statement provides some key insight. Since peonies and hydrangeas must be paired together, we now know that peonies, hydrangeas, and roses are not the universal flower. How? If peonies were included in every bouquet, then hydrangeas would be as well. That is a possibility until we recall that roses are only paired with one other flower. Peonies and hydrangeas come as a pair. Where one goes so must the other, thus potentially contradicting what is known about roses. The required pairing also excludes hydrangeas from being the universal flower. Similarly, because roses are only paired with one other flower, they cannot be in every bouquet because we learned that some flower types are paired together (i.e., peonies and hydrangeas) and would then violate the rule for roses.

From three statements, we've been able to extract a significant amount of information about how this flower shop composes its bouquets. And we still have more to evaluate. From the information given, we know that a recent bouquet included peonies, hydrangeas, and baby's breath. Based on our prior deductions, we know that peonies, hydrangeas, and roses are not the universal flower. That means that baby's breath must be included in every bouquet. When we check that conclusion against our known facts, we see that such a statement does not contradict the proposition that roses are only paired with one other kind of flower, nor what we know about peonies and hydrangeas. We have no restrictions for the use of baby's breath that would prevent it from being included in every bouquet. And when we re-examine the answers to this question, what do we see?

- **Choice A:** Only the baby's breath can be paired with roses. *This statement is true.* Roses are paired with only one other flower, thus excluding peonies and hydrangeas, and leaving only baby's breath.

- **Choice B:** Peonies, hydrangeas, and baby's breath are always sold together. *This statement is false.* While peonies and hydrangeas are always accompanied by baby's breath, baby's breath does not have to be sold together with the other two flowers. Of the flowers sold together, baby's breath is not always with peonies and hydrangeas.

- **Choice C:** No roses are ever sold with another flower. *This statement is false.* This directly contradicts information provided in the paragraph.

- **Choice D:** Baby's breath is always sold with peonies. *This statement is false.* While peonies will always be accompanied by baby's breath (and hydrangeas), similar to choice B, baby's breath will not always be accompanied by peonies. If this answer stated that all bouquets with peonies also have baby's breath, it would be logically valid.

- **Choice E:** Roses can only be sold with peonies. *This statement is false.* Roses can only be sold with one other flower; we know that peonies must be paired with hydrangeas and thus cannot accompany roses.

To arrive at those evaluations, we took some general steps that you'll see reflected again later on in this chapter.

1. We read the passage carefully.
2. We identified indicator words to isolate universal and more particular statements.
3. We paraphrased statements to dissect their meaning.
4. We worked with universal statements to determine what we knew about groups and their members.
5. We used the overlapping or exclusive elements of those groups to arrive at a valid conclusion.

Let's look at some further examples to see how this process unfolds in different situations. It is important to note that, while the concept behind solving logical reasoning questions is the same, each agency has its own style for how each question is presented. You will see examples that simulate questions and their phrasing from each test. However, remember that while the wording may differ, valid reasoning and the techniques to arrive at a conclusion are the same.

ATF Verbal Reasoning Example

The following example is written as you would read it on the Verbal Reasoning section of the ATF Special Agent Examination.

Ms. Price was not given a job as a director within the company. Ms. Price does have a law degree. Only persons with law degrees are hired as in-house counsel for the company. Not all persons hired by the company are lawyers. Some persons hired by the company do not have master's degrees. Only persons with master's degrees are given jobs as directors within the company.

From the information provided above, it can be validly concluded that:

A. Ms. Price does not have a master's degree.

B. Ms. Price was hired as in-house counsel for the company.

C. Some lawyers do not have master's degrees.

D. Some persons hired by the company are not given jobs as directors within the company.

E. All persons with master's degrees are given jobs as directors within the company.

Let's take a step-by-step approach to finding what we can validly conclude from the information we are given.

Step 1: Read the passage carefully.

Start by reading the paragraph carefully and thoroughly. Slow the pace of your reading way down if you are typically a fast reader. A helpful technique to employ is to mimic reading the passage aloud since the pace of the spoken word is slower than the pace of reading. Just be careful to silently read aloud. You won't be able to read aloud in an actual test environment.

Step 2: Identify indicator words.

In order to go about solving this question, it is important to take stock of all the indicator words available. Words like *only* and *not all* and *some* appear in this particular passage. We can focus on working with the more universal statements first, then work through the more particular, and paraphrase for simplicity. While simplifying, you may also discover that you're able to eliminate certain answers as they contradict the passage.

Step 3: Simplify indicator words and eliminate contradictory answers.

To make some of the words easier to comprehend, you can substitute their synonyms. For example, "Only persons with a law degree are hired as in-house counsel for the company," is really just, "All persons hired as in-house counsel for the company are persons with law degrees." However, this does not mean that all persons with law degrees are hired as in-house counsel for the company, and thus it is logically invalid to claim that Ms. Price was hired as in-house counsel for the company simply because she has a law degree. Therefore, we can eliminate choice B as a correct answer.

The same technique can be applied to simplify the final statement, "Only persons with master's degrees are given jobs as directors within the company." Ms. Price was not hired as a director within the company, but that does not mean that Ms. Price does not have a master's degree. The sentence simply states that all persons given jobs as directors within the company are persons with master's degrees but not that all persons with master's degrees are given directors positions. Thus, choices A and E are also incorrect.

Step 4: Assess corresponding premises.

Once you have simplified the sentences, you can begin to assess the given facts and how they relate to one another. When looking for corresponding premises, you're searching for two statements that possess a shared term. We can represent the different terms of the statements with S, P, and M. An S can be our minor premise, P the major premise, and M the connecting factor between the two premises that allows valid or invalid conclusions to be drawn. For instance, consider these two premises:

1. Not all persons hired by the company are lawyers.
2. Some persons hired by the company do not have master's degrees.

Recall that "not all" statements can also be worded as "some do not" statements. Let's reword the first premise so the common factor between the two premises is clearer.

1. Some persons hired by the company are not lawyers.
2. Some persons hired by the company do not have master's degrees.

Now, it's a bit clearer that the common factor (M) between these two premises is "persons hired by the company." S must then be "lawyers" and P must then be "persons with master's degrees." And so, the equation now looks like this:

1. Some M are not S.
2. Some M are not P.

While these two premises correspond with a common factor, no valid conclusion can be drawn from them. Nothing definitive can be said about lawyers or individuals with master's degrees. Nor can we conclude another "some" statement: that some lawyers do not have master's degrees. Thus, choice C must be incorrect.

There are two additional corresponding premises in this example that we need to examine:

1. Some persons hired by the company do not have master's degrees.

2. Only persons with master's degrees are given jobs as directors within the company; thus, all persons given jobs as directors within the company are persons with master's degrees.

If M is "persons with master's degrees," S is "persons hired by the company," and P is "persons given jobs as directors within the company," then the new equation looks like this:

1. Some S are not M.

2. All P are M.

Some things that are S are not M, but all things that are P are M. So, it must be true that some things that are S are not P. Therefore, it can be validly concluded that some persons that are hired by the company are not given jobs as directors within the company. **The correct answer is D.**

ICE Logical Reasoning Example

The following is a Logical Reasoning question similar to what you might find on the ICE Special Agent Test Battery.

A container shipped from Lithuania to Long Beach contains handguns bound for firearms dealers throughout the country. There are 9 mm, .38, and .45 caliber weapons. Customs agents learn that some, but not all, of the handguns included in the shipment are being brought into the country illegally and are bound for sale to street gangs. On further investigation, agents discover that all of the handguns shipped legally were made by Accurate Arms, while the illegal handguns were made by Choice Firearms. None of the smuggled handguns are .45 caliber.

From the information given above, it can be validly concluded that

A. Choice Firearms does not make .45 caliber handguns.

B. all of the smuggled handguns are .38 caliber.

C. Accurate Arms only makes .45 caliber handguns.

D. some of the smuggled weapons were made by Accurate Arms.

E. all .45 caliber handguns were shipped legally.

Let's take a closer look. Notice that the final sentence states that none of the smuggled handguns were .45 caliber. Even though all of the smuggled handguns were made by Choice Firearms, we do not know from the information given that Choice Firearms does not make .45 caliber handguns, just that none of the smuggled weapons were .45 caliber. This eliminates choice A as a valid conclusion. There is not enough information to validly conclude choice C either as nowhere in the information are we told what caliber the smuggled handguns were, just what they were not. Since the fourth sentence states that the Accurate Arms handguns were all shipped legally, choice D is incorrect as well. Notice again that the final sentence states that none of the smuggled handguns were .45 caliber. Because we know that .45 caliber weapons were present in the shipment, all of the .45 caliber weapons must have been shipped legally. Therefore, choice E is a valid conclusion. **The correct answer is E.**

FBI Logic-Based Reasoning Example

Let's look at one more example. The following is a Logic-Based Reasoning question similar to what you might find on the FBI Special Agent Exam.

> Edward is interested in purchasing a used truck. He visits a dealer and asks about the differences in cost between five similar trucks, each from a different manufacturer. If he learns that the below statements are true, then which of the response options also MUST be true?
>
> *The Ford truck is less expensive than the Dodge.*
>
> *The Chevrolet truck is less expensive than the GMC.*
>
> *The GMC is more expensive than the Dodge.*
>
> *The Nissan is more expensive than the Chevrolet.*
>
> **A.** The Chevrolet is the least expensive.
>
> **B.** The Ford is less expensive than the GMC.
>
> **C.** The Chevrolet is more expensive than the Ford.
>
> **D.** The GMC and the Nissan are the same price.
>
> **E.** The Dodge is less expensive than the Nissan.

Notice that this is an example of "If–Then" logic. Based on the information provided, the GMC truck is more expensive than the Dodge, and the Dodge is more expensive than the Ford. The Dodge is the key piece of information that allows us to compare the GMC and the Ford. With this information, the statement that the Ford is less expensive than the GMC is the only accurate choice. **The correct answer is B.**

QUANTITATIVE REASONING (ATF) AND ARITHMETIC REASONING (ICE)

The ATF Quantitative Reasoning part of the Special Agent Examination is divided into two sections. The ICE Special Agent Test Battery has one Arithmetic Reasoning section. While the structure of the two exams differs, you will find some of the same mathematical topics covered, including the following:

- Basic Algebra
- Ratios/Proportions
- Taxes
- Distance and Time
- Profit and Loss
- Money

ALERT

You will not be permitted to use a calculator on the actual exam. Practice solving arithmetic and quantitative reasoning questions using a pencil and scratch paper.

Quantitative Reasoning Section 1 (ATF)

Quantitative reasoning is a unique form of problem solving that requires the application of basic numeracy, critical thinking, and information literacy. It is the evaluation of real-world problems and solutions through the lens of numerical evidence. Test takers who understand this discipline should be able to interpret data, draw conclusions, and solve problems given certain information pertaining to individual scenarios.

Let's look at a quantitative reasoning question similar in structure to what you might find on the actual ATF Special Agent Examination.

> A team of ATF agents confiscated 300 individual packages of illegal tobacco products, valued at $195,000, that was likely to be sold on the black market. If all the packages of tobacco have the same value, what is the value of one package?
>
> **A.** $650
>
> **B.** $650.50
>
> **C.** $6,500
>
> **D.** $7,500
>
> **E.** $195,300

To solve, divide the total value of the tobacco ($195,000) by the number of individual packages (300) to find the value per package, as shown.

$$\frac{\$195,000}{300} = \$650$$

The value of one package is $650. **The correct answer is A.**

Quantitative Reasoning Section 2 (ATF)

The focus on this quantitative reasoning section of the test is on reasoning within verbal scenarios. You will be presented a passage with some type of numerical focus. This rarely equates to actual computation but rather numbers in commonplace situations. The answers are always TRUE or FALSE only, and you are asked to draw conclusions only from the data that is present in the passage.

Let's look at an example and follow a step-by-step process to determine whether the conclusion given in the question is true or false.

5

When baking a cake, you must be cognizant of the chemical process occurring within the oven. Ovens preheated to temperatures higher than 350 degrees render tough, crumbly-textured cakes due to the speed at which the water evaporates and the proteins coagulate. A crumbly cake can also be an indicator of excess flour or a lack of butter and eggs. Contrarily, ovens that are preheated to temperatures lower than 350 degrees are liable to create a gummy, pale cake with a sticky outer layer due to the lack of evaporation. The evaporation of water on the surface of the cake enables caramelization, which gives the cake its glazed, firm outer layer.

1. A finished cake with crumbly texture and a dry center was cooked at a temperature above 350 degrees.

   A. True

   B. False

Step 1: Identify and eliminate unnecessary information.

The first step in analyzing this passage is identifying unnecessary information and determining what key factors really contribute to the question being asked. In this case, the first sentence contains no necessary information. Neither does the last, as the evaporation of water and the caramelization of the cake do not play a role in the context of this question.

Step 2: Locate relational numbers.

The second step is to take notice of relational numbers that might pertain to the question being asked. In this case, the only numbers referenced are the temperatures of the oven. The question specifically states that the cake was cooked "above 350 degrees." In the second sentence of the passage, it reads that "ovens preheated to temperatures over 350 degrees render tough, crumbly textured cakes," which coincides with the information presented in the question.

Step 3: Connect key words/phrases.

Lastly, it is prudent to keep an eye out for key words and phrases that might indicate relation to the question. Key words seen in both the question and passage are "crumbly texture" and "dry." While the second sentence does say that ovens cooked at temperatures over 350 are liable to be crumbly and dry, the third sentence says that a "crumbly cake can also be an indicator of excess flour or a lack of butter and eggs."

Step 4: Analyze for TRUE/FALSE.

Let's take another look at the question. The question states that "A finished cake with a crumbly texture and a dry center was cooked at a temperature above 350 degrees." While the second sentence affirms that this could be a possibility, the third sentence asserts that it could also be crumbly for another reason. **Thus, the correct answer is False.**

TIP

When choosing between the two answers, remember that if you select true, it must be true <u>all</u> the time. Otherwise, the answer is false.

Arithmetic Reasoning (ICE)

For the arithmetic reasoning test, you do not need to understand intricate mathematical operations or memorize complicated formulas. You can solve the problems arithmetically or by using some simple algebra. Each problem is presented as a short verbal description of a situation that includes some numerical facts. You must read the problem to determine what the question is asking. If a series of calculations will be required, you do not want to stop short of the answer because you misinterpreted the question. Likewise, you do not want to waste time going beyond what is asked. Once you have determined what the question asks, you must settle on the best route for arriving at the answer and set the problem up accordingly. Finally, you must perform the calculations.

Let's look at an arithmetic reasoning question similar to what you would find on the ICE Special Agent Test Battery.

> Agent Youngs is moving from the Atlanta office to the Los Angeles office. If she drives at a rate of 65 miles per hour and the drive is 3,276 miles, how many days should she allocate for her drive?
>
> **A.** 1 day
>
> **B.** 2 days
>
> **C.** 4 days
>
> **D.** 5 days
>
> **E.** none of these

To solve, start by dividing the number of miles by the number of miles per hour:

$$\frac{3,276}{65} = 50.4 \text{ hours}$$

Then divide that number by 24:

$$\frac{50.4}{24} = 2.1 \text{ days} \approx 3 \text{ days}$$

Since there is 0.1 of a day left, the drive will go into a third day, thus Agent Youngs will need to budget 3 days for her drive. Notice that 3 days is not an answer choice provided. Since the fifth answer choice is always *none of these*, it is important that you calculate your answer from start to finish. **The correct answer is E.**

INVESTIGATIVE REASONING (ATF ONLY)

How well you perform on investigative reasoning questions directly correlates to your strength in reading. Reading speed is not crucial. Accuracy and careful attention to each detail of the reading passage and the statements are essential to scoring high. You can go back and reread and recheck as often as you like while answering these questions. Do not rush through in an effort to get to the questions. Take notes of key events and names as you read through.

> ⚠️ **ALERT**
>
> The Arithmetic Reasoning section of the ICE Exam has a fifth multiple-choice answer option that reads "E. none of these." It is important that you perform all calculations carefully because an estimate or an approximation may lead you to choose the wrong answer.

Clear thinking and total concentration are the keys to doing well on this significant portion of the exam. You have the time to contemplate the true meaning and the implications of each statement, so ask yourself the following questions:

- Is this fact? Can the fact be substantiated?
- Is the statement based on hearsay?
- Is the statement pure conjecture?
- How reliable is the source of the evidence?
- Does the person have a motive for making this statement?

Note time sequences and interrelationships of events. Consider interpersonal relationships, as well, as you try to determine which statements support the questions. Remain detached from the situation. You might disagree with the actions taken by the agent in regard to handling evidence or questioning witnesses. Don't let such opinions enter into the situation. Concentrate on the description of the events as they are reported, the statements made by witnesses, and the questions that must be supported by statements. In short, be analytical, objective, and careful.

Let's look at an example similar in format to what you will see on the ATF Special Agent Examination.

Example Investigative Reasoning Passage and Question Set

On October 30th, the Belton First National Bank discovered that the $3,000 it had received that morning from the Greenville First National Bank was in counterfeit 10-, 20-, and 50-dollar bills. The genuine $3,000 had been counted by Greenville First National bank clerk Iris Stewart the preceding afternoon. They were packed in eight black leather satchels and stored in the bank vault overnight. Greenville First National clerk Brian Caruthers accompanied carriers James Clark and Howard O'Keefe to Belton in an armored truck. Belton First National clerk Cynthia Randall discovered the counterfeit bills when she examined the serial numbers of the bills.

In the course of the investigation, the following statements were made:

1. *Gerald Hathaway, clerk of the Greenville bank, told investigators that he had found the bank office open when he arrived to work on the morning of October 30th. The only articles that appeared to be missing were eight black leather satchels of the type used to transport large sums of money.*

2. *Jon Perkins, head teller of the Greenville bank, told investigators that he did not check the contents of the black leather satchels after locking them in the vault around 4:30 p.m., on October 29th.*

3. *Henry Green, janitor of the Greenville bank, said that he noticed Jon Perkins leaving the bank office around 5:30 p.m., one-half hour after the bank closed on October 29th. He said that Perkins locked the door.*

4. *A scrap of cloth, identical to the material of the carriers' uniforms, was found caught in the seal of one of the black leather satchels delivered to Belton.*

5. *Brian Caruthers, clerk, said he saw James Clark and Howard O'Keefe talking in a secretive manner in the armored truck.*

5

TIP

When answering investigative reasoning questions, clear thinking and total concentration are key. Set aside emotions, opinions, and judgments. Be analytical, objective, and careful.

6. *Thomas Stillman, Greenville bank executive, identified the eight black leather satchels containing the counterfeit money that arrived at the Belton First National Bank as the eight satchels that had disappeared from the bank office. He had noticed a slight difference in the linings of the satchels.*

7. *Virginia Fowler, bank accountant, noticed two 10-dollar bills with the same serial numbers as the lost bills in a bank deposit from Ferdinand's Restaurant of Greenville.*

8. *Vincent Johnson, manager of Ferdinand's Restaurant, told police that Iris Stewart frequently dined there with her boyfriend.*

1. Which one of the following statements best indicates that satchels containing the counterfeit bills were substituted for satchels containing genuine bills while they were being transported from Greenville to Belton?

   A. Statement 1
   B. Statement 3
   C. Statement 4
   D. Statement 5
   E. Statement 7

2. Which one of the following statements best links the information given in Statement 1 with the substitution of the counterfeit bills?

   A. Statement 2
   B. Statement 3
   C. Statement 4
   D. Statement 5
   E. Statement 6

3. Which one of the following statements, along with Statement 7, best indicates that the substitution of the counterfeit bills casts suspicion on at LEAST one employee of the Greenville bank?

   A. Statement 1
   B. Statement 2
   C. Statement 3
   D. Statement 5
   E. Statement 8

Answers and Explanations

Notice that the first question asks you to choose the statement that best supports information that you are given in the passage. The second question asks you to choose the statement that supports information given in another statement. The third question asks you to choose the statement that along with another statement casts doubt. You may also encounter questions that ask you to pick two statements that best support information given in the passage. The intent of this section of the examination is to test your investigative abilities using real-life scenarios. The correct answers along with explanations follow.

1. **The correct answer is C.** The armor carriers had the greatest opportunity to substitute counterfeit bills for real ones during the transportation procedure. Statement 4 strongly links the carriers to the crime. The scrap of material caught in the seal of one of the satchels is identical to the material of the carrier's uniforms.

2. **The correct answer is E.** Statement 1 establishes that eight satchels were missing from Greenville Bank. Statement 6 identifies the satchels that arrived at the Belton Bank as the missing satchels.

3. **The correct answer is E.** Statement 7 establishes that two stolen 10-dollar bills were spent at Ferdinand's Restaurant. Statement 8 identifies a bank employee as a frequent diner at Ferdinand's Restaurant. This statement casts suspicion on the bank employee but does not prove complicity.

WRITING SKILLS ASSESSMENT (ICE ONLY)

5

The Writing Skills Assessment tests your proficiency with standard written English. If you are a native English speaker, this section should be fairly self-explanatory. If you learned English after your first language, this section will help you hone in on areas that may be more confusing. Most adults can benefit from an English refresher, whether English is their first language or not.

The Writing Skills Assessment can be found only on the ICE Special Agent Test Battery. The questions are in a multiple-choice format. You will be tested on grammar, punctuation, capitalization, spelling, sentence organization, and paragraph organization.

You do not need to go back and relearn all the grammar that was taught in school. Most of the questions on Writing Skills Assessment cover basic grammatical and sentence structure concepts including:

- Verb tense
- Word choice
- Adjectives/Adverbs
- Nouns

However, some areas of grammar are more difficult to recall since we either don't use them every day, or they are areas of struggle for most people. It is important to familiarize yourself with the following trickier concepts that may be included in the test:

- **Capitalization**—This includes proper nouns and abbreviations.
- **Commas**—This is the most difficult concept for all learners. Review rules around the Oxford comma, commas for subordinate clauses, and commas for adverbial phrases.
- **Homophones**—It is common to use words that sound the same but have different spellings and meanings incorrectly. This is true whether you are native speaker or English is not your first language. Review common homophones such as the ones that follow:
  - do, due, dew
  - to, two, too
  - there, their, they're
  - where, wear
  - here, hear

Remember, you are not penalized for wrong answers. If you find that you do not know the answer, try the following:

1. Eliminate the obviously wrong answers. This usually constitutes half of the answers provided.
2. Make an educated guess with the remaining answers.
3. If all else fails, simply guess! Since you are NOT penalized for incorrect answers, it is in your best interest to guess. You may just guess right!

Let's take look at some of the concepts you will be tested on, along with examples similar in format to what you will find on the actual test itself.

Grammar

Questions dealing with grammar involve reading a sentence and then choosing a change that corrects the given sentence. In other words, you'll be employing proper grammar. On the actual exam, you will be given directions to choose the one option that represents a change that should be made to correct the sentence. Changes will be underlined for clarity. The fifth option will always be worded as *no correction is necessary*. The following is an example of how this type of question is presented.

> After completing an investigation, each agent that worked on the case is required to individually submit an summary report.
>
> A. Change an to a
> B. Change submit to submits
> C. Change individually to individual
> D. Change report to reports
> E. No correction is necessary

A and *an* are article adjectives used in front of a noun. *An* is only used when the noun after it begins with a vowel sound. For example, *an* orange NOT *a* orange. Since the word *summary* begins with a consonant, we need to change *an* to *a* for this sentence to be grammatically correct. **The correct answer is A.**

Punctuation

You will also encounter questions on the actual exam that ask you to choose the sentence that is correctly punctuated. Correct punctuation includes commas, end marks, semicolons, colons, periods, etc. You will be asked to choose the one sentence from four options that is correct.

ALERT
Some of the questions on the Writing Skills Assessment will provide a fifth option indicating that no correction is necessary. Be careful as this is sometimes the case!

1. A. Under normal circumstances, disinfectant products are restocked every two to for weeks; however, we have been stocking them daily this past month.

B. Under normal circumstances, disinfectant products are restocked every two to four weeks; however; we have been stocking them daily this past month.

C. Under normal circumstances, disinfectant products are restocked every two to four weeks; however, we have been stocking them daily this past month.

D. Under normal circumstances, disinfectant products are restocked every to to four weeks; however, we have been stocking them daily this past month.

The sentences shown in choices A and D contain homophone errors. In choice A, the word *for* should be *four*. In choice D, *to* should be *two*. Choice B has a semicolon after the word *however* instead of a comma. Choice C lacks the homophone errors of the other choices and is punctuated correctly with a comma placed after *however*. **The correct answer is C.**

Capitalization

This type of question will ask you to choose the one option that demonstrates correct capitalization. Once again, you will be given four choices, but only one of the choices will contain proper capitalization. Be on the lookout for the proper capitalization at the beginning of a sentence, in abbreviations, with proper nouns, and with phrases. The following is similar to what you might find on the actual exam.

1. A. The US Immigration and Customs Enforcement (ICE) has relocated Special Agent Brown to their Guam office after the events of September 11, 2001.

B. The US Immigration and Customs Enforcement (ice) has relocated Special Agent Brown to their Guam Office after the events of September 11, 2001.

C. The US Immigration and Customs Enforcement (ICE) has relocated Special Agent brown to their Guam Office after the events of September 11, 2001.

D. The US Immigration and Customs Enforcement (ICE) has relocated Special Agent Brown to their Guam Office after the events of september 11, 2001.

Proper nouns including organizations, professional titles, and countries must be capitalized. In addition, months must be capitalized. Choice B does not capitalize ICE. Choice C should have Brown capitalized. September should be capitalized in choice D. The only sentence that contains the correct capitalization is choice A. **The correct answer is A.**

Spelling

You will also encounter questions that ask you to choose the answer option that contains the correct spelling of the missing word. The question will look similar to the following:

Alexis decided to _____ around the streets downtown to kill time before her bus arrived.

A. wunder

B. wonder

C. wander

D. waunder

E. wounder

For this type of question, you will not only need to know the correct spelling of a word, but also the correct word for the sentence context. In this case, the words in choices A, D, and E are spelled incorrectly. This leaves us with *wander* and *wonder*, two homophones that sound the same but have different meanings. *Wonder* means "to think about something." *Wander* means "to go idly about." **The correct answer is C.**

Sentence Organization

Sentence organization questions focus on the correct and logical arrangement of sentences within a paragraph. This includes a well-constructed topic sentence, the use of transition terms (e.g., next, then, finally) to move the reader through the text, and a conclusion that pulls it all together. In addition, paying attention to details, with the broader topic opening the paragraph and supporting details following is best practice from an organizational perspective. The directions will ask you to select the correct sentence order to form a clear, concise, and coherent paragraph. Five answer options are given, with the fifth option always being *no correction is necessary*. An example follows.

1. Although there are hundreds of agencies, the government itself is divided into three broad branches—executive, legislative, and judicial.

2. The federal government is made up of hundreds of agencies that all work together for the good of the country.

3. Overall, the government is a series of smaller agencies divided and housed under larger branches, with the overarching title of government connecting them all together.

4. Within the executive branch are all of the special agent positions that are responsible for ensuring safety of US citizens.

A. 4–1–2–3

B. 3–1–2–4

C. 1–4–3–2

D. 2–1–4–3

E. no correction is necessary

Sentence 2 is a topic sentence and presents the broadest amount of information comparatively. Sentence 1 narrows down the topic to the three branches of the government. Sentence 4 narrows down even further to special agents. Sentence 3 uses the term *overall*, which indicates a concluding sentence. **The correct answer is D.**

Paragraph Organization

You will also encounter a section on the exam that focuses on the correct and logical arrangement of paragraphs to construct a professional document. Again, you will be asked to select the correct order with the fifth answer option being *no correction is necessary*.

1. Next, your family must carefully select a dog that works well for all your members. Everyone should meet the dog prior to adopting it. Ask questions from the agency or breeder. How well does this dog get along with children? Is it ok to leave the dog alone during the day? What is the typical activity level for the breed? These questions will help to assess if the dog is the right fit for you and your family.

2. Owning a dog is not a simple undertaking. It involves many tasks, both short-term and long-term, many of which go overlooked. Home preparation, proper animal selection, and daily care are all vital components to contemplate before embarking on this journey. If a family dives head-first into this journey unprepared, the results can be catastrophic.

3. Finally, it is time to bring the dog home! Now the real work begins. Developing a daily and weekly chore chart for dog care is a terrific way to ensure proper treatment of your new family member. Daily walks, a feeding schedule, and weekly cleaning of personal space are all necessary. All your hard work will pay off as you, your family, and your pup adjust to a new life together.

4. First, it is important to assess your house for the addition of a pet. Does your current set up allow a pet to move freely? Where will the dog sleep at night? Where will it be allowed to roam during the day? Establishing house rules and preparing your home must preclude the actual animal selection.

A. 3–4–2–1

B. 4–2–1–3

C. 2–4–1–3

D. 1–4–3–2

E. no correction is necessary

Paragraph 2 houses the thesis, "Home preparation, proper animal selection, and daily care are all vital components to contemplate before embarking on this journey." The rest of the paragraphs break down this thesis section by section. The transition word *First* in Paragraph 4 indicates that this is the next paragraph following the thesis. Paragraph 1 begins with another transition word, *Next*, and Paragraph 3 is obviously the last paragraph due to the word *Finally*. **The correct answer is C.**

FIGURAL REASONING (FBI ONLY)

Figural Reasoning questions only appear on the FBI Special Agent Exam. Designed to test your ability to use problem solving and reasoning skills, this type of question contains images that include a sequence of shapes and patterns. These visually sequenced shapes and patterns require you to analyze the following:

1. How are the three images sequenced in a row connected to each other?

2. How are the three images in each series changing—e.g., are they building on each other, separating into smaller pieces, combining in a logical fashion, etc.?

Using information from the first two sequenced series provided, your goal is to identify the sequence or pattern, and then determine the shape or image that logically fits the missing piece.

This type of puzzle can be difficult at first. The sequences and patterns will always go from left to right, row by row. If you start with identifying the various changes that are occurring for each series, it will make it easier to figure out the missing piece of the final sequence. Let's take a look at an example to illustrate.

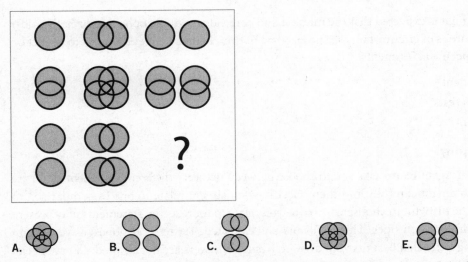

Each sequence in each row is a combination of shapes, specifically circles. Let's look at the first row. The first image is a single shape, and the last image is two of the same shape, side-by-side. The middle image overlaps the two shapes side-by-side. The second row reveals the same sequential pattern. The first image is a single shape of two vertically overlapping gray circles. The last image duplicates the first image side-by-side. The middle image overlaps the four circles. Based on this sequential pattern, the final series has two untouching circles on the left, so the duplicate would be four untouching circles on the right. To verify that this is the correct choice, you simply check the middle, which shows four partially touching circles, which would fulfill the identified pattern. **The correct answer is B.**

CHARACTER AND PERSONALITY ASSESSMENTS (FBI ONLY)

The FBI places additional importance on assessing the character and personality of candidates. It's not enough to test well or to ace the in-person interview and become a special agent. The best candidates possess a unique set of character-based skills and personality traits that set them apart from others. To measure these additional skill-sets, the FBI incorporates questions that assess not only character, but personality and interests as well as judgment in specific situations.

The focal point of these assessments is to see how well you will fit in with the mission of the agency and maintain its core values. Questions will focus upon the following core values, among others:

- Having integrity
- Being a team player
- Having leadership skills
- Having sound judgment
- Being compassionate
- Being respectful
- Being honest
- Being trustworthy
- Being responsible/accountable
- Being obedient

The standards are high, and it is expected that the mission and core values will be upheld, especially under the most stressful and rigorous of circumstances. The last part of this chapter will review what to expect on the following three FBI-specific assessments:

1. Personality Assessment
2. Preferences and Interests
3. Situational Judgment

Personality Assessment

This part of the FBI Special Agent Exam asks you to choose between two very different statements. You are instructed to read each statement carefully and then select how much you relate to one in comparison to the other. At times it may be difficult to choose which one you relate to more as the statements may present topics that you connect with on both sides. This is normal and expected. Try to be as honest as you can in marking the corresponding letter that best fits your answer. Neutral answers are not allowed, so pay special attention to your choices. There are no right or wrong answers as the answers are based on your personal characteristics. The following is an example of this type of question.

Statement A: I enjoy trying new things, even if they seem scary or unfamiliar.	**Statement B:** It is important to me that all people in a conversation are heard and respected.

A. I Agree with Statement A.

B. I Slightly Agree with Statement A.

C. I Slightly Agree with Statement B.

D. I Agree with Statement B.

Preferences and Interests

This part of the FBI Special Agent Exam is designed to gauge your true preferences and interests against the job duties experienced on a day-to-day basis. You will be presented with a series of statements where you will need to choose how strongly you agree or disagree with the statements. It is important to answer honestly and not to "read into" a statement in an effort to figure out what the FBI is looking for. Trying to manipulate your answers will only make it more difficult for the hiring committee to assess your job readiness as well as to get to know you during this introductory phase. You will encounter questions similar to the following:

When working on a team, I am liable to take on the organizational component of the planning tasks.

A. Strongly Agree

B. Agree

C. Neither Agree nor Disagree

D. Disagree

E. Strongly Disagree

Situational Judgment

In this part of the FBI Special Agent Exam, you will be presented with a series of scenarios that relate to common human behavior topics and situations you would likely encounter in a typical work environment. There are no right or wrong answers for each scenario, although at times it may feel that way. Your job is to answer genuinely, as these scenarios may happen to you during your time as a special agent. The best method is to read through the scenario two to three times and then formulate your own answer before you look at the answer options. Then, examine the options provided and choose the response option that is most consistent with how you would actually respond.

ALERT

Personality, preferences and interest, and situational judgment questions appear on the FBI test only. These questions are not scored based on a traditional multiple choice scoring system. Answer these questions to the best of your ability, being as honest as possible.

The following is a a sample scenario similar to what will be presented on the actual exam.

5

You were recently promoted to a supervisory role at your field office. You are the youngest supervisor in a tri-state region, and you are receiving a lot of flak from your fellow supervisory coworkers. During a routine supervisory staff meeting, you ask for suggestions on how to improve the morale during the current state of quarantine due to a recent pandemic. Agent Klaus stands up and says, "Maybe you could entertain us a bit to get our spirits up!" The remaining five agents laugh but are clearly feeling a bit awkward after the outburst. What would you MOST likely do?

A. Say nothing but make a note to keep a close eye on Agent Klaus moving forward.

B. Immediately reprimand Agent Klaus, stating that that type of unprofessional behavior is not behooving of an FBI special agent based on the agency's core values.

C. Pull Agent Klaus aside privately and discuss proper time and place for the type of behavior displayed.

D. Submit a formal verbal warning to Agent Klaus for insubordinate behavior.

E. Fill out a written reprimand detailing the behavior, meet with Agent Klaus to discuss, have both parties sign, and then turn it over to HR to administer repercussions.

Summing It Up

- ATF, ICE, and FBI each have their own separate agency-specific special agent exams. However, there is some overlap in the types of questions you will encounter as well as agency-specific testing requirements.

  - All three special agent exams will contain logical reasoning type questions.
  - The ATF and ICE exams will contain quantitative and/or arithmetic reasoning questions.
  - The ATF exam contains an investigative reasoning section.
  - The ICE exam contains a writing skills assessment.
  - The FBI exam contains a figural reasoning sequential pattern assessment as well as character assessments that measure personality, preferences and interests, and situational judgment.

- **Logical reasoning questions** assess your ability to draw valid conclusions based upon the facts of a situation. This type of question is also referred to as Verbal Reasoning or Logic-Based Reasoning, depending upon which exam you are taking.

- In logical reasoning, many relationships can be deduced from the presence of **indicator words** that have specific purposes in the statement of facts in logical discourse. To reason validly, special attention must be paid to the use of words, their order, and their relationships with other statements.

  - Statements that include words such as *all* or *every* suggest that what is true of one group or category is true of another. However, these statements are not commutative; not everything that is true for the second group is true of the first group.

○ Statements that use *no* and *none* function as absolutes. A statement that uses the word *no* implies that there is no overlap between the two groups or categories indicated. This means that if one thing is true for one group, it is never true of the other; if one thing is true of the second group, then it is also never true of the first.

○ "Some" statements imply that a connection does exist, but they do not imply that some connection does not.

○ "Not all" statements (also worded as "some do not") imply that parts of one group do not apply to the second group.

○ There are statements that use sentential logic—logical statements that use "If–then." This form of logic asserts that if one thing is true, then another thing must be true.

○ The indicator word *only* is similar to *all* in the sense that it implies a concrete connection. If only members of the first group belong to the second group, then that must mean that all things belonging to the second group are within the first group. However, this does not mean that all things belonging to the first group are the second group.

○ "If and only if" statements imply that one thing is true if and only if another condition is true.

- Keep in mind the following steps as you answer logical reasoning questions:

  1. Read the passage carefully.

  2. Identify indicator words to isolate universal and more particular statements.

  3. Paraphrase statements to dissect their meaning.

  4. Work with universal statements to determine what you know about groups and their members.

  5. Use overlapping or exclusive group elements to arrive at a valid conclusion.

- You will encounter **quantitative reasoning questions** on the ATF Special Agent Examination, and **arithmetic reasoning questions** on the ICE exam. While the structure of the two exams differs, you will find some of the same mathematical topics covered, including the following:

  ○ Basic Algebra

  ○ Ratios/Proportions

  ○ Taxes

  ○ Distance and Time

  ○ Profit and Loss

  ○ Money

- **Quantitative reasoning** is a unique form of problem solving that requires the application of basic numeracy, critical thinking, and information literacy. It is the evaluation of real-world problems and solutions through the lens of numerical evidence.

- For those quantitative reasoning questions that ask you to choose from **true/false** options, keep in mind the following:

  1. Identify and eliminate unnecessary information.

  2. Locate relational numbers.

  3. Connect key words/phrases.

  4. Analyze for true/false.

- For the **arithmetic reasoning** test, you do not need to understand intricate mathematical operations or memorize complicated formulas. You can solve the problems arithmetically or by using some simple algebra.

- You will encounter **investigative reasoning questions** on the ATF test only. You will be asked to read a passage and examine a series of statements based on the passage. Then, based on the description of the events as they are reported, the statements made by witnesses, and the questions that must be supported by statements, you must choose the best answer. Here are some helpful questions to ask yourself as you answer this type of question:

  - Is this fact? Can the fact be substantiated?
  - Is the statement based on hearsay?
  - Is the statement pure conjecture?
  - How reliable is the source of the evidence?
  - Does the person have a motive for making this statement?

- The **Writing Skills Assessment** on the ICE Special Agent Test Battery tests your proficiency with standard written English. Basic grammatical and sentence structure concepts will be tested, including verb tense, word choice, adjectives, adverbs, and nouns. You will also be tested on proper capitalization, punctuation, sentence order, and paragraph order.

- **Figural reasoning questions** only appear on the FBI Special Agent Exam. These questions are designed to test your ability to identify a shape or image that logically fits the pattern given.

- The FBI places a heavy emphasis on an applicant's character. Unique to this exam are sections based on assessing your **personality, preferences and personal interests** as they relate to the job responsibilities, and **situational judgment**. These assessments are not graded but serve as a measurement to make sure you are the best fit for the job opportunity.

Chapter 6

Mathematics Review

OVERVIEW

- Basic Arithmetic
- Factors and the Greatest Common Factor
- Fractions
- Decimals
- Percentages
- Ratios and Proportions
- Calculating Rate Problems Using Distance and Time
- Calculating Work Rate Problems
- Solving for Unknown Quantities
- Expressing Word Problems as Equations
- Calculating the Area of an Object
- Summing It Up

Throughout your career as a Special Agent—whether with the ATF, ICE, or FBI—math will be in integral part of your day-to-day operations. Therefore, it is imperative that you have a firm grasp of several mathematical concepts ranging from simple addition and calculating the area of an object to finding the value of an unknown variable. The following chapter provides review of these essential mathematical concepts. Use the following information to improve your speed and confidence for these core topics prior to your exams.

BASIC ARITHMETIC

Basic arithmetic constitutes those core skills you have been using since you first started learning math in elementary school—addition, subtraction, multiplication, and division. As these skills have been established and reinforced over decades, review will occur through their use in other equations. It is important, however, for you to use these core skills often. Repeated use builds both speed and accuracy. Additionally, despite the ubiquitous presence of mobile devices with scientific calculators, the ability to solve math equations without relying on technology is a valuable skill.

As part of this refresher, here are some common mathematical terms you will encounter:

- **Whole number:** A whole number is any integer divisible by itself and 1. For example:

$$1, 2, 3, 5, 100, 10{,}000$$

- **Fraction:** A fraction represents part of a whole number.

$$\frac{1}{2}, \frac{5}{12}, \frac{5}{16}, \frac{11}{32}$$

- **Improper fraction:** An improper fraction is a fraction where the numerator is greater than the denominator.

$$\frac{7}{4}, \frac{12}{8}, \frac{177}{10}$$

- **Mixed number:** A mixed number is a combination of a whole number and a fraction and is a simplified version of an improper fraction.

$$\frac{7}{4} = 1\frac{3}{4}$$

$$\frac{12}{8} = 1\frac{1}{2}$$

$$\frac{177}{10} = 17\frac{7}{10}$$

- **Prime number:** A number that is only divisible by itself and 1. Number pairs, like (7, 13), that don't have any number other than 1 in common, are termed **relatively prime**.

FACTORS AND THE GREATEST COMMON FACTOR

Factors are whole numbers that are multiplied together to produce another number. For example, the factors of the number 36 are 1, 2, 3, 4, 6, 9, 12, 18, and 36. The pairs of factors of 36 are: 1 and 36, 2 and 18, 3 and 12, 4 and 9, and 6 and 6.

The term **greatest common factor (GCF)** refers to the largest number that can be factored into two numbers cleanly (that is, without a remainder). For example, the GCF of 10 and 15 is 5. For 10 and 20, the GCF is 10.

Example: Find the GCF for (12, 8)

Solution: Factors for 12: 1, 2, 3, 4, 6, 12

Factors for 8: 1, 2, 4, 8

The **common factors**—i.e., the factors common to both sets of numbers—for 12 and 8 are 1, 2, and 4. The greatest (largest) of the group is 4, so 4 is the GCF of (12, 8).

Example: Find the GCF for (28, 56)

Solution: Factors for 28: 1, 2, 4, 7, 14, 28

Factors for 56: 1, 2, 4, 7, 8, 14, 28, 56

The greatest common factor the two numbers share is 28.

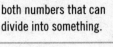

TIP
Don't be confused by the term **greatest common divisor**. A divisor and a factor have the same meaning. They are both numbers that can divide into something.

FRACTIONS

Fractions indicate parts of a whole. A fraction consists of a numerator and a denominator.

$$\frac{3}{4} \quad \begin{array}{l} \leftarrow \text{numerator} \rightarrow \\ \leftarrow \text{denominator} \rightarrow \end{array} \quad \frac{7}{8}$$

The **denominator** tells you how many equal parts the object or number is divided into, and the **numerator** indicates the number of parts represented.

Example: Divide a baseball game, a football game, and a hockey game into convenient numbers of parts. Write a fraction to represent each situation.

1. If a pitcher played two innings, how much of the whole baseball game did he play?

2. If a quarterback played three quarters of a football game, how much of the whole game did he play?

3. If a goalie played two periods of a hockey game, how much of the whole game did he play?

Solution 1:   A baseball game has nine parts (each an inning). The pitcher pitched two innings. Therefore, he played $\frac{2}{9}$ of the game. The denominator represents the nine parts the game is divided into; the numerator represents the two parts played by the pitcher.

Solution 2:   Similarly, there are four quarters in a football game, and a quarterback playing three of those quarters plays in $\frac{3}{4}$ of the game.

Solution 3:   There are three periods in a hockey game, and the goalie played in two of them. Therefore, he played in $\frac{2}{3}$ of the game.

Adding and Subtracting Fractions

To add fractions with the same denominators, add the numerators and keep the common denominator.

Example: Add $\frac{1}{4} + \frac{3}{4} + \frac{3}{4}$.

Solution: When the denominators are the same, add the numerators to arrive at the answer.

If you end up with an improper fraction, simplify into a mixed number.

$$\frac{1}{4} + \frac{3}{4} + \frac{3}{4} = \frac{7}{4} = 1\frac{3}{4}$$

To find the difference between two fractions with the same denominators, subtract the numerators, leaving the denominators alone.

Example: Find the difference between $\frac{7}{8}$ and $\frac{3}{8}$.

Solution: $$\frac{7}{8} - \frac{3}{8} = \frac{4}{8} = \frac{1}{2}$$

To add or subtract fractions with different denominators, find the common denominator. A **common denominator** is a number that can be divided by the denominators of all the fractions in the problem without a remainder.

Example: Find a common denominator for $\frac{1}{4}$ and $\frac{1}{3}$.

Solution: Multiply the denominators to get $4 \times 3 = 12$. 12 can be divided by both 4 and 3:

$$\frac{1}{4} \text{ is equivalent to } \frac{3}{12}$$

$$\frac{1}{3} \text{ is equivalent to } \frac{4}{12}$$

$$\frac{3}{12} + \frac{4}{12} = \frac{7}{12}$$

Therefore:

$$\frac{1}{4} + \frac{1}{3} = \frac{7}{12}$$

Seven-twelfths is in its simplest form because 7 and 12 do not have a whole number (other than 1) by which they are both divisible.

Example: Add $\frac{3}{8}$, $\frac{5}{6}$, $\frac{1}{4}$, and $\frac{2}{3}$.

Solution: Find the common denominator.

$$\frac{3}{8} = \frac{9}{24} \quad (24 \div 8 = 3); (3 \times 3 = 9)$$

$$\frac{5}{6} = \frac{20}{24} \quad (24 \div 6 = 4); (4 \times 5 = 20)$$

$$\frac{1}{4} = \frac{6}{24} \quad (24 \div 4 = 6); (6 \times 1 = 6)$$

$$\frac{2}{3} = \frac{16}{24} \quad (24 \div 3 = 8); (8 \times 2 = 16)$$

Now add the fractions:

$$\frac{9}{24} + \frac{20}{24} + \frac{6}{24} + \frac{16}{24} = \frac{51}{24}$$

Note that the answer is an improper fraction—that is, the numerator is greater than the denominator. To rewrite the answer as a mixed number, divide the numerator by the denominator and express the remainder as a fraction.

$$\frac{51}{24} = 51 \div 24 = 2\frac{3}{24} = 2\frac{1}{8}$$

Multiplying and Dividing Fractions

When multiplying fractions, multiply numerators by numerators and denominators by denominators.

$$\frac{3}{5} \times \frac{4}{7} \times \frac{1}{5} = \frac{3 \times 4 \times 1}{5 \times 7 \times 5} = \frac{12}{175}$$

Try to work with numbers that are as small as possible. You can make numbers smaller by dividing out common factors. Do this by dividing the numerator of any one fraction and the denominator of any one fraction by the same number.

$$\frac{\overset{1}{\cancel{3}}}{\cancel{4}_{2}} \times \frac{\overset{1}{\cancel{2}}}{\cancel{9}_{3}} = \frac{1 \times 1}{2 \times 3} = \frac{1}{6}$$

In this case, we divided the numerator of the first fraction and the denominator of the second fraction by 3, while the denominator of the first fraction and the numerator of the second fraction were divided by 2.

To divide by a fraction, multiply by the reciprocal of the divisor.

$$\frac{3}{16} \div \frac{1}{8} = \frac{3}{\cancel{16}_{2}} \times \frac{\overset{1}{\cancel{8}}}{1} = \frac{3}{2} = 1\frac{1}{2}$$

To convert a fraction to a decimal, follow through on the division.

$$\frac{4}{5} = 4 \div 5 = 0.8$$

DECIMALS

Decimals are a way of writing fractions using tenths, hundredths, thousandths, and so forth. If you can count money, make change, or understand a batting average, decimals should present no problem. The key to solving decimal addition and subtraction problems is keeping the decimal points in line.

Incorrect decimal alignment:

$$173.75$$
$$+124.22$$

Correct decimal alignment:

$$173.75$$
$$+124.22$$

While addition and subtraction of decimals should present no problems, there are a few things to keep in mind when it comes to multiplication and division of decimals.

Example: $1.482 \times 0.16 =$

Solution: Remember that you have decimals in the problem. This is important because when you multiply decimals, the placement of the decimal point in the solution is dependent on the sum of the places to the right of the decimal point in both the multiplier and number being multiplied. Simplify by removing the decimal points:

$$1482 \times 16 = 23{,}712$$

Now, reinsert the decimal point. Remember, the placement of the decimal point is dependent on the sum of the places to the right of the decimal point in both the multiplier and number being multiplied.

$$1.482 \times 0.16 = 0.23712$$

You can also think of it this way:

$$1.482 \leftarrow \text{three decimal places}$$
$$\times \ 0.16 \leftarrow \text{two decimal places}$$
$$8892$$
$$14820$$
$$0.23712 \leftarrow \text{five decimal places}$$

You cannot divide a number by a decimal, so for division problems you will move the decimal to the right the same number of places for each set of numbers. Here is a demonstration, using the previous equation:

$$0.23712 \div 0.16 =$$

Move the decimal point two places to the right:

$$23.712 \div 16 = 1.482$$

Fortunately, with division you do not need to shift the decimal point back to where it was; your divisor must be a whole number. Here is another example:

$$7,512 \div 0.06 =$$
$$751,200 \div 6 = 125,200$$

Check your math:

$$125,200 \times 0.06 = 7,512$$

PERCENTAGES

One percent is one hundredth of something (*cent* = 100). One percent of $1.00, then, is one cent. Using decimal notation, we can write one cent as $0.01, five cents as $0.05, twenty-five cents as $0.25, and so forth.

There is a relationship between decimals, fractions, and percentages. The following will help you to convert numbers from one of these forms to another:

1. To change a percentage to a decimal, remove the percent sign (%) and divide the number by 100.

$$25\% = \frac{25}{100} = 0.25$$

2. To change a decimal to a percentage, multiply by 100 and add the percent sign (%).

$$0.25 = 0.25 \times 100 = 25\%$$

3. To change a percentage to a fraction, remove the % sign and use that number as your numerator, with 100 as your denominator.

$$25\% = \frac{25}{100} = \frac{1}{4}$$

4. To change a fraction to a percentage, multiply by 100 and add the percent sign (%).

$$\frac{1}{4} \times 100 = 25\%$$

Example: Find 1% of 200.

Solution: 1% of 200 is 1/100, or 0.01 of 200.

Using decimal notation, we can calculate one percent of 200 by multiplying:

$$200 \times 0.01 = 2$$

Using decimal notation, we write one-tenth of one percent as 0.001, the decimal number for one thousandth. If you remember that a percent is one hundredth of something, you can see that one tenth of that percent is equivalent to one thousandth of the whole.

6

NOTE

Decimal expressions are considered mixed numbers, but a percentage is not. Percentage is not limited to comparing other numbers to 100. You can divide any number into hundredths and talk about percentage.

The following table shows some common percentage and fractional equivalents you should remember.

Percent	Equivalent Fraction	Equivalent Decimal
10%	$\frac{1}{10}$	0.10
12.5%	$\frac{1}{8}$	0.125
20%	$\frac{1}{5}$	0.20
25%	$\frac{1}{4}$	0.25
$33\frac{1}{3}\%$	$\frac{1}{3}$	$0.33\overline{3}$
50%	$\frac{1}{2}$	0.50
$66\frac{2}{3}\%$	$\frac{2}{3}$	$0.66\overline{6}$
75%	$\frac{3}{4}$	0.75

To find a percent of a number, change the percent to a decimal and multiply the number by it.

Example: What is 5% of 80?

Solution: 5% of 80 = 80 × 0.05 = 4

To find out what a number is when given a percent of it, change the percent to a decimal and divide the given number by it.

Example: 5 is 10% of what number?

Solution: 5 ÷ 0.10 = 50

To find what percent one number is of another number, create a fraction by placing the part over the whole. Simplify the fraction if possible, then rename it as a decimal (remember the fraction bar means *divided by*, so divide the numerator by the denominator), and rename the answer as a percent by multiplying by 100, moving the decimal point two places to the right.

Example: 4 is what percent of 80?

Solution: $\frac{4}{80} = \frac{1}{20} = 0.05 = 5\%$

Percent of Change

A **percent of change** is the relative change between an old value and a new value, expressed as a percentage of the old value. For example, a 10% discount on a $60 restaurant bill means you pay $6 less, or $54. Conversely, a 10% increase on that same bill means you pay $66. Sales tax is another example of a percent of change.

To calculate percent of change, you need a good understanding of decimals, percentages, and fractions.

For this, we use the percent of change formula.

$$\frac{\% \text{ change}}{100} = \frac{\text{difference}}{\text{original \#}}$$

To get the new value, we need two pieces of information. Looking at the restaurant bill above, we know the original price is $60, and the discount is ten percent.

$$\frac{10}{100} = \frac{x}{60}$$

From here, we cross-multiply:

$$\frac{10 \times 60}{100 \times x} = \frac{600}{100x}$$

Then solve for x.

$$600 = 100x$$
$$6 = x$$

Subtract this from the original price to find the new price.

$$\$60 - \$6 = \$54$$

You can use the same formula to calculate the percent of change between two numbers. Using the previous example, we know the original price was $60 and the new price is $54. Enter this information into the percent of change formula, cross multiply, and solve for x.

$$\frac{x}{100} = \frac{(60 - 54)}{60}$$
$$\frac{x}{100} = \frac{6}{60}$$
$$60x = 600$$
$$x = 10$$

The difference is 10%.

RATIOS AND PROPORTIONS

Ratios show the relationship between two or more items. For example, if three out of every ten armed robbers are apprehended within the first 24 hours, then the ratio would be 3 : 10, or three arrests for every ten robberies.

Example: Write a ratio showing the number of tires (excluding the spare) on a car.

Solution: There are four tires on a car, so the ratio is 4 : 1.

Example: There are 1.8 autos for every household in the US.

Solution: 1.8 : 1

Proportioning is a way to show relations between two or more ratios. For example, you can use proportions to find out how many books you need to read each month if your goal is to read 100 books in 12 months. You can also use proportions to learn how a set number of items are distributed among multiple locations.

Example: You have a goal of reading 100 books over the next 12 months. How many books do you need to read each month?

Solution: Write out the proportion, with x representing the unknown quantity.

$$\frac{x}{1} = \frac{100}{12}$$

Cross-multiply both fractions:

$$\frac{12(x)}{1} = \frac{(1)100}{12}$$
$$12x = 100$$

Solve for x:

$$\frac{12x}{12} = \frac{100}{12}$$
$$x = 8.3$$

Example: Ten thousand case files for the Denver Field Office are stored between three locations scattered throughout the region, including 3,000 active case files located at the field office itself. The remaining files are stored at field offices in Cheyenne and Colorado Springs in the ratio of 4 : 6. How many files are stored in Cheyenne and Colorado Springs, respectively?

Solution: First, find how many files are *not* stored at the Denver field office:

$$10,000 - 3,000 = 7,000 \text{ files}$$

The ratio of 4 : 6 tells us that of every ten files, four are stored in Cheyenne and six are stored in Colorado Springs. To find the number of files stored in Cheyenne, set up a proportion:

$$\frac{x}{7,000} = \frac{4}{10}$$

Cross multiply both fractions:

$$\frac{(10)x}{7,000} = \frac{(7,000)4}{10}$$
$$10x = 28,000$$

Solve for x:

$$\frac{(10)x}{10} = \frac{28,000}{10}$$
$$x = 2,800$$

Now we know there are 2,800 files in Cheyenne, with the remainder (7,000 – 2,800 = 4,200) in Colorado Springs.

CALCULATING RATE PROBLEMS USING DISTANCE AND TIME

These problems require that you find the speed, or rate, that something happens over a given distance and time. For example, you might need to calculate how fast Special Agent Grimsdale was driving when she traveled from Milwaukee to Madison, Wisconsin, a 79-mile drive, in 45 minutes. The basic formula for solving this type of problem is *distance = rate × time*, or $d = r \times t$.

Example: Special Agent Grimsdale drove 79 miles in 45 minutes. How fast was she driving?

Solution: To calculate rate using distance and time, use this formula: $r = \dfrac{d}{t}$, where *r* is rate (in miles per hour), *d* is distance (in miles), and *t* is time (in hours).

$$r = \frac{79}{0.75}$$

Solve for *r*:

$$r = 79 \div 0.75 = 105.3$$

Special Agent Grimsdale drove at a rate of 105 miles per hour.

You can use this formula to solve for distance or time, as well.

Example: How far did Agent Walker travel when driving 45 mph for five hours?

Solution: Use the formula $r = \dfrac{d}{t}$:

$$45 = \frac{d}{5}$$

Multiply both sides by 5:

$$(5)45 = \frac{d}{5}(5)$$
$$225 = d$$

Agent Walker traveled 225 miles.

Example: Driving at an average speed of 65 mph, how long did Agent Benson take to drive from San Francisco to Los Angeles, a driving distance of 383 miles?

Solution: Use the formula $r = \dfrac{d}{t}$:

$$65 = \frac{383}{t}$$

Multiply both sides by *t*:

$$(t)65 = \frac{383}{t}(t)$$
$$65t = 383$$

Divide both sides by 65:

$$t = \frac{383}{65} = 5.89$$

Agent Benson drove from San Francisco to Los Angeles in 5.89 hours.

6

NOTE

To find how many minutes are in a fractional or decimal number of hours, multiply by 60. For 0.89 hours, for example, multiply by 60: 0.89 × 60 = 53 minutes. You may also have questions asking you to compare two different equations sharing a constant value.

CALCULATING WORK RATE PROBLEMS

Work rate problems ask you to determine how long it would take to complete a job at a given rate.

Example: As part of an ongoing investigation, Agent Miller needs to review 35 case files. After four hours, she has finished five files. How long will it take Agent Miller to review the remaining 30 files?

Solution: Use a proportion to solve:

$$\frac{4}{5} = \frac{x}{30}$$

Cross-multiply, then solve for *x*:

$$5x = 4(30)$$
$$5x = 120$$
$$x = \frac{120}{5}$$
$$x = 24$$

Example: Agent Thomason has been ordered to supervise the building of a berm along a 200-mile length of border frequented by smugglers. For the first hour, he has two bulldozers at his disposal, and combined they can build up to two miles of earthen berm every 45 minutes. At hour 2, seven more bulldozers show up to help. Assuming the same rate, how long will it take to complete the full 200 miles?

Solution: First, find how much berm each bulldozer can build in one hour. We know it takes two bulldozers 45 minutes to create two miles of berm, so it is easy to determine that one bulldozer can create one mile of berm in 45 minutes. Knowing that, we can calculate how much berm (*x*) one bulldozer can create in one hour:

$$\frac{1}{0.75} = \frac{x}{1}$$

Cross multiply and solve for *x*:

$$0.75x = 1$$
$$\frac{0.75}{0.75}x = \frac{1}{0.75}$$
$$x = 1.33$$

So it takes one bulldozer one hour to create 1.33 miles of berm. From this, we know that in two hours two bulldozers can complete 5.33 miles of berm, leaving 194.67 miles to build.

Next, calculate how long it will take nine bulldozers to build 194.67 miles of berm at this same rate. To do this, divide 194.67 (berm remaining) by 9 (number of bulldozers) multiplied by 1.33 (miles of berm per hour):

$$194.67 \div 9(1.33) = 16.26$$

Now add back the initial two hours the first two bulldozers worked for the first 5.33 miles of berm. This yields 18.26 hours. When converted and rounded, that's 18 hours and 16 minutes that are needed for the bulldozers to construct 200 miles of berm.

SOLVING FOR UNKNOWN QUANTITIES

You are probably familiar with the word **variable**, meaning something that is unknown. Not every math problem will have all of the values you need to solve the problem expressed. Some will have variables that you must solve in order to complete the problem. Let's look at an example.

Example: The cost at the register for a pack of cigarettes is $5.25. If the tax on a pack of cigarettes is 17%, what was the cost for the pack, pre-tax?

Solution: We want to find the original cost of the pack (x), and we know that the total cost of the pack including the 17% tax is $5.25. We can write this as:

$$5.25 = x(1 + 0.17)$$

Solve for x:

$$5.25 = x(1 + 0.17)$$
$$5.25 = 1.17x$$
$$\frac{5.25}{1.17} = \frac{1.17x}{1.17}$$
$$4.4872 = x$$

Rounding to the nearest cent, the cost per pack is $4.49, with an additional $0.76 in added tax.

Example: Special Agent Fisher rents a car and drives from Spokane, Washington to Cheyenne, Wyoming, a 933-mile drive. He rents the car for four days at $56.00/day. The rental includes 100 miles per day, and each mile past that is $0.20. How much ($x$) did Special Agent Smith pay for the rental?

Solution: The cost (r) for the car itself is easy enough: $r = \$56.00 \times 4 = \$224.00$. We also know that the rental includes 100 miles per day, meaning Smith is responsible for only 533 miles of the drive ($933 - 400 = 533$). We know the rate per mile is $0.20, so we can find the cost for mileage (m) by multiplying the mileage by the cost per mile:

$$m = 533 \times \$0.20$$
$$m = \$106.60$$

Add this to the rental cost (r) for the total cost for the vehicle:

$$x = \$224.00 + \$106.60$$
$$x = \$330.60$$

Special Agent Fisher paid $330.60 for the vehicle rental.

EXPRESSING WORD PROBLEMS AS EQUATIONS

In the previous examples, we converted several word problems into equations, but let's look at a few more. The most common types of word problems are distance/rate/time and work problems.

Example: Two hikers start walking from the city line at different times. The second hiker, whose speed is 4 miles per hour, starts 2 hours after the first hiker, whose speed is 3 miles per hour. Determine the amount of time and distance that will be covered by the time that the second hiker catches up with the first.

Solution 1: Since the first hiker has a 2-hour head start and is walking at the rate of 3 miles per hour, he is 6 miles from the city line when the second hiker starts.

$$\text{Rate} \times \text{Time} = \text{Distance}$$

Subtracting 3 miles per hour from 4 miles per hour gives us 1 mile per hour or the difference in the rates of speed of the two hikers. In other words, the second hiker gains 1 mile on the first hiker every hour.

Because there is a 6-mile difference to cut down and it is cut down 1 mile every hour, the second hiker will need 6 hours to overtake his companion. In this time, he will have traveled $4 \times 6 = 24$ miles. The first hiker will have been walking 8 hours, since he had a 2-hour head start, $8 \times 3 = 24$ miles.

Solution 2: Another way to solve distance (or mixture) problems is to organize all of the data in a chart. For distance problems, make columns for rate, time, and distance and separate lines for each moving object. In the problem about the two hikers, the chart technique works like this:

STEP 1: Draw the chart.

	Rate	×	Time	=	Distance
Hiker 1					
Hiker 2					

STEP 2: Since the problem states that Hiker 1 is traveling at 3 miles per hour and Hiker 2 is traveling at 4 miles per hour, enter these two figures in the rate column.

	Rate	×	Time	=	Distance
Hiker 1	3 mph				
Hiker 2	4 mph				

STEP 3: The problem does not tell us how long each hiker traveled, but it does say that Hiker 1 started 2 hours before Hiker 2. Therefore, if we use the unknown x to represent the number of hours Hiker 2 traveled, we can set Hiker 1's time as $x + 2$. Enter these two figures in the time column.

	Rate	×	Time	=	Distance
Hiker 1	3 mph		$x + 2$		
Hiker 2	4 mph		x		

STEP 4: Using the formula $D = R \times T$, we can easily find each hiker's distance by multiplying the figures for rate and time already in the chart.

For Hiker 1: $3(x + 2) = 3x + 6$

For Hiker 2: $4(x) = 4x$

	Rate	×	Time	=	Distance
Hiker 1	3 mph		$x + 2$		$3x + 6$
Hiker 2	4 mph		x		$4x$

STEP 5: When the two hikers meet, each will have covered the same distance. Using this information, we can set up an equation:

Distance covered by Hiker 1		Distance covered by Hiker 2
$3x + 6$	=	$4x$

Solving this equation for x, we find that $x = 6$. This means that Hiker 1 has walked for $6 + 2 = 8$ hours when Hiker 2 catches up to him.

STEP 6: Because Hiker 1 started 2 hours earlier than Hiker 2, Hiker 2 will have walked for 6 hours to catch up to Hiker 1.

STEP 7: Using this information, we can determine that Hiker 1 walked 8 hours at 3 miles per hour to cover 24 miles. Hiker 2 walked for 6 hours at 4 miles per hour to cover the same 24 miles.

Example: How far can a man drive into the country if he drives out at 40 miles per hour, returns over the same road at 30 miles per hour, and spends 8 hours away from home, including a 1-hour stop for lunch?

Solution: Set up a chart and fill in the rate (miles per hour) for the trip out and the return trip.

Let x be the time for trip out.

Total driving time is $8 - 1 = 7$ hours.

Therefore, time for return trip is $7 - x$ hours.

	Rate	×	Time	=	Distance
Going	40		x		$40x$
Return	30		$7 - x$		$210 - 30x$

You can then calculate the distance by multiplying the terms for rate and time, and then solve for time:

$$40x = 210 - 30x$$
$$70x = 210$$
$$x = 3 \text{ hours}$$

Using the formula $R \times T = D$:

$$40 \text{ mph} \times 3 \text{ hours} = 120 \text{ miles}$$

CALCULATING THE AREA OF AN OBJECT

Area is the space enclosed by a plane (flat) figure. A rectangle is a plane figure with four right angles. Opposite sides of a rectangle are of equal length and are parallel to each other. To find the area of a rectangle, multiply the length of the base of the rectangle by the length of its height. Always use square units to express area.

$A = bh$

$A = 9 \text{ ft.} \times 3 \text{ ft.}$

$A = 27 \text{ sq. ft.}$

3 ft.

9 ft.

A square is a rectangle in which all four sides are the same length. You find the area of a square by squaring the length of one side, which is the same as multiplying the square's length by its width.

$A = s^2$

$A = 4 \text{ in.} \times 4 \text{ in.}$

$A = 16 \text{ sq. in.}$

4 in.

4 in.

A triangle is a three-sided plane figure. You find the area of a triangle by multiplying the base by the altitude (height) and dividing by two.

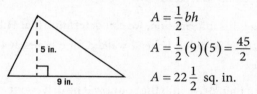

$A = \frac{1}{2}bh$

$A = \frac{1}{2}(9)(5) = \frac{45}{2}$

$A = 22\frac{1}{2} \text{ sq. in.}$

5 in.

9 in.

A circle is a perfectly round plane figure. The distance from the center of a circle to its rim is its radius. The distance from one edge to the other through the center is its diameter. The diameter is twice the length of the radius.

Pi (π) is the ratio between a circle's circumference and its diameter, a mathematical value equal to approximately 3.14, or $\frac{22}{7}$. Pi (π) is frequently used in calculations involving circles.

You find the area of a circle by squaring the radius and multiplying it by π. You may leave the area in terms of pi unless you are told what value to assign π.

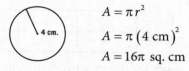

$A = \pi r^2$

$A = \pi (4 \text{ cm})^2$

$A = 16\pi \text{ sq. cm}$

4 cm.

6

TIP

Don't confuse the two formulas for calculating the circumference and the area of circles. A good way to keep them straight is to remember the square in πr^2. It should remind you that area must be in square units.

Summing It Up

- Arithmetic reasoning and quantitative reasoning questions are presented in word problem form. The path to the correct answer may be as simple as performing basic arithmetic, or it may include converting information into an equation and solving for an unknown variable.

- Basic arithmetic factors into all math problems and includes addition, subtraction, multiplication, and division.

- You must be familiar with the following terms:

    ○ **Whole number:** Any integer divisible by itself and 1.

    ○ **Fraction:** A part of a whole number that consists of a **numerator** and a **denominator**, the top and bottom, respectively.

    ○ **Improper fraction**: A fraction where the numerator is greater than the denominator.

    ○ **Mixed number:** A combination of a whole number and a fraction that is a simplified version of an improper fraction.

- **Factors** are whole numbers that are multiplied together to produce another number. The **greatest common factor (GCF)** of two numbers is the largest number that can be divided into each without creating a remainder.

- Keep in mind the following when working with **fractions**:

    ○ To reduce a fraction, divide out the common factor from the top and bottom.

    ○ To add and subtract, the fractions must have the same denominator.

    ○ To find a **common denominator**, multiply the denominators by one another and then reduce the final fraction as needed.

    ○ To multiply fractions, you must multiply numerators by numerators and denominators by denominators.

    ○ To divide fractions, multiply the first fraction by the reciprocal of the second.

- Keep in mind the following rules when working with **decimals**:

    ○ When adding or subtracting, make sure to align the decimal places.

    ○ When multiplying, the placement of the decimal point in the solution is dependent on the sum of the places to the right of the decimal point in *both* the multiplier and the number being multiplied.

    ○ For division problems, the divisor must be a whole number. You will need to move the decimal point to the right the same amount of places for each set of numbers.

- A **percentage** represents a value out of 100. In other words, a percentage equals a part divided by a whole. Percentages can be easily changed to decimals and fractions. The opposite is also true.

    ○ The **percent of change** between two numbers can be found by dividing the difference between the two numbers and the original value.

6

- A **ratio** is a relationship between two values, often expressed as a fraction.
- A **proportion** comprises two ratios that are equal.
- The $D = RT$ formula is used to find distance, rate, and time; with two of those values, you can always find the third.
- **Work rate problems** require you to find how long a job requires given a certain rate; similar to distance, rate, and time, you'll need to know at least two values to find a third (time, work rate, and total work to be completed).
- Calculating the **area** (internal space) of 2D shapes requires specific formulas; you need to know the formulas for at least rectangles, squares, triangles, and circles.

6

PART IV
PRACTICE TESTS

PRACTICE TEST 1: ATF SPECIAL AGENT EXAMINATION

The following is a sample practice test that contains the types of questions found on the ATF Special Agent Examination. It's divided into the following three parts:

- Part A—Verbal Reasoning
- Part B—Quantitative Reasoning
- Part C—Investigative Reasoning

If you decide to time yourself, you have 100 minutes to complete this practice test. Use this time limit to gauge your comfort level under time constraints and your level of mastery of the types of questions found in the exam. The actual test session is approximately four hours long for two tests: the ATF Special Agent Examination and the ATF Special Agent Applicant Assessment.

After you have completed this practice test, check your answers against the answer keys located after Part C. Detailed answer explanations and applicable step-by-step mathematical breakdowns are provided.

Remember, you are not allowed to use a calculator, and there is no penalty for guessing.

PRACTICE TEST 1: ATF SPECIAL AGENT EXAMINATION ANSWER SHEET

Part A—Verbal Reasoning

1. Ⓐ Ⓑ Ⓒ Ⓓ Ⓔ   6. Ⓐ Ⓑ Ⓒ Ⓓ Ⓔ   11. Ⓐ Ⓑ Ⓒ Ⓓ Ⓔ
2. Ⓐ Ⓑ Ⓒ Ⓓ Ⓔ   7. Ⓐ Ⓑ Ⓒ Ⓓ Ⓔ   12. Ⓐ Ⓑ Ⓒ Ⓓ Ⓔ
3. Ⓐ Ⓑ Ⓒ Ⓓ Ⓔ   8. Ⓐ Ⓑ Ⓒ Ⓓ Ⓔ   13. Ⓐ Ⓑ Ⓒ Ⓓ Ⓔ
4. Ⓐ Ⓑ Ⓒ Ⓓ Ⓔ   9. Ⓐ Ⓑ Ⓒ Ⓓ Ⓔ   14. Ⓐ Ⓑ Ⓒ Ⓓ Ⓔ
5. Ⓐ Ⓑ Ⓒ Ⓓ Ⓔ   10. Ⓐ Ⓑ Ⓒ Ⓓ Ⓔ   15. Ⓐ Ⓑ Ⓒ Ⓓ Ⓔ

Part B—Quantitative Reasoning

1. Ⓐ Ⓑ Ⓒ Ⓓ Ⓔ   9. Ⓐ Ⓑ Ⓒ Ⓓ Ⓔ   17. Ⓐ Ⓑ Ⓒ Ⓓ Ⓔ   25. Ⓐ Ⓑ
2. Ⓐ Ⓑ Ⓒ Ⓓ Ⓔ   10. Ⓐ Ⓑ Ⓒ Ⓓ Ⓔ   18. Ⓐ Ⓑ Ⓒ Ⓓ Ⓔ   26. Ⓐ Ⓑ
3. Ⓐ Ⓑ Ⓒ Ⓓ Ⓔ   11. Ⓐ Ⓑ Ⓒ Ⓓ Ⓔ   19. Ⓐ Ⓑ Ⓒ Ⓓ Ⓔ   27. Ⓐ Ⓑ
4. Ⓐ Ⓑ Ⓒ Ⓓ Ⓔ   12. Ⓐ Ⓑ Ⓒ Ⓓ Ⓔ   20. Ⓐ Ⓑ Ⓒ Ⓓ Ⓔ   28. Ⓐ Ⓑ
5. Ⓐ Ⓑ Ⓒ Ⓓ Ⓔ   13. Ⓐ Ⓑ Ⓒ Ⓓ Ⓔ   21. Ⓐ Ⓑ   29. Ⓐ Ⓑ
6. Ⓐ Ⓑ Ⓒ Ⓓ Ⓔ   14. Ⓐ Ⓑ Ⓒ Ⓓ Ⓔ   22. Ⓐ Ⓑ   30. Ⓐ Ⓑ
7. Ⓐ Ⓑ Ⓒ Ⓓ Ⓔ   15. Ⓐ Ⓑ Ⓒ Ⓓ Ⓔ   23. Ⓐ Ⓑ
8. Ⓐ Ⓑ Ⓒ Ⓓ Ⓔ   16. Ⓐ Ⓑ Ⓒ Ⓓ Ⓔ   24. Ⓐ Ⓑ

Part C—Investigative Reasoning

1. Ⓐ Ⓑ Ⓒ Ⓓ Ⓔ   6. Ⓐ Ⓑ Ⓒ Ⓓ Ⓔ   11. Ⓐ Ⓑ Ⓒ Ⓓ Ⓔ
2. Ⓐ Ⓑ Ⓒ Ⓓ Ⓔ   7. Ⓐ Ⓑ Ⓒ Ⓓ Ⓔ   12. Ⓐ Ⓑ Ⓒ Ⓓ Ⓔ
3. Ⓐ Ⓑ Ⓒ Ⓓ Ⓔ   8. Ⓐ Ⓑ Ⓒ Ⓓ Ⓔ   13. Ⓐ Ⓑ Ⓒ Ⓓ Ⓔ
4. Ⓐ Ⓑ Ⓒ Ⓓ Ⓔ   9. Ⓐ Ⓑ Ⓒ Ⓓ Ⓔ   14. Ⓐ Ⓑ Ⓒ Ⓓ Ⓔ
5. Ⓐ Ⓑ Ⓒ Ⓓ Ⓔ   10. Ⓐ Ⓑ Ⓒ Ⓓ Ⓔ   15. Ⓐ Ⓑ Ⓒ Ⓓ Ⓔ

PRACTICE TEST 1: ATF SPECIAL AGENT EXAMINATION

100 minutes—60 questions

Part A—Verbal Reasoning

> **DIRECTIONS:** In each of these questions, you will be given a paragraph that contains all the information necessary to infer the correct answer. Use **only** the information provided in the paragraph. Do not make any assumptions or introduce information beyond what is presented. Also, assume that all information given in the paragraph is true, even if it conflicts with some fact known to you. Only one correct answer is possible based on the information in the paragraph.

1. ATF special agents believe there is a gun smuggling operation in an apartment complex in a middle-class neighborhood. Since the activity typically takes place during the night, there is concern for the safety of the residents in their homes. For a warrant to be issued, the agents need to establish probable cause of contraband, stolen items, and/or evidence of a crime based on facts and circumstances. The agents have been staking out the apartment complex for two months, and there has been suspicious activity surrounding the people who enter and leave the premises. Although none of the agents ever saw illegal firearms, the lead agent believes he has enough evidence to secure a warrant based solely on the facts that they have had surveillance for two months and there were suspicious people going in and out of the apartment complex.

   From the information provided above, it can be validly concluded that:

   A. The request for a search warrant will be granted because the agents have provided enough information for probable cause.

   B. The request for a search warrant will be granted because the agents had enough evidence when they provided surveillance footage.

   C. The request for a search warrant will be denied because the agents have violated the reasonable right to privacy.

   D. The request for a search warrant will be denied because there is insufficient evidence for probable cause.

   E. The request for a search warrant will be denied because there is no probable cause for the search warrant.

2. Agents are required to use government vehicles for official business. Agents must be performing duties when driving the vehicles. Agents do not have to be on duty if the vehicle is used for official business. Agents may use government vehicles for personal business if they are on duty and making a stop that is not out of their direction of travel.

From the information provided above, it can be validly concluded that:

A. Government vehicles may be used for personal matters if agents are not working and do not deviate from their routes of travel.

B. An agent who is off duty may not drive a government vehicle for personal business or official business.

C. Using a government vehicle for strictly personal matters is prohibited.

D. On-duty agents may use only government vehicles to perform their duties as government officials.

E. When driving a government vehicle, an agent need not be on duty or performing any kind of working assignment.

3. Stefan was convicted of a liquor license misdemeanor two years ago, and his license was revoked. He has since applied for another liquor license in a different state. Agent Harris has reviewed the file and is aware of the lengthy process for recertification for this first-time offender. Although Stefan realizes that he has the misdemeanor, he feels he will meet the three-year criteria to recertify for the permit.

From the information provided above, it can be validly concluded that:

A. Stefan will be granted a probationary license.

B. Stefan will be granted the license because this is his only misdemeanor.

C. Stefan will be denied because his misdemeanor is only 2 years old.

D. Stefan will be denied because there is sufficient evidence for his license to remain revoked.

E. Stefan will be denied because he moved to another state.

4. ATF agents must be at least 21 years of age. The day immediately preceding an individual's 37th birthday is the last day to be referred for selection consideration. However, the age restriction may not apply if the individual is a preference-eligible veteran or is currently serving or has previously served in a federal civilian law enforcement position. There are other criteria that these individuals may have to meet.

From the information provided above, it can be validly concluded that:

A. All candidates that are applying must be 36 years old.

B. None of the candidates can be above 37 years of age.

C. Every candidate who is preference-eligible can be considered for selection consideration as an ATF agent.

D. At least some preference-eligible veterans and some currently serving law enforcement officers or those who have previously served in a federal civilian law enforcement position may not have the age restriction.

E. None of the 40-year-old preference-eligible veterans may apply.

5. Dragona, a key witness in a court case, is afraid to respond to Agent Hammons' questioning regarding the Pino family's alleged illegal firearms trafficking operations. Dragona maintains her silence, though she does reveal to Agent Hammons that her family's life has been threatened by Alberto, the Pino family bodyguard, if she testifies. There is concern that Alberto's actions are an obstruction of justice, which is defined as an act that "corruptly or by threats or force, or by any threatening letter or communication, influences, obstructs, or impedes, or endeavors to influence, obstruct, or impede, the due administration of justice." The assistant US attorney offers a witness relocation program that can provide a layer of security for the witness prior to the trial.

From the information provided above, it can be validly concluded that:

A. Agent Hammons can arrest Dragona for refusing to testify due to obstruction of justice.

B. Agent Hammons can arrest Alberto for obstruction of justice.

C. Agent Hammons can have Dragona removed from the trial.

D. Agent Hammons can arrange to have the family put into protective custody after Dragona testifies.

E. Agent Hammons can invite Dragona to speak in exchange for family protection.

6. A key witness was set to testify against the defendant on a felony charge for an illegal alcohol business conducted near a public school. The defendant was the older brother of the key witness. Once on the stand, the witness decided not to testify against his brother. After conferring with ATF agents in attendance and looking at other evidence, the assistant US attorney filed a petition stating that the witness was in contempt of court. The witness asserted that he was within his rights to plead the Fifth Amendment. Even after invoking the Fifth Amendment, witnesses may be forced to testify, by law.

From the information provided above, it can be validly concluded that:

A. A witness can be pardoned from testifying by invoking Fifth Amendment rights.

B. All witnesses who assert Fifth Amendment rights will be found in contempt of court.

C. If a witness pleads the Fifth Amendment, then the witness cannot be held in contempt of court.

D. Some witnesses may be forced to testify after invoking the Fifth Amendment.

E. No witness shall be compelled to testify against their will.

7. Agent Splice arrests Trinity during a raid of illegal transport of alcohol to avoid taxation. Although Trinity does not say much to Agent Splice during the arrest proceedings, one of her closest and most highly regarded associates, Trudy, passionately states that Trinity told her that she "uses this route several times a year to transport the alcohol." At trial, Trudy's statement is submitted into evidence, but the defense claims it is hearsay. Although hearsay, as a general rule, is not allowed as evidence, there are exemptions for consideration. The prosecution states that the statement is with exemption because it was made by the party's agent or employee on a matter within the scope of that relationship and while it existed.

From the information provided above, it can be validly concluded that:

A. All hearsay statements are considered evidence.

B. If the hearsay statement meets the exemption criteria, then it will be considered with exemption.

C. Some hearsay will be omitted because it was asserted by a co-conspirator.

D. Hearsay statements are inadmissible due to lack of witness credibility.

E. As a general rule, hearsay statements are not admissible under any circumstances.

8. Marko was a witness in a trial involving a former firearms dealer who was also his friend. For this, Marko was not prosecuted for his involvement in the deal and was given immunity. After trial, Special Agent Tupps found out from the dealer, who was found guilty, that Marko was involved in a firearm deal a month prior with an associate of his former friend. After much discussion with Agent Tupps, the prosecutor charged Marko for his involvement in this crime. According to Marko's defense attorney, he cannot be charged for a crime in which he was given immunity because it was similar to the charges of the first firearms dealing case.

From the information provided above, it can be validly concluded that:

A. Marko will not be charged because his immunity extends into this case.

B. Marko will not be charged because this case is related to the case where he received immunity.

C. Marko will not be charged because his involvement in this crime was more than 30 days ago.

D. Marko will be charged because this case is unrelated to the case where he received immunity.

E. Marko will be charged because the statute of limitations of immunity has not expired.

9. Twenty ATF agents with ten years' experience along with their supervisory agent were mandated by senior office management to attend a weekend training session in a city in Virginia and then report the outcomes for further review. At this training session, the topics of gun control and better communication among the major agencies were discussed as these were the challenges the agents selected as being most important in their field. Upon return, programs and innovative ideas were discussed with the supervisory agent and approved by senior office management. By the end of sixty days, none of the programs or innovative ideas were implemented.

From the information provided above, it can be validly concluded that:

A. The supervisory agent has the responsibility to implement the programs and ideas since they were approved.

B. Since the supervisory agent attended the training session, this agent is ultimately responsible for implementing all approved programs and innovative ideas.

C. The supervisory agent is required to implement all approved programs and innovative ideas.

D. The supervisory agent was only required to attend the training session with the agents.

E. Senior management has ultimate responsibility and is required to ensure that all office protocols are followed.

10. Norbert had been on the run from ATF agents for quite some time but was recently apprehended in South Carolina where he has been hiding out for the past several years. He was charged with numerous felony counts of federal firearm crimes. During the investigation, it was noted that Norbert had stolen property from an acquaintance in North Carolina 24 months earlier and that there was a civil lawsuit being filed. Although felony crimes in North Carolina do not have a statute of limitations, there is a 2-year statute of limitations for civil matters. The attorney for Norbert's acquaintance is still planning to file the civil lawsuit with a notation that the clock against the 2-year statute of limitations began on the date of Norbert's apprehension, not on the date the property was stolen.

From the information provided above, it can be validly concluded that:

A. The request for the civil lawsuit will be granted because the statute of limitations has not been reached.

B. The request for the civil lawsuit will be denied because the statute of limitations expired.

C. The request for the civil lawsuit will be denied because the evidence has deteriorated.

D. The request for the civil lawsuit will be denied because civil lawsuits do not supersede felony charges.

E. The request for the civil lawsuit will be denied because there will be no way Norbert can pay for the damages incurred to the property.

11. When a critical domestic incident occurs, the Department of Justice (DOJ) stands ready to immediately provide a law enforcement response and has the authority to combine resources from different agencies to accomplish a mission. The DOJ has primary jurisdiction over the agencies it involves. Several ATF and FBI agents organized a siege on a compound harboring a cult organization and their leader, Daniel, who was known to hide illegal firearms. With evidence mounting, fear of a shootout, and the potential harming of innocent lives, the DOJ directed both sets of agents to proceed together into the compound to recover the illegal firearm cache. During the recovery process, a shootout occurred, and many innocent people were killed. Both ATF and FBI agencies believe that they had jurisdiction over the handling of the siege.

From the information provided above, it can be validly concluded that:

A. The FBI had the primary jurisdiction and are best equipped to handle the situation because they cover a broad spectrum of responsibilities in their agency.

B. The ATF had the primary jurisdiction because they are the only agency that regulates the explosives industry.

C. Neither the FBI nor ATF had the primary jurisdiction because the DOJ can combine the efforts and responsibilities that each agency has to offer to accomplish its mission.

D. Both the FBI and ATF were not equipped to complete the mission of the siege independently.

E. The DOJ was out of line for combining efforts between the agencies.

12. Agent Jensen and his wife, Margaret, attend a graduation party for their 17-year-old neighbor, Max. Paula and Josiah, Max's parents and the party's hosts, serve beer and wine. The parents figure that, if Max and his friends are going to drink, it is better for Max and his friends to drink alcohol in their home and under supervision. Agent Jensen makes a comment to Max's parents indicating that underage drinking is against the law and adults who offer alcohol to minors could be charged for underage drinking. He then asks them to put away the alcohol. Unbeknownst to all in the house, one of the teenage guests, who is under the influence, leaves the party. While driving down Highway 192 in Florida, the teen guest collides with and severely injures a pedestrian.

From the information provided above, it can be validly concluded that:

A. Agent Jensen was an accessory to the vehicular accident because he was aware there was alcohol being served at the party.

B. Paula and Josiah had knowledge that someone under the influence left the party.

C. Max's parents are not responsible for the vehicular accident since it happened after the teen left the party.

D. The teen will not be charged with underage drinking because it was provided by an adult in a position of authority.

E. Paula and Josiah will face charges in the vehicular accident because they were the ones that provided the underage teen alcohol at the party.

13. All ATF agents and staff working within the organization are bound by a confidentiality agreement, in and outside of the agency. They have a duty to keep information, documents, and any work-related issues discreet. Severe consequences are often a result of breaking the confidentiality agreement. In a big profile case, there were visitors from other agencies invited to meet with the ATF agents and staff. While retrieving information, Agent Glenn left his file case open on his desk. The next day, sensitive information was leaked to the media. This compromised the integrity of the case, and the case was no longer viable. If suspension is a possible severe consequence for the agency to use, then agents who break the confidentiality agreement may be at risk of being suspended.

From the information provided above, it can be validly concluded that:

A. Agent Glenn will be liable for severe consequences because he intentionally violated the confidentiality agreement by leaving the file case open on his desk.

B. Agent Glenn will be liable for severe consequences because he walked away from his desk and left his file case open, knowingly violating the confidentiality agreement.

C. Agent Glenn will be liable for severe consequences because it was his responsibility to ensure that the integrity of the case remained intact.

D. Agent Glenn will not be liable for severe consequences because the confidentiality agreement is practiced by all who occupy the building.

E. Agent Glenn will not be liable because it is reasonable to expect that all who enter the building are expected to sign and abide by the agency's confidentiality agreements.

14. During a raid to seize an illegal shipment of firearms, Agent Lester arrested and handcuffed Monte, a suspected illegal firearms seller. A shootout occurred during the arrest, injuring a fellow agent. At this time, Monte told Agent Lester where to find one of the crates of illegal firearms. Monte was asked to stay quiet and was taken to the patrol car. While Agent Lester retrieved the crate, another agent drove Monte to the field office to be interrogated, completing due process along the way. At the pre-trial hearing, Monte's attorney motioned to have the crate of illegal firearms deemed inadmissible because his client's Miranda rights were read after his client revealed where the crate was located, thereby violating his client's due process. The district attorney stated that the law of due process requires that officers read Miranda rights to a suspect in custody prior to their questioning or interrogation.

From the information provided above, it can be validly concluded that:

A. The judge will grant the motion because due process was not completed in a timely manner.

B. The judge will grant the motion because Monte's Miranda rights were read after he was interrogated.

C. The judge will deny the motion because Monte's Miranda rights were not required at the time of his arrest.

D. The judge will deny the motion because Monte's Miranda rights did not supersede the safety of the agents at the time of the shootout.

E. The judge will deny the motion because Monte revealed the location of the crate voluntarily before due process was completed and he was officially questioned.

15. The Catalano sisters run several illegal firearms operations from their private properties located in the southeastern area of the United States. The sisters are informed that their Georgia warehouse has experienced an enormous explosion. While on the scene of the investigation, the ATF agents are told by warehouse workers that there are additional warehouses in other states that are storing illegal firearms. The Fourth Amendment provides privacy safeguards to the sisters; however, if circumstances justify a search and there is probable cause to believe evidence will be found, then law enforcement is permitted under the Fourth Amendment to conduct a search of private property without a warrant. The sisters, believing that they are legally within their Fourth Amendment rights to privacy, quietly instruct the workers at the other properties to dispose of the firearms immediately. Based on the circumstances and the probable cause of the existence of firearms, ATF agents from Florida, South Carolina, and Tennessee converge on the property locations for each of the states without a search warrant to seize the firearms.

From the information provided above, it can be validly concluded that:

A. The sisters' Fourth Amendment rights to privacy were violated.

B. The sisters' Fourth Amendment rights to privacy were violated only in Georgia.

C. The sisters' Fourth Amendment rights to privacy were violated only in Florida, South Carolina, and Tennessee.

D. The sisters' Fourth Amendment rights were not violated because there was insufficient information to conclude that evidence would not be removed or destroyed before a warrant could be obtained.

E. The sisters' Fourth Amendment rights were not violated because there was sufficient information to conclude that evidence would be removed or destroyed before a warrant could be obtained.

Part B—Quantitative Reasoning

Section 1

DIRECTIONS: In Part B—Quantitative Reasoning, you will have to solve problems formulated in both verbal and numeric form. For Section 1, Questions 1–20, solve the problem using the information provided. You may not use a calculator; however, scratch paper is permitted.

---

1. Special Agent Sean has to conduct 50 interviews per month to reach a goal of 400 interviews completed in order to solve a case. How long in months will it take Special Agent Sean to reach the goal of 400 completed interviews?

   A. 8 weeks

   B. 32 weeks

   C. 7 months

   D. 8 months

   E. 24 months

2. The ATF reported a balanced budget of $675,000. By the end of the fiscal year, the bureau had only expensed $595,000. How much of a surplus did ATF have?

   A. $20,000

   B. $80,000

   C. $100,000

   D. $120,000

   E. $1,270,000

3. Levi made twice as many explosives-related arrests as Skip. Ted made 6 explosives-related arrests, which is 10 less than Levi. How many explosives-related arrests did Skip make?

   A. 4

   B. 5

   C. 8

   D. 20

   E. 38

4. An ATF reconnaissance vehicle holds 200 gallons of fuel. If it is three-fourths full, how many gallons of fuel is in the fuel tank?

   A. 50 gallons

   B. 125 gallons

   C. 150 gallons

   D. 200 gallons

   E. 533 gallons

5. The ATF issues an average of 90 arrest warrants per month. What is the average amount of arrest warrants issued over a five-year period?

    A. 540

    B. 1,080

    C. 4,500

    D. 5,400

    E. 10,800

6. Special Agent Lee led the ATF team's effort to recover 50,590 pounds of explosives found in a tractor trailer and another 44,200 pounds of explosives found in a converted bus. How much heavier are the explosives in the tractor trailer?

    A. 4,390 pounds

    B. 4,700 pounds

    C. 6,390 pounds

    D. 6,700 pounds

    E. 94,790 pounds

7. Each agent must purchase a minimum of 5 pairs of uniform pants for $36 each and 5 uniform shirts for $25 each. How much will each agent spend if they only adhere to the minimum purchasing requirements?

    A. $61

    B. $180

    C. $269

    D. $280

    E. $305

8. Two Special Agents drove by car to execute a search warrant and make an arrest. They left Tallahassee, Florida on Tuesday at 9:30 a.m. and arrived in Newark, New Jersey at 2 p.m. Friday afternoon. How long did the drive take them?

    A. 4.5 hours

    B. 28.5 hours

    C. 52.5 hours

    D. 76 hours

    E. 76.5 hours

9. ATF Agent Linda Taxin was cataloguing firearms in the evidence room. There were 10 more knives than brass knuckles and twice as many guns as brass knuckles. If she catalogued 14 knives, how many guns were there?

   A. 4

   B. 8

   C. 14

   D. 24

   E. 28

10. The cell phone provider for the federal government charges a monthly rate of $13.75 plus $0.25 a minute per international call. How many international minutes were billed if the monthly bill was $45.25?

    A. 67 minutes

    B. 85 minutes

    C. 126 minutes

    D. 142 minutes

    E. 152 minutes

11. Agents Scollin and Donahue made a pact to bring their lunches and save the money for a surprise going away party for their supervisor at the end of the quarter. Agent Scollin started with $60 and Agent Donahue started with $120. If Agent Scollin saves $7 a day and Agent Donahue saves $5 a day, how long will it be before both agents have saved the same amount of money?

    A. 10 days

    B. 15 days

    C. 30 days

    D. 28 days

    E. 40 days

12. ATF headquarters allows agents to drive agency vehicles to personal locations as long as it is en route to a business-related location. If Agent Johnson drives 1,687 miles during the week, including the 28-mile round trip to the bank three times, how many total business-related miles did he drive?

    A. 1,261 miles

    B. 1,600 miles

    C. 1,603 miles

    D. 1,620 miles

    E. 1,659 miles

13. Agent Aphols has been working at the Atlanta field office for 7.25 years. What is this amount in months?

    A. 84 months

    B. 87 months

    C. 88 months

    D. 89 months

    E. 90 months

14. The going rate for a new work truck is $45,750 plus tax. If the current tax rate on all vehicle purchases is 7.5%, what will the final sale price be?

    A. $3,431.25

    B. $34,312.50

    C. $42,318.75

    D. $49,181.25

    E. $343,125

15. There are four windows on the front of the field office. Each window measures 24 inches by 36 inches. How many feet total is the perimeter of all four windows?

    A. 20 feet

    B. 24 feet

    C. 40 feet

    D. 42 feet

    E. 45 feet

16. It is 1,743 miles from the field office to Washington, D.C. How many gallons of gas will it take to drive to Washington, D.C., if the work truck gets 28 miles to the gallon?

    A. 62

    B. 62.25

    C. 63.25

    D. 123

    E. 124

17. When balancing the budget, Agent Frans realizes there is a surplus of $3,750. The field office needs a new printer that costs $250 and three office chairs at a cost of $74.50 each. How much surplus will be left after completing all of these purchases?

    A. $3,276.50
    B. $3,426.50
    C. $3,500
    D. $3,520
    E. $3,526.50

18. In the winter, the sun sets in California at 5:37 p.m. and rises at 7:02 a.m. How many minutes are between the sunset and the sunrise?

    A. 325 min.
    B. 625 min.
    C. 725 min.
    D. 780 min.
    E. 805 min.

19. Agent Rodriguez has made 75 arrests this month. This is 85% less than Senior Agent Krupps. How many arrests did Agent Krupps complete this month?

    A. 60 arrests
    B. 120 arrests
    C. 155 arrests
    D. 370 arrests
    E. 500 arrests

20. If a stakeout begins at 7 p.m. on Friday night and lasts for 37 hours, what day and time will it end?

    A. 7 a.m. Saturday
    B. 8 p.m. Saturday
    C. 7 a.m. Sunday
    D. 8 a.m. Sunday
    E. 8 p.m. Sunday

Section 2

> **DIRECTIONS:** Section 2 focuses on verbal abilities related to numbers. Read each scenario carefully and then evaluate each conclusion using the following options:
>
> - True, which means that you can infer the conclusion from the facts presented.
>
> - False, which means that the conclusion cannot be true given the facts presented.

Questions 21–23 are based on the following information.

The National Minimum Drinking Age Act established a federally recognized minimum drinking age of 21 that all states must adhere to if they wish to receive federal funding. However, the Twenty-First Amendment reserves the right of each state to make their own laws regulating the consumption and distribution of alcohol within their own borders.

It is estimated that merely 5 states have not taken advantage of this exception. Of the 45 states that have made exceptions to the minimum legal drinking age (MLDA), 11 states excuse consumption by minors for educational purposes, 16 states allow medical exemptions, and only 4 states have made the exception for law enforcement or employment purposes. There are also exceptions in 17 states that protect minors who have been under the influence from prosecution in cases where they are meaning to seek medical aid for a fellow minor who has fallen ill due to alcohol consumption.

More than half of all the states (26) make exceptions for minors to consume alcohol for religious purposes. This would apply in situations like drinking wine at church. Native American reservations are considered domestic independent sovereigns and are responsible for setting their own rules and regulations independently from federal law. However, they are still required to adhere to state laws and regulations dealing with alcohol consumption.

21. If an inebriated minor were to seek medical assistance for a fellow minor with alcohol poisoning, both minors would be protected from legal prosecution under the Twenty-First Amendment.

    A. True

    B. False

22. Drinking wine in church is not legally permissible for minors in all states, despite it being a religious ceremony.

    A. True

    B. False

23. If a 16-year-old were to drink alcohol on a Native American reservation, it would be legally permissible under United States federal law because Native American reservations are domestic independent sovereigns, they do not adhere to the MLDA, and the 16-year-old is within his or her rights.

    A. True

    B. False

Part IV

Questions 24–26 are based on the following information.

Massachusetts is one of 11 states in the US that has legalized both the medicinal use of marijuana and decriminalized possession of it in small amounts. However, there are limits to this legalization. Similar to alcohol, marijuana purchase, use, and possession are all restricted to adults over the age of 21. Unlike alcohol, however, the purchase, use, and possession of marijuana is limited to certain environments and amounts.

Any person over 21 is allowed possession of up to one ounce of marijuana for recreational use anywhere in the Commonwealth, but they are allowed to keep up to ten ounces in their private residence. If anyone over the age of 18 but under the age of 21 is found with up to two ounces of marijuana on their person, they will receive a civil citation for $100. Likewise, if anyone below the age of 18 is found to be in possession of up to two ounces of marijuana, they will also receive a noncriminal, civil citation for $100, and they will be required to attend a court-approved drug awareness program.

These new laws also extend to the cultivation of marijuana plants within a household. Up to six but no more than 12 plants may be grown in a single household, but the possession of such plants will not disqualify any one person from civil participation. They may not be disqualified from receiving financial aid, public housing, public financial assistance, or a driver's license or becoming a foster parent/adoptive parent.

24. Under Massachusetts law, any person found to be in possession of up to 10 ounces of marijuana in their private household is within their rights as a Massachusetts citizen.

   A. True
   B. False

25. A 17-year-old found to be in possession of one ounce of marijuana will be issued a civil citation, fined $100, and will be required to attend a court-approved drug awareness program.

   A. True
   B. False

26. A 16-year-old boy found to be in possession of two ounces of marijuana might be fined $100 and required to complete a court-approved drug awareness program, but he may not be denied his driver's license.

   A. True
   B. False

Questions 27–30 are based on the following information.

The Gun Control Act of 1968 codifies that certain categories of people are not allowed to purchase firearms from a registered dealer. These categories include and are not limited to criminal history, age, fugitive status, addiction history, mental health, citizenship status, and whether or not they have been dishonorably discharged from the military. Background checks for the purchase of guns have prevented more than three million people in these categories from obtaining firearms. This does not, however, extend to those who have been identified by public health researchers as a risk for public endangerment. Convicted felons with violent or gun-related misdemeanors are allowed to purchase, as well as those with addiction histories, convicted juvenile offenders, and those who suffer from extreme mental illnesses and disabilities.

According to a study done in California, those convicted on a charge involving a gun-violence misdemeanor are seven times more likely to be charged again following a handgun purchase than someone who has no prior criminal history. Similarly, those who were arrested before the age of 18 were 38% more likely to be arrested again by the time they were 26 for crimes relating to gun-violence. Substance abusers also have a higher likelihood of engaging in dangerous activity when in possession of a firearm. Research shows that gun owners are more likely to drive under the influence, while non-gun-owners are not. Although federal law prohibits unlawful users or addicts of a controlled substance to be in possession of a gun, such individuals often go unreported; involvement in illegal use and/or selling of such substances is often associated with heightened risk of gun violence. Federal law also fails to prevent suspected terrorists from purchasing firearms. Out of 2,477 attempted firearm purchases made by those on the terrorist watchlist, the FBI only managed to halt 212 (9%) because they were categorically blocked from making such deals. Legally, however, being on the terrorist watch list does not disqualify a person from being able to purchase guns.

Of course, there are also age restrictions on the purchase of firearms from both licensed and unlicensed dealers. Those who are licensed firearm dealers may sell handguns to anyone over the age of 21; however, those who are unlicensed may sell to those they have reasonable cause to believe are over the age of 18. Both ages are lessened when it comes to rifles and shotguns—licensed dealers may sell to those over the age of 18, while unlicensed persons may sell, deliver, or transfer to anyone of any age.

27. All persons with a criminal record dating to before they were 18 are arrested again for gun violence by the age of 26.

    A. True

    B. False

28. More than three million people who are categorically blocked from purchasing firearms have been blocked from purchasing firearms.

    A. True

    B. False

29. Anyone under the age of 18 may purchase, use, or transfer a rifle from an unlicensed person.

    A. True

    B. False

30. Despite the fact that those on the terrorist watch list are categorically unable to purchase guns legally, the FBI was only able to stop 212 of 2,477 attempted gun purchases made by those on the terrorist watchlist.

    A. True

    B. False

PART C—Investigative Reasoning

> **DIRECTIONS:** Read the paragraph and statements carefully. Then answer the questions that follow the investigative situation. You may refer to the paragraph and statements as often as needed.

Questions 1–8 are based on the following paragraph and statements.

The aspiring candidate, Z, had strong, well-defined positions and a personality that attracted many and just as forcefully irritated others. His supporters were visible and audible throughout the country; his detractors were just as evident. As the convention neared, Z and his remaining worthwhile competitors, X and Y, campaigned vigorously about the country. In one major city, only days before a scheduled debate among the three, the daily newspaper published a paid advertisement warning of dire consequences to the party and to the nation if Z were to be the party's candidate but made no specific threats against any one person. On the same day, a message arrived at Z's local headquarters and another at a radio station. These messages made direct threats against Z's person and his family. Z's advisers suggested that he bow out of this debate, but Z refused to succumb to pressure and threats.

In the course of the investigation, the following statements were made:

1. *Lanetta Jefferson, an employee in the newspaper's advertising department, stated that two days before the ad appeared, a man with a squeaky voice had called and asked many questions about sizes of ads and relative costs but had not placed an order.*

2. *Lin Kagawa of the newspaper's mailroom stated that the ad had not arrived in the mail but had been slipped through a door slot during the night.*

3. *Anna Appleton, advertising manager of the newspaper, stated that the correct payment, in cash, accompanied the copy for the advertisement.*

4. *Joe Jenkins, a volunteer in Z's headquarters, stated that upon opening the office he had found the threats in an envelope that had been pushed under the door.*

5. *Padma DeLomba, a forensic expert, stated that the advertisement and the threat appeared to have come from the same typewriter.*

6. *Riley Meltzer of the radio station stated that the threat received at the station was made by telephone and that the caller was a woman.*

7. *LaDrea Mawes, a well-known opponent of Z, stated that she had been in another city on business when the threats were delivered.*

8. *Agnes Kirby, a supporter of Y, stated that the ad and threats were planted by Z's own committee to elicit extra sympathy for Z and to cast vague suspicions about his opponents.*

9. *Bobby Jones, a homeless person who had previously been a patient in a mental hospital, stated in his squeaky voice that he was responsible for the ad and threats.*

10. *Veronique Yin, a police informer, stated that she could not name her sources but that a sniper would be stationed in a basement apartment along the route usually taken from the airport to the hotel at which Z would be staying.*

1. Which statement clearly demands action by local police and by Secret Service?

   A. Statement 1
   B. Statement 6
   C. Statement 8
   D. Statement 9
   E. Statement 10

2. Which two statements indicate that more than one person was involved in the intimidation attempt?

   A. Statements 1 and 3
   B. Statements 1 and 5
   C. Statements 1 and 6
   D. Statements 5 and 9
   E. Statements 6 and 9

3. Which statement constitutes an alibi?

   A. Statement 3
   B. Statement 7
   C. Statement 8
   D. Statement 9
   E. Statement 10

4. Which statement is likely to be of LEAST use in this investigation?

   A. Statement 1
   B. Statement 3
   C. Statement 5
   D. Statement 8
   E. Statement 9

5. Which statement indicates that the threat-maker is aware of federal mail fraud law?

   A. Statement 1
   B. Statement 4
   C. Statement 7
   D. Statement 9
   E. Statement 10

6. Which statement, along with Statement 3, indicates that at least part of the intimidation scheme was planned rather than spontaneous?

   A. Statement 1
   B. Statement 2
   C. Statement 4
   D. Statement 5
   E. Statement 7

7. Which statement links the advertisement and the threats to the same typewriter?

   A. Statement 1
   B. Statement 3
   C. Statement 5
   D. Statement 6
   E. Statement 7

8. Which statement offers a clue that is probably just coincidental?

   A. Statement 3
   B. Statement 5
   C. Statement 6
   D. Statement 7
   E. Statement 9

Questions 9–15 are based on the following paragraph and statements.

Charlie Horton was very upset. His monthly credit card bill had just arrived in the mail with a total far in excess of any charges he could even imagine. Sorting through the printed bill, he found six unaccountable charges payable to four different gun shops in Texas, a state he had never traveled to. In addition, Mr. Horton did not own a gun permit and was a vehement supporter for stricter gun control, maintaining that guns should only be in the hands of law enforcement. Mr. Horton looked in his wallet and found that his credit card was right there in its usual slot. His wife produced her credit card as well. Evidently, the guns had been purchased either online or over the phone. Mr. Horton immediately called the bankcard company to cancel his cards. Next, he opened an online investigation to dispute the charges related to the gun purchases. Finally, he called the police. The local police told Mr. Horton that the matter was out of their jurisdiction because the card had not been stolen. Mr. Horton called the FBI, which referred him to the Secret Service, which deals with credit card fraud, and to the Bureau of Alcohol, Tobacco, and Firearms because firearms apparently had been ordered under a false name.

In the course of the investigation, the following statements were made:

1. *Charlie Horton stated that he usually bought gas at Bill's Service Center where the attendant took his card into the office to run it through the machine.*

2. *Mrs. Horton stated that she often had lunch with her friend Lily Bell at the Pickwick Tea Room and occasionally forgot to sign her receipts.*

3. *Jimmy Horton, age 15, stated that he had placed a telephone order for tickets to a hockey game and had given his father's credit card number over the telephone.*

4. *Anwar Amin who pumped gas at Bill's Service Center stated that Harvey Brilliant, who also worked at Bill's, frequently complained that the machine had errors when certain cards were swiped, requiring Brilliant to manually put in the credit card number. On occasion, Brilliant would simply write the number down to speed up the process if the line was long. Amin claimed to never have noticed Brilliant destroying the paper with the card number on it after the transaction.*

5. *Martha Brilliant, Harvey's mother, stated that Harvey had always been a good, hardworking boy but that she did not much care for a new group of friends with whom he had been spending his free time.*

6. *Maria Gerardi, waitress at the Pickwick Tea Room, stated that Mrs. Horton was a nice lady but a stingy tipper.*

7. *Joyce Shigekawa, supervisor at the ticket agency that handled sports tickets for the community, stated that all the telephone operators in her employ had been fully investigated and were bonded.*

8. *Ginny Chen, an operator at the ticket agency, stated that her co-worker, Peggy Kowalski, seemed to wear an expensive new outfit nearly every day.*

9. *Tony Pisano, owner of Hunters' Supply Depot of Laramie, Texas, stated that he adhered strictly to the law in filling orders for guns and ammunition.*

10. *Peter van Rijn, manager of Buy Rite Liquors, stated that he was applying for a gun permit because many young toughs in the neighborhood suddenly seemed to have acquired guns, and he was feeling very vulnerable.*

9. Which statement, along with Statement 3, might link Jimmy Horton's activities to the misuse of his father's card?

   A. Statement 4

   B. Statement 5

   C. Statement 7

   D. Statement 8

   E. Statement 10

10. Which statement should prove LEAST helpful to the investigators?

    A. Statement 2

    B. Statement 5

    C. Statement 6

    D. Statement 7

    E. Statement 9

11. Which statement is most likely to cause the investigators to concentrate their search for the perpetrator of the credit card fraud right in Horton's hometown?

    A. Statement 1

    B. Statement 3

    C. Statement 5

    D. Statement 8

    E. Statement 10

12. Which statement is most likely to remove suspicion from Peggy Kowalski?

    A. Statement 3

    B. Statement 4

    C. Statement 7

    D. Statement 8

    E. Statement 9

13. Which two statements, along with Statement 3, describe risky practices that the Hortons can avoid for future purchases?

    A. Statements 1 and 2

    B. Statements 1 and 4

    C. Statements 2 and 6

    D. Statements 4 and 9

    E. Statements 9 and 10

14. Which single statement casts the greatest suspicion on Harvey Brilliant?

    A. Statement 1

    B. Statement 4

    C. Statement 5

    D. Statement 9

    E. Statement 10

15. Which statement might draw state investigators into this case?

    A. Statement 3

    B. Statement 5

    C. Statement 7

    D. Statement 9

    E. Statement 10

ANSWER KEYS AND EXPLANATIONS

Part A—Verbal Reasoning

1. D	**4.** D	**7.** B	**10.** A	**13.** C
2. C	**5.** B	**8.** D	**11.** C	**14.** E
3. C	**6.** D	**9.** E	**12.** E	**15.** E

1. **The correct answer is D.** The agent did not gather enough facts or circumstances that there were illegal firearms in the apartment. According to the information given, the agents needed to establish probable cause of contraband, stolen items, and/or evidence of a crime based on facts and circumstances. In this case, there was no evidence of contraband or anyone seen with any contraband, so it can be validly concluded that the request for a search warrant will be denied because there is insufficient evidence for probable cause. Thereby, choices A and B can be eliminated as there is not enough evidence for probable cause and, although helpful, surveillance footage alone is not enough evidence to attain a search warrant without other credible sources. Choice C is an invalid conclusion because the agents have not violated the reasonable right to privacy as the surveillance is outside the building. Choice E can be eliminated because the reason for the denial would be based on insufficient evidence, not a total lack of probable cause.

2. **The correct answer is C.** The government vehicle can be used for personal matters, but there are certain limitations. Agents must be on duty and making a stop that is not out of their direction of official travel. Therefore, to use a government vehicle for only personal reasons would be a violation of policy. Thus, it can be validly concluded from the information given that using a government vehicle for strictly personal matters is prohibited. The second sentence

invalidates choice A. Choice B is only partially true. Use off duty is allowed, but only for official business matters. There is not enough information to reach the conclusion in choice D. The second sentence invalidates choice E.

3. **The correct answer is C.** Based on the information given (specifically the last sentence), it can be validly concluded that Stefan will be denied because his misdemeanor is only 2 years old. It cannot be inferred from the information given that he will be granted a probationary license, so choice A can be eliminated. Choice B is not a valid conclusion because there is not enough additional information given regarding the three-year criteria that needs to be met after being convicted of a misdemeanor. Further, choice D is invalid because the paragraph does not present any evidence at all. There is no information to support the conclusion in choice E.

4. **The correct answer is D.** The third sentence of the paragraph contains the information needed to understand the answer. It states that "the age restriction may not apply if the individual is a preference-eligible veteran or is currently serving or has previously served in a federal civilian law enforcement position." Therefore, it can be validly concluded that the age restriction may not apply to these candidates. Thus, choices A and B cannot be valid because it's possible that the age restriction does not apply to all candidates. There is not enough information given to say that choices C and

D are valid conclusions. There may be other reasons why a preference-eligible veteran and current or previous federal civilian law enforcement candidate may not be considered. Age is not the sole deciding factor.

5. **The correct answer is B.** The paragraph defines obstruction of justice as an act that "corruptly or by threats or force, or by any threatening letter or communication, influences, obstructs, or impedes, or endeavors to influence, obstruct, or impede, the due administration of justice." This clearly relates to Alberto's behavior and not Dragona's, so it can be validly concluded that Agent Hammons can arrest Alberto—not Dragona as choice A indicates—for obstruction of justice. Choice C doesn't make sense as the paragraph states that Dragona is a key witness. For choice D to be valid, the family would need to be placed into protective custody or witness protection *before* the trial, not after. There is not enough information given to validly conclude that Agent Hammons can, or will, invite Dragona to speak in exchange for family protection, thus eliminating choice E as a valid conclusion.

6. **The correct answer is D.** According to the last sentence of the paragraph, a witness may be forced, by law, to testify even though the witness may have pleaded the Fifth. Therefore, it can be validly concluded that some witnesses may be forced to testify and some may not. This effectively eliminates choice E as a valid conclusion. There is not enough information to support the conclusion that a witness can be pardoned from testifying by invoking Fifth Amendment rights (choice A). There is also not enough information to conclude that witnesses who plead the Fifth Amendment cannot be held in contempt of court (choice C).

7. **The correct answer is B.** Based on the information included in the paragraph, hearsay, as a general rule, is not allowed as evidence, but there are exemptions. The last sentence provides criteria under which a hearsay statement can be considered. So it can be inferred that if the hearsay statement meets the exemption criteria, then it will be considered with exemption. The fourth sentence invalidates choice A. There is no information to support the conclusions in choices C and D. Choice E is incorrect because, according to the information given, there are exemptions.

8. **The correct answer is D.** Based on the given information, Marko was involved in two separate incidents that occurred a month apart. Marko was given immunity for his witness testimony in one incident, but since the other crime was disclosed after the trial *and* the crime was committed a month prior, it stands to conclude that his immunity would not extend to his involvement in this second crime. Therefore, it is reasonable to infer that Marko will be charged in the second crime because this case is unrelated to the case where he received immunity. This eliminates choices A and B. There is not enough information given to reach the conclusions provided in choices C and E.

9. **The correct answer is E.** By following the chain of command given, it stands that senior office management supersedes the supervisory agent. If senior management is able to mandate the training, then it can be reasonably concluded that senior management can also mandate how the office is managed and is required to ensure that all office protocols are followed. Therefore, it is the responsibility of senior office management, who supersedes the supervisory agent, to ensure the programs and

innovative ideas are implemented. This eliminates choices A and B. The paragraph does not expand upon who is in charge of implementation, so there is not enough information given to infer the conclusion reached in choice C. Choice D is not true as the first sentence states that the agents, along with the supervisory agent, were required to attend the training *and* report the outcomes.

10. **The correct answer is A.** If it is true that the clock against the statute of limitations started on the date of apprehension rather than on the date the crime was committed, then the statute of limitations on the crime has not been reached. Based on the information given, there is nothing to indicate to the contrary. Therefore, it is reasonable to validly conclude that the request for the civil suit will be granted. This eliminates choice B. There is not enough information given to reach the conclusions provided in choices C, D, and E.

11. **The correct answer is C.** Based on the information given, the DOJ has the authority to combine resources from different agencies to elicit a response to a mission. Therefore, it can be inferred that the DOJ has primary jurisdiction. This eliminates choices A and B. There is not enough information given to determine whether or not the FBI or ATF were equipped to carry out the siege independently. Choice E doesn't make sense because the first sentence of the paragraph states otherwise.

12. **The correct answer is E.** Paula and Josiah knowingly and voluntarily provided alcohol to underage minors. The accident is a direct result of their actions, so charges do apply. Choice A is incorrect because Agent Jensen did not serve the alcohol and also directed the parents to put it away. Choice B is incorrect because sentence 4 specifically

states that no one knew that the teen left. The opposite of choice C is true; Max's parents would be responsible for their part in the accident due to the intoxication. The opposite of choice D is true as well. The teen will be charged with underage drinking as the law applies to both the adults that offered it and the minor that drank it.

13. **The correct answer is C.** It is reasonable to conclude that by leaving the open file on his desk and walking away, Agent Glenn did not act responsibly nor did he maintain the integrity of the case. Therefore, he violated the confidentiality agreement he knew he was bound by when he signed it. However, choices A and B are incorrect because the paragraph does not state that Agent Glenn *intentionally* violated the confidentiality agreement. Although all ATF agents are bound by the confidentiality agreement, choice D is incorrect because this does not automatically extend to all that occupy the building; remember, there were visitors present. Choice E is incorrect because there is no mention of having to sign a document upon entrance.

14. **The correct answer is E.** Based on the information given, Monte revealed the location of one of the crates of illegal firearms to Agent Lester during the shootout. He was not questioned or interrogated for this information. In fact, once Monte revealed the location of the crate, Agent Lester advised Monte to be quiet and another agent completed due process before Monte was interrogated. Based on the requirements of due process the DA specifies in the last sentence, the only valid conclusion that can be reached is that the judge will deny the motion to dismiss the evidence because Monte's statement was made voluntarily and interrogation had not yet commenced.

15. **The correct answer is E.** The Fourth Amendment does permit searches and seizures that are reasonable. In practice, this means that law enforcement may override privacy concerns and conduct a search of you, your home, barn, car, boat, office, personal or business documents, bank account records, trash barrel, etc. if the police have probable cause to believe they can find evidence that you committed a crime and a judge issues a warrant, or the particular circumstances justify the search without a warrant first being issued. Because of the explosion at their Georgia property, the sisters' Fourth Amendment rights are no longer justified on *any* of their private properties. This eliminates choices A, B, and C. Choice D is incorrect because, as the paragraph states, the Catalano sisters specifically requested that the firearms at all locations be removed.

Part B—Quantitative Reasoning

1. D	**7.** E	**13.** B	**19.** E	**25.** A
2. B	**8.** E	**14.** D	**20.** D	**26.** A
3. C	**9.** B	**15.** C	**21.** B	**27.** B
4. C	**10.** C	**16.** B	**22.** A	**28.** A
5. D	**11.** C	**17.** A	**23.** B	**29.** A
6. C	**12.** C	**18.** E	**24.** B	**30.** B

1. **The correct answer is D.** Divide the number of complete interviews (400) by the number of interviews conducted per month (50).

$$400 \div 50 = 8 \text{ months}$$

   It will take 8 months for Special Agent Stanley to reach the goal of 400 completed interviews.

2. **The correct answer is B.** "Expensed" indicates what was spent and "surplus" indicates what was left over. Subtract the number spent from the budgeted number to see how much of a surplus ATF had.

$$\$675{,}000 - \$595{,}000 = \$80{,}000$$

3. **The correct answer is C.** Breakdown the information by person and write equations to solve. Start with Ted who had 6 explosives-related arrests.

   Ted: 6

   Levi: 6 + 10 = 16

   Skip: 16 ÷ 2 = 8

4. **The correct answer is C.** Multiply the capacity of the fuel tank by three-fourths.

$$\frac{200}{1} \times \frac{3}{4} = 150$$

5. **The correct answer is D.** Multiply the average number of arrests per month (90) by the number of months in 5 years.

$$x = 90 \times (12 \times 5)$$
$$x = 90 \times 60$$
$$x = 5{,}400$$

6. **The correct answer is C.** Subtract the weight of the bus from the weight of the tractor trailer.

$$50{,}590 - 44{,}200 = 6{,}390 \text{ pounds}$$

7. **The correct answer is E.** Multiply the number of minimum pairs for each piece of clothing by their price, then add the results.

$$5 \times \$36 = \$180$$
$$5 \times \$25 = \$125$$
$$\$180 + \$125 = \$305$$

8. **The correct answer is E.** Calculate three 24-hour periods from Tuesday to Wednesday, Wednesday to Thursday, and Thursday to Friday at 9:30 a.m.

$$24 \times 3 = 72 \text{ hours}$$

   Now calculate the time from Friday at 9:30 a.m. to 1:30 p.m. and 1:30 p.m. to 2 p.m., then add the hours to see how long the drive took.

$$9{:}30 \rightarrow 1{:}30 = 4 \text{ hours}$$
$$1{:}30 \rightarrow 2{:}00 = 0.5 \text{ hours}$$

$$72 + 4 + 0.5 = 76.5 \text{ hours}$$

9. **The correct answer is B.** Breakdown the information by evidence type and write equations to solve. Start with the fact that Agent Taxin catalogued 14 knives, then calculate how many brass knuckles there were, then solve to see how many guns were in the evidence room.

Knives: 14

Brass knuckles: 14 – 10 = 4

Guns: 4 × 2 = 8

10. **The correct answer is C.** Subtract the monthly rate from the monthly bill and divide the resulting number by 0.25 to find out how many international minutes were billed.

$$\$45.25 - \$13.75 = \$31.50$$
$$\$31.50 \div 0.25 = 126$$

11. **The correct answer is C.** Create an equation using the variable x as the number of days and solve as follows:

$$60 + 7x = 120 + 5x$$
$$7x - 5x = 120 - 60$$
$$2x = 60$$
$$x = \frac{60}{2}$$
$$x = 30$$

It will take 30 days for both agents to save the same amount of money.

12. **The correct answer is C.** Find the total number of miles driven to and from the bank and subtract it from the total amount of miles driven during the week.

$$60 + 7x = 120 + 5x$$
$$7x - 5x = 120 - 60$$

13. **The correct answer is B.** Multiply the number of years worked by 12.

$$7.25 \times 12 = 87$$

14. **The correct answer is D.** Multiply the going rate for a new work truck by the tax rate. Then add the resulting number to the cost.

$$\$45,750 \times 0.0750 = 3,431.25$$
$$\$45,750 + \$3,431.25 = \$49,181.25$$

15. **The correct answer is C.** The perimeter of a rectangle is found by adding up the length of all four sides. First, find the perimeter of one window.

$$p = l + w + l + w$$
$$p = 2(l) + 2(w)$$
$$p = 2(24) + 2(36)$$
$$p = 48 + 72$$
$$p = 120$$

To find the perimeter of all four windows, multiply by 4.

$$120 \times 4 = 480$$

The total perimeter of the four windows is 480 inches. However, the question is asking for feet, not inches. To solve, divide by 12 to convert the inches to feet.

$$\frac{480}{12} = 40 \text{ ft.}$$

16. **The correct answer is B.** Divide the distance from the field office to Washington, D.C., by the number of miles per gallon.

$$1,743 \div 28 = 62.25 \text{ gallons}$$

17. **The correct answer is A.** Add the cost of the purchases and subtract from the surplus.

$$\$250 + 3(\$74.50) = \$473.50$$
$$\$3,750 - \$473.50 = \$3,276.50$$

18. **The correct answer is E.** Start by counting the number of hours between 5:37 p.m. and 6:37 a.m. Then multiply the result by 60 to convert to minutes.

$$5\text{:}37 \text{ p.m.} \to 6\text{:}37 \text{ a.m.} = 13 \text{ hrs}$$
$$13 \times 60 = 780 \text{ min.}$$

Next, count the minutes between 6:37 a.m. and 7:02 a.m. and add the two results to solve.

$$6\text{:}37 \text{ a.m.} \to 7\text{:}02 \text{ a.m.} = 25 \text{ min.}$$
$$780 + 25 = 805 \text{ min.}$$

19. **The correct answer is E.** Subtract 85 from 100 to get the percentage of arrests made by Agent Rodriguez.

$$100 - 85 = 15\%$$

Let x = arrests made by Krupps. Solve as follows:

$$0.15x = 75$$
$$x = 75 \div 0.15$$
$$x = 500$$

20. **The correct answer is D.** We know that there are 24 hours in a day, so the first 24 hours of the stakeout occurred from 7 p.m. Friday to 7 p.m. Saturday. By subtracting 24 hours from 37 we find that the stake-out continued 13 more hours from 7 p.m. Saturday. The time the stakeout ended can be computed as follows:

7 p.m. Saturday + 12 hours = 7 a.m. Sunday

7 a.m. Sunday + 1 hour = 8 a.m. Sunday

21. **The correct answer is B.** Only 17 states excuse the consumption of alcohol by a minor in cases where that minor is seeking medical attention.

22. **The correct answer is A.** It is only legally permissible in 26 states.

23. **The correct answer is B.** Native American reservations still adhere to state laws and regulations.

24. **The correct answer is B.** Not "any person." This law is restricted to persons who are over the age of 18.

25. **The correct answer is A.** According to the passage, if anyone below the age of 18 is found to be in possession of up to two ounces of marijuana, they will receive a noncriminal, civil citation for $100, and they will be required to attend a court-approved drug awareness program.

26. **The correct answer is A.** No person may be disqualified from receiving a driver's license due to drug possession in Massachusetts.

27. **The correct answer is B.** Not "all persons" are certain to be arrested again. They are simply 38% more likely.

28. **The correct answer is A.** Background checks have blocked more than 3 million people from purchasing firearms.

29. **The correct answer is A.** Unlicensed persons are able to transfer or sell rifles and/or shotguns to persons of any age.

30. **The correct answer is B.** Those on the terrorist watch list are not legally barred from purchasing firearms.

Part C—Investigative Reasoning

1. E	4. D	7. C	10. C	13. A
2. C	5. B	8. E	11. E	14. B
3. B	6. A	9. D	12. C	15. D

1. **The correct answer is E.** A police informer must always be taken seriously. The sniper threat may or may not be related to the threats received by the candidate's headquarters and by the radio station, but it must be thoroughly checked by a door-to-door search of basement apartments along the route and possibly averted by change of the route.

2. **The correct answer is C.** Statement 1 ties the newspaper ad to a man with a squeaky voice. Statement 6 indicates that the phone statement was made by a woman.

3. **The correct answer is B.** In Statement 7, LaDrea Mawes' assertion that she was out of town on business at the time that the threats were delivered represents an alibi, albeit not a very good one. From this paragraph and these statements, there is no evidence to connect Mawes with the threats, but her being out of town when they were delivered does not preclude her involvement in their preparation.

4. **The correct answer is D.** Agnes Kirby's statement (Statement 8) is an expression of her own opinion and nothing more.

5. **The correct answer is B.** Use of the mail to transmit a real threat subjects the threat-maker to conviction and penalties for mail fraud in addition to violation of the civil rights of the victim. Statement 4 indicates that the envelope that contained the threats had been pushed under the door at the headquarters. The threat-maker is aware of the law and wants to expose himself as little as possible to legal action.

6. **The correct answer is A.** In Statement 1, the ad placer called the newspaper to determine exact costs for the ad he wished to place so as to avoid the detection that would come through billing. Then he paid cash so as to eliminate the possibility of being traced through a check.

7. **The correct answer is C.** Statement 5 identifies both written communications as having been produced on the same typewriter.

8. **The correct answer is E.** In Statement 9, Bobby Jones's squeaky-pitched voice is a clue that may be a coincidence. Statements 1 and 6 cast doubt that the treat-maker worked alone; however, Bobby Jones's claim of responsibility must be checked out even if his involvement seems highly unlikely.

9. **The correct answer is D.** Peggy Kowalski's impressive wardrobe implies unlimited funds. It is possible that Peggy, in taking Jimmy's ticket order and credit card number, made note of the number and used it to place telephone orders for clothing. Peggy's occupation exposes her to many credit card numbers and instant suspicion, so her using the card number is unlikely, though possible.

10. **The correct answer is C.** The fact that a waitress considered Mrs. Horton to be pleasant even though a poor tipper really has no bearing on the case.

11. **The correct answer is E.** The liquor store operator's comment that guns had suddenly appeared in the neighborhood points to the perpetrator of credit card fraud as remaining in the area and as distributing firearms to his or her friends.

12. **The correct answer is C.** The fact that telephone operators who were privy to patrons' credit card numbers were investigated and bonded adds to the unlikelihood that Peggy Kowalski is the guilty party.

13. **The correct answer is A.** The practices described in Statements 1 and 2 are risky but avoidable for future purchases. Mr. Horton can reduce his fraud risk when he buys gas by taking the card into the gas station office himself and then watching the attendant swipe the card through the machine. Mrs. Horton can make some changes to the end of her lunch routine, such as asking her friend to remind her to sign the receipt, to help her remember.

14. **The correct answer is B.** Amin's statement that Harvey Brilliant often manually inputted credit cards into the machine by writing down the card number on a separate piece of paper and did not destroy them is, if true, a damaging statement and must be thoroughly investigated.

15. **The correct answer is D.** One gun dealer stated that he acted within the law in selling guns, but, because guns were obtained from four gun shops by one person, Texas authorities must look into the case to be certain that all four transactions were made in accordance with Texas law.

PRACTICE TEST 2: ICE SPECIAL AGENT TEST BATTERY

The following is a sample practice test that contains the types of questions found on the actual ICE Special Agent Test Battery. It's divided into the following three parts:

- Part A—Logical Reasoning
- Part B—Arithmetic Reasoning
- Part C—Writing Skills Assessment

If you decide to time yourself, each part has a recommended time limit. Use this time limit to gauge your comfort level under time constraints and your level of mastery of the types of questions found in the test battery.

After you have completed the practice test, check your answers against the answer keys located after Part C. Detailed answer explanations and applicable step-by-step mathematical breakdowns are provided.

Remember, you are not allowed to use a calculator, and there is no penalty for guessing.

PRACTICE TEST 2:
ICE SPECIAL AGENT
TEST BATTERY

PRACTICE TEST 2: ICE SPECIAL AGENT TEST BATTERY ANSWER SHEET

Part A—Logical Reasoning

1. Ⓐ Ⓑ Ⓒ Ⓓ Ⓔ   6. Ⓐ Ⓑ Ⓒ Ⓓ Ⓔ   11. Ⓐ Ⓑ Ⓒ Ⓓ Ⓔ   16. Ⓐ Ⓑ Ⓒ Ⓓ Ⓔ
2. Ⓐ Ⓑ Ⓒ Ⓓ Ⓔ   7. Ⓐ Ⓑ Ⓒ Ⓓ Ⓔ   12. Ⓐ Ⓑ Ⓒ Ⓓ Ⓔ   17. Ⓐ Ⓑ Ⓒ Ⓓ Ⓔ
3. Ⓐ Ⓑ Ⓒ Ⓓ Ⓔ   8. Ⓐ Ⓑ Ⓒ Ⓓ Ⓔ   13. Ⓐ Ⓑ Ⓒ Ⓓ Ⓔ   18. Ⓐ Ⓑ Ⓒ Ⓓ Ⓔ
4. Ⓐ Ⓑ Ⓒ Ⓓ Ⓔ   9. Ⓐ Ⓑ Ⓒ Ⓓ Ⓔ   14. Ⓐ Ⓑ Ⓒ Ⓓ Ⓔ   19. Ⓐ Ⓑ Ⓒ Ⓓ Ⓔ
5. Ⓐ Ⓑ Ⓒ Ⓓ Ⓔ   10. Ⓐ Ⓑ Ⓒ Ⓓ Ⓔ   15. Ⓐ Ⓑ Ⓒ Ⓓ Ⓔ   20. Ⓐ Ⓑ Ⓒ Ⓓ Ⓔ

Part B—Arithmetic Reasoning

1. Ⓐ Ⓑ Ⓒ Ⓓ Ⓔ   6. Ⓐ Ⓑ Ⓒ Ⓓ Ⓔ   11. Ⓐ Ⓑ Ⓒ Ⓓ Ⓔ   16. Ⓐ Ⓑ Ⓒ Ⓓ Ⓔ
2. Ⓐ Ⓑ Ⓒ Ⓓ Ⓔ   7. Ⓐ Ⓑ Ⓒ Ⓓ Ⓔ   12. Ⓐ Ⓑ Ⓒ Ⓓ Ⓔ   17. Ⓐ Ⓑ Ⓒ Ⓓ Ⓔ
3. Ⓐ Ⓑ Ⓒ Ⓓ Ⓔ   8. Ⓐ Ⓑ Ⓒ Ⓓ Ⓔ   13. Ⓐ Ⓑ Ⓒ Ⓓ Ⓔ   18. Ⓐ Ⓑ Ⓒ Ⓓ Ⓔ
4. Ⓐ Ⓑ Ⓒ Ⓓ Ⓔ   9. Ⓐ Ⓑ Ⓒ Ⓓ Ⓔ   14. Ⓐ Ⓑ Ⓒ Ⓓ Ⓔ   19. Ⓐ Ⓑ Ⓒ Ⓓ Ⓔ
5. Ⓐ Ⓑ Ⓒ Ⓓ Ⓔ   10. Ⓐ Ⓑ Ⓒ Ⓓ Ⓔ   15. Ⓐ Ⓑ Ⓒ Ⓓ Ⓔ   20. Ⓐ Ⓑ Ⓒ Ⓓ Ⓔ

Part C—Writing Skills Assessment

1. Ⓐ Ⓑ Ⓒ Ⓓ Ⓔ   6. Ⓐ Ⓑ Ⓒ Ⓓ Ⓔ   11. Ⓐ Ⓑ Ⓒ Ⓓ   16. Ⓐ Ⓑ Ⓒ Ⓓ
2. Ⓐ Ⓑ Ⓒ Ⓓ Ⓔ   7. Ⓐ Ⓑ Ⓒ Ⓓ Ⓔ   12. Ⓐ Ⓑ Ⓒ Ⓓ Ⓔ   17. Ⓐ Ⓑ Ⓒ Ⓓ Ⓔ
3. Ⓐ Ⓑ Ⓒ Ⓓ Ⓔ   8. Ⓐ Ⓑ Ⓒ Ⓓ Ⓔ   13. Ⓐ Ⓑ Ⓒ Ⓓ Ⓔ   18. Ⓐ Ⓑ Ⓒ Ⓓ Ⓔ
4. Ⓐ Ⓑ Ⓒ Ⓓ Ⓔ   9. Ⓐ Ⓑ Ⓒ Ⓓ   14. Ⓐ Ⓑ Ⓒ Ⓓ Ⓔ   19. Ⓐ Ⓑ Ⓒ Ⓓ Ⓔ
5. Ⓐ Ⓑ Ⓒ Ⓓ Ⓔ   10. Ⓐ Ⓑ Ⓒ Ⓓ   15. Ⓐ Ⓑ Ⓒ Ⓓ   20. Ⓐ Ⓑ Ⓒ Ⓓ Ⓔ

PRACTICE TEST 2: ICE SPECIAL AGENT TEST BATTERY

Part A—Logical Reasoning

40 minutes—20 questions

> **DIRECTIONS:** For Questions 1–20, select the only answer that *can* be validly concluded or the only answer that *cannot* be validly concluded from the related paragraph. Using only the information provided in the paragraph, make a logical conclusion based on what is presented. Assume all the information in the paragraph is true, even if it conflicts with some fact known to you.

1. All H-1B professionals are noncitizens that are granted work visas under US employers. Mr. Jones is an H-1B dependent employer, meaning his H-1B professional employees comprise 15 percent of his full-time equivalent employees. Some H-1B dependent employers are subject to additional rules. No H-1B dependent employers that hire H-1B workers who are paid at least $60,000 per year or have at least a master's degree in a specialty related to their field are subject to additional rules. Mr. Jones pays his H-1B professional employees $55,000 per year, but they all have master's degrees in their field of specialty.

   From the information given above, it can be validly concluded that

   A. Mr. Jones is not subject to any additional rules.

   B. all H-1B dependent employers pay their H-1B employees less than $55,000 per year.

   C. some H-1B professionals are citizens of the US.

   D. no H-1B dependent employers hire H-1B professionals who have less than a master's degree in their field of specialty.

   E. Mr. Jones is subject to all additional rules.

2. The Immigration Marriage Fraud Amendment of 1986 (IMFA) is a law that aims to prevent illegal marriages for the sake of "green cards." Under this law, all US citizens who wish to enter into a marriage license with foreign nationals must undergo a two-year period of "conditional permanent residence." If they should not complete this two-year period, their marriage will be found unlawful, and no green card shall be issued to the foreign national party. After such a period of time, an Immigration and Naturalization Service (INS) agent must determine whether or not the marriage is a sham. Some marriages are found to be shams if the party does not open a joint bank account, file joint tax returns, or join a gym together. In the event that the INS pronounces the marriage to be a sham, no green card shall be issued.

From the information given above, it can be validly concluded that

A. no green card shall be issued in an instance where the couple does not open a joint bank account together.

B. all individuals who undergo the entire two-year period of "conditional permanent residence" will be issued a green card.

C. no individuals who undergo a one-year period of "conditional permanent residence" will be issued a green card.

D. some individuals who do not join a gym together are issued a green card.

E. some individuals who do not undergo the entire two-year period of "conditional permanent residence" will be issued a green card.

3. The Immigration Reform and Control Act of 1986 (IRCA) provided amnesty for certain groups of people within the United States. All undocumented immigrants who had arrived before January 1, 1982 were provided amnesty under the IRCA, as well as all Cuban and Haitian refugees. However, the IRCA also established the precedent that no amnesty would be given to employers for knowingly hiring undocumented immigrants. Abel was granted amnesty under the IRCA.

From the information given above, it can be validly concluded that

A. all undocumented immigrants were granted amnesty under the IRCA.

B. Abel had arrived in the country before January 1, 1982.

C. all undocumented immigrants granted amnesty under the IRCA were Cuban and Haitian immigrants.

D. Abel did not knowingly hire undocumented immigrants.

E. some persons who hired undocumented immigrants were granted amnesty under the IRCA.

4. "Right to be forgotten" laws are provisions that give individuals and corporations the right to request that their private information be deleted from certain online resources. Only the European Union (EU) uses and enforces "right to be forgotten" laws. Only citizens of the EU have the right to request their information be forgotten. Some companies that are based in the US are international companies that operate in the EU and are thus subject to all EU laws. Google is a US-based company that operates in the EU.

From the information given above, it can be validly concluded that

A. not all corporations based in the EU are subject to "right to be forgotten" laws.

B. all corporations subject to "right to be forgotten" laws are based in the EU.

C. no corporation based in the US is subject to "right to be forgotten" laws.

D. a US citizen could request for Google to forget their information under the "right to be forgotten" laws.

E. Google is subject to "right to be forgotten" laws.

5. Privacy rights for children on social media sites are limited to parental supervision and consent. No site whose target audience includes children under the age of 13 can collect personal information about a child without first providing written disclosure of the site's practices and obtaining written parental consent. Posting crude or otherwise indecent pictures of children online is considered obscene and is illegal. However, there are no laws pertaining to children's privacy on social media in cases where the parents infringe upon those rights in nonobscene ways.

From the information given above, it can be validly concluded that

A. in order to collect personal information about a child under the age of 13, an online site must only obtain written parental consent.

B. a parent who wishes to post pictures or online data about their child must first provide written consent of their doing so.

C. all sites whose target audience includes children under the age of 13 are within their rights to collect obscene data on those children as long as they provide written disclosure and obtain parental consent.

D. a parent who wishes to post a nonobscene picture of their child online is within their rights to do so.

E. an online site whose target audience is children under the age of 13 is within their rights to collect nonobscene personal information about a child without parental consent.

6. The owner of a coffee shop only sells their honey brew on Saturdays and Sundays. This honey brew is sold with a bamboo straw. Only cold coffees are sold with bamboo straws. Some cups of honey brew sell for $4.00. Some coffees sold by this coffee shop are sold for $3.45.

   From the information given above, it can be validly concluded that

   A. all coffees sold for $4.00 are cold coffees.

   B. the honey brew is a cold coffee.

   C. only coffees sold for $4.00 are sold with bamboo straws.

   D. some cold coffees are sold for $3.45.

   E. no coffees sold for $3.45 are honey brew.

7. Under the Civil Asset Forfeiture Reform Act (CAFRA), all persons whose properties are identified as having been used for smuggling or to conceal illicit activities are subject to a notice of seizure. Still, not all persons who are subject to a notice of seizure are aware of smuggling or illicit activities occurring within their property. If the government does not provide a proper notice of seizure that is in accordance with CAFRA regulations, then the government is required to return property to the person from whom it was seized. However, only in situations where the property seized was not in the legal possession of the person from whom it was seized is the government not required to return that property.

   *From the information given above, it **CANNOT** be validly concluded that*

   A. the government is required to return property to the person from whom it was seized if and only if the government does not provide proper notice of seizure.

   B. the government is not required to return property to the person from whom it was seized in situations where there was no notice of seizure if and only if that person was not the legal possessor of the property seized.

   C. not all persons whose property is seized without proper notice of seizure are due the return of their property.

   D. no person whose property is seized under CAFRA is due the return of their property if the property seized is not that person's legal possession.

   E. some persons whose properties are identified as having been used for smuggling or concealing illicit activities are aware of smuggling or the concealing of illicit activities occurring within their property.

8. The Intelligence Reform and Terrorism Prevention Act of 2004 (IRTPA) addresses international cooperation on the separate but related issues of human trafficking, alien smuggling, and terrorist travel. While some countries do not cooperate with one another on human trafficking cases, all countries experience human trafficking within their borders. Oftentimes, crimes of this nature involve some form of passport or visa fraud, which prompts the participation of both domestic and international law enforcement agencies.

From the information given above, it can be validly concluded that

   A. most countries that experience human trafficking do not cooperate with one another.

   B. some countries that experience human trafficking within their borders do not cooperate with one another on cases of human trafficking.

   C. IRTPA only addresses international cooperation on issues relating to human trafficking.

   D. all countries that experience human trafficking cooperate with one another on cases that involve human trafficking.

   E. all crimes related to human trafficking involve some form of passport or visa fraud, which prompts the participation of both domestic and international law enforcement agencies.

9. Some instances of involuntary servitude are not considered peonage. All instances where a person is compelled to work against their will through the use of force, the threat of force, or the threat of legal coercion are considered instances of involuntary servitude. To be sure, there are some cases of involuntary servitude in which the laborer being held against their will receives a wage, so wage is not a determinant of whether or not an instance can be considered involuntary servitude. Only instances that are considered peonage are instances where the servitude is tied to an unpaid debt.

*From the information given above, it **CANNOT** be validly concluded that*

   A. some instances that are considered involuntary servitude are instances where the person being held against their will does not receive a wage.

   B. some instances that are considered peonage are instances where the person being held against their will does receive a wage.

   C. all instances of work compelled by threat of force are involuntary servitude.

   D. no instances of involuntary servitude are instances where the servitude is tied to an unpaid debt.

   E. some instances of peonage are not instances where the servitude is tied to an unpaid debt.

10. Mrs. Smith is responsible for stealing a cultural heritage object that is worth $200,000. Stealing, receiving, concealing, exhibiting, and disposing of an object of cultural heritage are all considered trafficking of cultural property. Objects of cultural heritage are defined as objects that are more than 100 years old and worth in excess of $5,000 or simply worth at least $100,000. Some crimes related to the trafficking of cultural property are not crimes in which an object of cultural heritage was stolen.

From the information given above, it can be validly concluded that

A. Mrs. Smith is responsible for trafficking of cultural property.

B. Mrs. Smith is not responsible for stealing an object of cultural heritage.

C. all objects of cultural heritage are worth at least $100,000.

D. some objects that are over 100 years old and worth at least $5,000 are not objects of cultural heritage.

E. receiving an object of cultural heritage is not considered trafficking of cultural property.

11. Some violent acts of conflict intended to harm another nation or people are not acts of terrorism. If an act of conflict is committed between two or more nations or military forces, then that act is considered an act of war. No military force includes persons who have been designated as members of a foreign terrorist organization. Some persons that have been designated as members of foreign terrorist organizations commit violent acts of conflict.

From the information given above, it can be validly concluded that

A. if an act is not considered an act of war, then it was not an act of conflict between two or more nations or military forces.

B. not all military forces include persons designated as members of foreign terrorist organizations.

C. some foreign terrorist organizations do not commit acts of conflict.

D. all violent acts of conflict intended to hurt another nation or people are acts of terrorism.

E. only persons that have been designated as members of foreign terrorist organizations are not allowed in military forces.

12. The Computer Fraud and Abuse Act (CFAA) was enacted chiefly for the purpose of combating the abuse of technology and prohibiting the unauthorized use of a computer or the use of a computer in excess of authorization. The most recent updates made to CFAA assert that the maximum sentence for obtaining national security information by such means is 10 years in federal prison and 20 years for repeat offenders. Not all persons sentenced to 20 years are guilty of obtaining national security information. The penalty for attempting or conspiring to commit such crimes is also 10 years in federal prison.

*From the information given above, it **CANNOT** be validly concluded that*

A. some persons sentenced to 10 years in federal prison are not guilty of obtaining national security information.

B. all persons sentenced to 20 years in prison are repeat offenders guilty of obtaining national security information.

C. a person guilty of unauthorized use of a computer is in violation of the CFAA.

D. a person who attempts to obtain national security information will receive the same penalty as a person who succeeds in obtaining national security information.

E. a person only guilty of conspiring to obtain national security information is given the penalty of 10 years in prison.

13. As technology has continued to advance, the ways in which it can be abused have similarly evolved. Before the Electronic Communications Privacy Act (ECPA), there were no laws forbidding the interception of private computer, digital, and electronic communications. Some interceptions of private computer, digital, and electronic communications are legal. If the person intercepting the communication medium is protected under the Foreign Intelligence Surveillance Act (FISA), then they are not guilty of violating the ECPA. Edward is not protected under FISA.

From the information given above, it can be validly concluded that

A. Edward is guilty of violating ECPA.

B. not all interceptions of private computer, digital, and electronic communications are legal.

C. if Edward were to illegally intercept a communication medium, he would be guilty of violating the ECPA.

D. if Edward were to illegally intercept a communication medium, he would not be guilty of violating ECPA.

E. if a person is not guilty of violating the ECPA, then they must be protected under FISA.

14. In issues of securities fraud, it is always important to note the intention of the accused. A person is guilty of securities fraud if and only if that person intentionally employs fraudulence or deceit in connection with the purchase of a security. Not all instances of fraudulence or deceit involve the omission of necessary facts. However, some instances of securities fraud involve the omission of necessary facts.

From the information given above, it can be validly concluded that

A. all instances of fraudulence or deceit with intent in connection with the purchase of a security are instances of securities fraud.

B. a person is guilty of securities fraud if and only if that person intentionally omits necessary facts related to the purchase of security.

C. no instances of securities fraud occur without the omission of necessary facts.

D. some instances of securities fraud do not intentionally employ omission of necessary facts.

E. some instances of securities fraud involve fraudulence or deceit.

15. Some instances of fraud are instances of insider trading. Only security breaches that involve the buying and selling of stocks from within an organization can be considered insider trading. In some instances of insider trading, "tipping" is a method used to exchange information to those who would misuse it. Not all insider trading occurs within stock markets and the like, but some occurs within corporations themselves.

From the information given above, it can be validly concluded that

A. insider trading occurs if and only if there is a breach in security involving "tipping."

B. only in insider trading is the method of "tipping" utilized.

C. all instances of fraud are instances of insider trading.

D. some security breaches that involve the buying and selling of stock utilize the method of "tipping."

E. no security breaches that utilize the method of "tipping" occur within stock markets and the like.

16. Andrea is involved in a play in which her character breaks the fourth wall with the audience. She told her friends that she was in a musical, but according to her director, no play can be a musical. A musical is defined as a piece of performance in which music is an essential part of the storytelling. Some musicals involve characters that are self-aware and break the fourth wall by interacting with the audience.

    From the information given above, it can be validly concluded that

    A. some pieces of performance in which music is an essential part of the storytelling involve characters that are self-aware and break the fourth wall.

    B. all plays involve a character that is self-aware and breaks the fourth wall.

    C. only musicals involve characters that are self-aware and break the fourth wall by interacting with the audience.

    D. not all pieces of storytelling in which the music is an essential part of the storytelling are musicals.

    E. some musicals are plays.

17. After Kate entrusted the management of her bank account to her friend, she accused him of embezzlement when money was stolen from the account. A crime can be considered embezzlement if and only if the embezzler was entrusted with the assets of the victim before appropriating them. All instances where assets are appropriated are considered theft. Not all instances where assets are appropriated are considered embezzlement.

    From the information given above, it can be validly concluded that

    A. Kate's friend committed theft, not embezzlement.

    B. some instances of theft are instances of embezzlement.

    C. some instances of theft are not instances of embezzlement.

    D. Kate's friend is guilty of embezzlement.

    E. no instances where assets are appropriated are considered embezzlement.

18. A person who offers payment to a figure of authority in order to influence their decision-making is participating in bribery. Under the Foreign Corrupt Practices Act (FCPA), it is illegal to pay, offer to pay, or promise pay to a foreign government official in order to influence their decision-making. Some persons guilty of violating the FCPA can receive up to five years in prison. Miranda offered to pay but did not pay a figure of authority within the United States in order to influence certain decisions being made in the future.

    From the information given above, it can be validly concluded that

    A. Miranda is guilty of violating the FCPA and can therefore receive up to five years in prison.

    B. all persons guilty of bribery can receive up to five years in prison.

    C. if a person is guilty of bribery, then they are guilty of violating the FCPA.

    D. Miranda is guilty of participating in bribery.

    E. all persons guilty of violating the FCPA can receive at least 5 years in prison.

Practice Test 2

19. Alex was born in the American Samoa and Swain Islands, but he is not a US citizen. Both US citizens and US nationals are persons who owe loyalty to the United States, but some US nationals are not US citizens. All persons who were born in or who had parents that were born in outlying possessions of the United States are considered US nationals. The American Samoa and Swain Islands are outlying possessions of the United States.

*From the information given above, it **CANNOT** be validly concluded that*

A. Alex was born in an outlying possession of the United States.

B. Alex is a US national.

C. all US nationals are persons born in the American Samoa and Swain Islands.

D. all persons who had parents born in the American Samoa and Swain Islands are US nationals.

E. not all US nationals are US citizens.

20. The Deferred Action for Childhood Arrivals (DACA) is an exercise in prosecutorial discretion that defers threat of deportation for some young undocumented immigrants. All persons protected under DACA are given work authorization in the United States. However, because DACA is not a piece of federal legislation, no person protected under DACA is given permanent legal status in the United States. If a person does not renew their status as a person protected under DACA every two years, then that person will be deported.

From the information given above, it can be validly concluded that

A. if a person does renew their status as a person protected under DACA every two years, then that person will not be deported.

B. some persons protected under DACA are not given work authorization in the United States.

C. all persons given work authorization in the United States are given permanent legal status in the United States.

D. only those protected under DACA can be deported.

E. all persons that are deported are persons that failed to renew their status as a person protected under DACA every two years.

Part B—Arithmetic Reasoning

25 minutes—20 questions

DIRECTIONS: For Questions 1–20, a mathematical question is presented in the form of a word problem. You must extrapolate the data and compute the correct answer based on the information provided. If the exact answer is not given as one of the response choices, select *E. none of these.*

1. A company provides matching stocks for each employee. The price of one share of a stock fell $4 each day for 10 days. If the original price of the stock was $57, what was the price after the 10 days?

   A. $4

   B. $7

   C. $17

   D. $40

   E. none of these

2. From sea level, a truck ascends a hill at a rate of 30 feet per minute. Where is the truck in relation to sea level 5 minutes after it starts ascending?

   A. 35 feet

   B. 80 feet

   C. 150 feet

   D. 180 feet

   E. none of these

3. The tires on all of the ICE cars need to be replaced. There are currently 357 vehicles in the fleet, 49 cars and 308 trucks. How many tires need to be replaced?

   A. 196

   B. 504

   C. 1,232

   D. 1,428

   E. none of these

4. After a long day of work, ICE Agent Lopez accidentally gets lost on the way home from work. He drives 17 miles in the wrong direction from the office before he turns around. If his home is 38 miles from the office, how many total miles did he have to drive to get home that night?

   A. 21

   B. 34

   C. 55

   D. 76

   E. none of these

5. Supervisor Magbee has been working at the Atlanta office for 26 years. If she began working for ICE when she was 29 years old, how old will she be on her next birthday?

   A. 27

   B. 30

   C. 55

   D. 56

   E. none of these

6. A canister of disinfectant spray has a diameter of 5 inches and a height of 12 inches. What is the volume, in cubic inches?

   A. 75 cubic inches

   B. 180 cubic inches

   C. 235.6 cubic inches

   D. 240.5 cubic inches

   E. none of these

7. During an evening stakeout, the temperature drops 37 degrees. If the current temperature is now −13 degrees Fahrenheit, what was the temperature when the stakeout began?

   A. −40°F

   B. −37°F

   C. 24°F

   D. 40°F

   E. none of these

8. In an effort to stay in shape, Agent Dreski has decided to create a personalized workout routine. Each weekday, he does 12 pushups, 40 jumping jacks, 60 lunges, and 10 high kicks. How many total lunges will he complete after 2 weeks?

   A. 140

   B. 168

   C. 400

   D. 840

   E. none of these

9. An alleged smuggler is booked wearing a total of 12 rings. Six are diamond solitaires, 2 are 24-karat gold bands, and 4 are silver bands. An ICE officer wants to examine the rings before talking with the suspect. What is the probability that the officer will choose a 24-karat gold band from the evidence bag?

   A. $\dfrac{1}{6}$

   B. $\dfrac{1}{4}$

   C. $\dfrac{1}{3}$

   D. $\dfrac{1}{2}$

   E. none of these

10. An ICE vehicle brakes at a rate of 16 feet per second. If a stoplight is 500 feet away, how many seconds must the driver allow for in order to safely stop the vehicle before reaching the light?

   A. 14.25 seconds

   B. 25 seconds

   C. 30.5 seconds

   D. 31.25 seconds

   E. none of these

11. Agent Khalid arrives to work early. After he swipes his key card to open the front door, he must head to the alarm to disarm it and then go back to the front door to confirm that it closed properly. If the distance from the front door to the alarm is 27 feet, how many feet must he travel to disarm the alarm and then go back to the front door?

   A. 13.5 ft.

   B. 27 ft.

   C. 40.5 ft.

   D. 54 ft.

   E. none of these

12. An ICE field office building in Colorado is 140 feet tall. The height of the main training center building in Georgia is 56 feet. The highest point of the New York field office is 350 feet. How much taller is the highest point of the New York building from the top of the training center?

   A. 84 ft.

   B. 294 ft.

   C. 336 ft.

   D. 406 ft.

   E. none of these

13. If four is added to the difference when $20x$ is subtracted from $-28x$, the result is 102. What is the value of x?

    A. -2.04

    B. -2.4

    C. 2.125

    D. 2.40

    E. none of these

14. ICE agents confiscated x pounds of cocaine with an estimated value of $5 per pound. At the same time, the agents confiscated 15 pounds of marijuana valued at $2 per pound. Find the total number of pounds of both confiscated narcotics if the average value per pound is $3.50.

    A. 15 lbs.

    B. 26.25 lbs.

    C. 30 lbs.

    D. 55 lbs.

    E. none of these

15. Cyber investigators track and destroy 250 hack attempts per hour of monitoring. How long will cyber investigators have to monitor cyberspace in order to track 1,000 hack attempts?

    A. 40 hours

    B. 4 hours

    C. 0.4 hours

    D. 0.25 hours

    E. none of these

16. During a training run to a nearby lighthouse, an ICE trainee noticed the lighthouse light blinks 20 times a minute. How long would it take the light to blink 1,000 times?

    A. 50 minutes

    B. 500 minutes

    C. 1,020 minutes

    D. 20,000 minutes

    E. none of these

17. Trainee Watkins earned a score of 60% on his first ICE test, a 68% on his second test, and a 91% on his third test. What is his average test score?

   A. 60%

   B. 68%

   C. 75%

   D. 87%

   E. none of these

18. The ratio of female to male agents in the Florida ICE office is 4 to 6. If there are 50 female agents, how many male agents are there?

   A. 33

   B. 75

   C. 200

   D. 750

   E. none of these

19. Trainee Doug earned scores of 83, 90, and 95 on his cybersecurity tests. What does he need to earn on his next cybersecurity test to have an arithmetic mean of 90?

   A. 87

   B. 90

   C. 92

   D. 96

   E. none of these

20. The large coffee pot in the break room holds 240 cups. It is three-fourths full. How many cups are in the pot?

   A. 60 cups

   B. 180 cups

   C. 240 cups

   D. 320 cups

   E. none of these

Part C—Writing Skills Assessment

25 minutes—20 questions

> **DIRECTIONS:** For Questions 1–5, select the one word that completes the sentence correctly.

1. It is important for every person on the investigation site to wear the proper color vest and name tag as this will provide clear _____ and access to enter the site.

   A. identification

   B. substitution

   C. location

   D. allocation

   E. modification

2. Although the posters and the loudspeaker _____ told all new recruits to meet at the cafeteria, three people went down to the stables.

   A. newspaper

   B. calendar

   C. announcements

   D. captain

   E. report

3. Alterations to any uniform must be completed by a(n) _____ tailor.

   A. certified

   B. unskilled

   C. verified

   D. cued

   E. clearly

4. First responders can easily find themselves in a _____ environment when there is a violent conflict between groups of people.

   A. calm

   B. hostile

   C. peaceful

   D. confused

   E. rough

5. Our next assignment for the Cultural Property, Arts, and Antiquities Investigations and Repatriations Program will be _____ in southeast Asia.

   A. stateside

   B. neighborhood

   C. cursive

   D. at home

   E. abroad

DIRECTIONS: For Questions 6–8, select the one option that represents a change that should be made to correct the sentence. If no change is needed, choose *E. No correction is necessary.*

---

6. After World War II, many Jewish familys struggled to stay safe.

   A. Change <u>struggled</u> to <u>struggle</u>

   B. Change <u>War</u> to <u>war</u>

   C. Change <u>familys</u> to <u>families</u>

   D. Change <u>World War II</u> to <u>world war II</u>

   E. No correction is necessary

7. The city of New York, which is made up of five burrows, is a unique city located in the northeastern region of the United States of America.

   A. Change <u>city of New York</u> to <u>City of New York</u>

   B. Change <u>northeastern</u> to <u>North Eastern</u>

   C. Change <u>burrows</u> to <u>boroughs</u>

   D. Change <u>York</u> to <u>york</u>

   E. No correction is necessary

8. Most people see know problem with white lies when they are used to protect someone.

   A. Change <u>white lies</u> to <u>White Lies</u>

   B. Change <u>protect</u> to <u>protecting</u>

   C. Change <u>are</u> to <u>is</u>

   D. Change <u>know</u> to <u>no</u>

   E. No correction is necessary

DIRECTIONS: For Questions 9–11, select the one option that is correctly punctuated.

9. **A.** The field office was incredibly busy today! human trafficking agents and Victims Assistance Specialists were intently focused on a high priority investigation.

   B. The field office was incredibly busy today: human trafficking agents and Victims Assistance Specialists were intently focused on a high priority investigation.

   C. The field office was incredibly busy today. Human trafficking agents and Victims Assistance Specialists were intently focused on a high priority investigation.

   D. The field office was incredibly busy today? human trafficking agents and Victims Assistance Specialists were intently focused on a high priority investigation

10. **A.** "Undercover field training starts tomorrow" said Agent Dwight.

    B. "Undercover field training starts tomorrow, said Agent Dwight."

    C. Undercover field training starts tomorrow, said Agent Dwight.

    D. "Undercover field training starts tomorrow," said Agent Dwight.

11. **A.** The agent discovered that cocaine was being smuggled into the US in boxes of childrens clothing.

    B. The agent discovered that cocaine was being smuggled into the US in boxes of childrens' clothing.

    C. The agent discovered that cocaine was being smuggled into the US in boxes of children's clothing.

    D. The agent discovered that cocaine was being smuggled into the US in boxes of childrens's clothing

DIRECTIONS: For Questions 12–14, select the one option that correctly spells the missing word in the sentence.

12. Please do not _____ any suspect a specific outcome to their case.

    A. garantee

    B. garanty

    C. garentee

    D. garyentee

    E. guarantee

13. Each agent will be given a complete uniform, which includes _____ garments, outerwear, head covering, and shoes.

    A. foundational

    B. fondational

    C. fundational

    D. funadtional

    E. fooduational

14. The hostile drug bust at the border has really had a negative _____ on Agent Wilkins.

    A. effeck

    B. affect

    C. afect

    D. effect

    E. auffec

DIRECTIONS: For Questions 15 and 16, select the one sentence that uses the correct capitalization.

---

15. A. Operation Stolen Promise is investigating Eat Our Profits organizers for claiming to feed the elderly affected by the coronavirus pandemic.

    B. Operation stolen promise is investigating Eat Our Profits organizers for claiming to feed the elderly affected by the coronavirus pandemic.

    C. Operation Stolen promise is investigating eat our Profits organizers for claiming to feed the elderly affected by the coronavirus pandemic.

    D. Operation stolen Promise is investigating Eat our Profits organizers for claiming to feed the elderly affected by the coronavirus pandemic.

16. A. Agent rhodes is assigned to man the Immigration and Customs Enforcement 24-hour hotline.

    B. Agent rhodes is assigned to man the Immigration and customs Enforcement 24-hour hotline.

    C. agent rhodes is assigned to man the Immigration and Customs Enforcement 24-hour Hotline.

    D. Agent Rhodes is assigned to man the Immigration and Customs Enforcement 24-hour hotline.

DIRECTIONS: For Questions 17 and 18, select the correct sentence order to form a clear, concise, and coherent paragraph. If no correction is necessary, choose *E. no correction is necessary.*

17.
1. Investigation group wrap up sessions are important especially for new agents.
2. It is their chance to ask questions and get clarification on processes.
3. This is also a time for seasoned agents to model thinking aloud.
4. Therefore, group wrap should happen after all investigations.

A. 4–2–3–1
B. 3–2–1–4
C. 2–3–1–4
D. 1–4–2–3
E. no correction is necessary

18.
1. During times of global pandemics, fraudulent people prey on vulnerable people.
2. When people are afraid, they can be easily manipulated.
3. In conclusion, ICE is seeking to protect people from falling prey to fraudulent organizations or people.
4. ICE's program, Operation Stolen Promise, constantly evaluates organizations to ensure that people are not exploited.

A. 1–2–4–3
B. 1–3–4–2
C. 4–3–2–1
D. 3–4–1–2
E. no correction is necessary

DIRECTIONS: For Questions 19 and 20, select the correct paragraph order to form a clear, concise, and coherent document. If no change to the paragraph order is necessary, choose *E. no correction is necessary.*

19.

1. At first glance, the cost of taking a cruise makes it seem to be an expensive vacation. Cruise prices listed as a per-person cost are often in the hundreds of dollars. The prices change based upon the number of days, size of room, and location on the ship. However, after careful analysis, it is clear that cruising is a very economical way to vacation.

2. While the cost is listed per person, it is an all-inclusive price. That means you do not have to come up with any additional funds for the essentials. Your room is completely paid for and comes with nightly turndown service that usually includes chocolates and towel origami. Your food is served buffet style. With all the essentials covered, what more do you need?

3. Entertainment is also good, extra fun on a vacation. If you choose to stay on-ship, all the entertainment is included, such as shuffleboard, arcade games, swimming, and karaoke. If you choose to go off-ship when docked, you can walk around for free or take a discounted tour. The only downside discovered during the investigation was with consuming LOTS of alcohol. Advice—monitor how much you drink.

4. It is clear that cruising is a cost-effective way to vacation because you pay for everything before you get on the ship. All your basic needs for the trip are paid for, with extras included, once on the ship. Entertainment on the ship is also included. Cruising is an economical way to vacation.

A. 1–3–4–2

B. 2–1–3–4

C. 4–3–2–1

D. 3–2–4–1

E. no correction is necessary

20.

1. Last August, the smuggling arms unit received a tip that an antique warehouse was storing and possibly selling illegal guns. A team of five agents was deployed to investigate and verify this tip. Two agents posed as a young married couple shopping for new home items. One agent posed as an antique dealer. Another two agents were hired to work at the warehouse, one as a salesperson and the other as a stock person. Their undercover identities allowed them to freely visit the warehouse.

2. After three weeks on site, the smuggling arms unit contacted the cultural artifacts team. Once members from the artifacts team were able to verify that the jade pieces, ivory tusks, and Van Gogh paintings were, in fact, authentic, arrests were made. While the initial tip did not yield an arrest for guns, it did help recover stolen artifacts from three countries.

3. After one week, the agents in the smuggling arms unit realized that they needed the help of the cultural artifacts team. When the agents posing as a young couple visited the warehouse, they observed several jade pieces and ivory tusks. The undercover art collector agent found three Van Gogh paintings. The warehouse owner indicated the paintings were replicas. The undercover agent tried to buy one of the paintings, but the warehouse owner refused to sell. These were the first signs something was wrong.

4. By the end of second week, the two agents who posed as employees were unable to find any signs of an illegal gun operation. However, they did notice unusual patterns of customers coming and going in the hours after closing. Many of the customers carried large heavy suitcases into the warehouse and exited with merchandise.

A. 1–3–4–2

B. 3–2–4–1

C. 4–3–1–2

D. 1–4–2–3

E. no correction necessary

ANSWER KEYS AND EXPLANATIONS
Part A—Logical Reasoning

1. A	**5.** D	**9.** E	**13.** C	**17.** C
2. C	**6.** B	**10.** A	**14.** A	**18.** D
3. D	**7.** E	**11.** A	**15.** D	**19.** C
4. E	**8.** B	**12.** B	**16.** A	**20.** A

1. **The correct answer is A.** Based on the information provided in the passage, it must be true that no H-1B dependent employers who hire H-1B professionals with master's degrees or higher in their field of specialty are subject to any additional rules. Mr. Jones is an H-1B dependent employer who only hires H-1B professionals with at least a master's degree in their field of specialty, so Mr. Jones is not subject to any additional rules.

2. **The correct answer is C.** Based on the information provided in the passage, it must be true that all persons wishing to receive a green card through a marriage contract must first undergo a two-year period of "conditional permanent residence." In this case, it is not so that a couple could undergo only a one-year period of "conditional permanent residence" and still receive a green card. Therefore, no individuals who undergo a one-year period of "conditional permanent residence" will be issued a green card.

3. **The correct answer is D.** Based on the information provided in the passage, it must be true that Abel was granted amnesty. It did not state what he was granted amnesty for. It was, however, stated that no people who knowingly hired undocumented immigrants were granted amnesty. Thus, Abel could not have knowingly hired undocumented immigrants.

4. **The correct answer is E.** Based on the information provided by the passage, it must be true that all corporations that operate in the EU are subject to EU laws. Google is a US based company that operates in the EU and, thus, it is subject to all EU laws. Therefore, Google is subject to the "right to be forgotten" laws.

5. **The correct answer is D.** Based on the information provided in the passage, it must be true that there are no laws pertaining to a child's privacy on social media in cases where the parents themselves post nonobscene pictures online. So, any parent who wishes to post a nonobscene picture of their child online is within their rights to do so.

6. **The correct answer is B.** Given the information provided in the passage, the only thing to be certain of is that honey brew is always sold with a bamboo straw, and all things that are sold with a bamboo straw are cold coffees. Therefore, honey brew must be a cold coffee.

7. **The correct answer is E.** Given the information provided in the passage, it must be true that all persons whose properties are identified as having been used for smuggling or the concealing of illicit activities are subject to a notice of seizure. However, some persons who are due notice of search and seizure are not aware of the smuggling or the concealing of illicit activities occurring within their property. The passage only allows that some are not aware or possibly

that none are aware. There is no indication that some are aware. Therefore, it cannot be validly concluded that some persons whose properties are identified as having been used for smuggling or concealing illicit activities are aware of smuggling or the concealing of illicit activities occurring within their property.

8. **The correct answer is B.** Given the information provided in the passage, it must be true that some countries do not cooperate with each other on cases related to human trafficking but that all countries have cases related to human trafficking. Therefore, it must be true that some countries that experience human trafficking within their borders do not cooperate with one another on those cases.

9. **The correct answer is E.** Given the information in the passage, all instances of peonage are related to an unpaid debt. Thus, it cannot be concluded that some instances of peonage are unrelated to an unpaid debt. Sentence 4 specifically states that only cases where involuntary servitude is tied to debt can be considered peonage.

10. **The correct answer is A.** Given the information provided in the passage, it must be true that stealing an object worth in excess of $100,000 is stealing an object of cultural heritage. It must also be true that stealing an object of cultural heritage is trafficking of cultural property. Mrs. Smith is responsible for stealing an object worth in excess of $100,000 and is, therefore, responsible for stealing an object of cultural heritage. Her crime is defined as trafficking of cultural property.

11. **The correct answer is A.** Given the information provided in the passage, it must be true that, if an act of conflict is committed between two or more nations or military forces, then that act is considered an act of war. Therefore, if an act is not considered an act of war, then it must not have been an act of conflict committed between two or more nations or military forces.

12. **The correct answer is B.** Based on the information in the passage, it must be true that not all persons sentenced to 20 years are repeat offenders guilty of obtaining national security information. So that must mean that a person sentenced to 20 years in prison is not necessarily guilty of obtaining national security information.

13. **The correct answer is C.** Given the information provided in the passage, it must be true that Edward is not protected under FISA. It must also be true that, if a person that is not protected under FISA were to illegally intercept a communication medium, then they would be guilty of violating the ECPA. If this is true, then if Edward were to illegally intercept a communication medium, he would be guilty of violating ECPA.

14. **The correct answer is A.** Given the information provided in the passage, it must be true that a person is guilty of securities fraud if and only if that person intentionally employs fraudulence or deceit in connection with the purchase of a security. It must then be true that all instances of fraudulence or deceit with intent in connection with the purchase of a security are instances of securities fraud.

15. **The correct answer is D.** Given the information provided in the passage, it must be true that, all things considered, insider trading is a security breach that involves the buying and selling of stocks within an organization. It must also be true that some instances of insider trading are instances that utilize the method of "tipping." Therefore, some security breaches that involve the buying and selling of stocks utilize the method of "tipping."

16. **The correct answer is A.** Given the information provided in the passage, it must be true that all musicals are defined as pieces of performance in which music is an essential part of the storytelling and that some musicals involve characters that are self-aware and break the fourth wall. If these things are true, then it must be true that some pieces of performance in which music is an essential part of the storytelling involve characters that are self-aware and break the fourth wall.

17. **The correct answer is C.** Given the information provided in the passage, it must be true that all instances where assets are appropriated are considered theft but that some such instances are not considered embezzlement. If this is true, then it must be true that some instances of theft are not instances of embezzlement.

18. **The correct answer is D.** Given the information provided in the passage, it must be true that a person who offers to pay a figure of authority in order to influence their decision-making is guilty of bribery. Miranda offered to pay, though she did not pay, a figure of authority within the United States in order to influence their decision-making and is therefore guilty of bribery.

19. **The correct answer is C.** Given the information provided in the passage, it must be true that the American Samoa and Swain Islands are outlying possessions of the United States and that all persons born in outlying possessions of the United States are US nationals. However, there is no logical premise given to suggest that all US nationals are persons born in the American Samoa and Swain Islands.

20. **The correct answer is A.** Given the information provided in the passage, it must be true that, if a person does not renew their status as a person protected under DACA every two years, then that person will be deported. In this case, it must be true that a person who does renew such status at the appropriate time will not be deported.

Part B—Arithmetic Reasoning

1. C	5. D	9. A	13. A	17. E
2. C	6. C	10. D	14. C	18. B
3. A	7. C	11. D	15. B	19. C
4. E	8. E	12. B	16. A	20. B

1. **The correct answer is C.** Multiply the number of dollars per day by the number of days and subtract that from the original price.

$$\$4 \times 10 = \$40$$
$$\$57 - \$40 = \$17$$

2. **The correct answer is C.** Multiply the number of feet per minute by the number of minutes.

$$30 \times 5 = 150 \text{ feet}$$

3. **The correct answer is A.** Multiply the number of cars times 4.

$$49 \times 4 = 196$$

4. **The correct answer is E.** Add the number of miles he took going the wrong direction to the distance from his house to his office.

$$17 \times 2 = 34$$
$$34 + 38 = 72$$

5. **The correct answer is D.** Add Magbee's original age to the number of years she has been working for ICE, then add 1 for her next birthday.

$$29 + 26 + 1 = 56$$

6. **The correct answer is C.** Use the volume formula for a cylinder.

$$V = \pi r^2 \times h$$
$$V = \pi (2.5)^2 \times 12$$
$$V = \pi \times 6.25 \times 12$$
$$V = 75\pi$$
$$V \approx 235.6 \text{ cubic inches}$$

7. **The correct answer is C.** Add 37 degrees to the current temperature.

$$-13 + 37 = 24 \text{ degrees Fahrenheit}$$

8. **The correct answer is E.** Since Agent Dreski only works out on weekdays, he will complete 5 workouts in one week and 10 workouts in two weeks. To solve, multiply the number of lunges Agent Dreski does each day by 10 to see how many lunges he will complete after two weeks.

$$60 \times 10 = 600$$

9. **The correct answer is A.** The probability of the officer choosing a 24-karat gold band is expressed as the number of bands divided by the total number of rings. If there are 24-karat gold bands among the 12 total rings, then the probability of choosing a gold band is calculated as follows:

$$\frac{2}{12} = \frac{1}{6}$$

10. **The correct answer is D.** To solve, divide the distance from the stoplight by the braking rate of the vehicle.

$$500 \div 16 = 31.25 \text{ sec}$$

11. **The correct answer is D.** Multiply the distance from the front door to the alarm (27 ft.) by 2.

$$27 \times 2 = 54 \text{ ft.}$$

12. **The correct answer is B.** Subtract the height of the highest point of the New York building from the height of the training center in Georgia.

$$350 - 56 = 294 \text{ ft.}$$

13. **The correct answer is A.** Rewrite the first part of the question, "If four is added to the difference when $20x$ is subtracted from $-28x$, the result is 102," into an equation then solve for x.

$$(-28x + -20x) + 4 = 102$$
$$-48x + 4 = 102$$
$$-48x = 102 - 4$$
$$-48x = 98$$
$$x = -\frac{98}{48}$$
$$x = -\frac{49}{24}$$
$$x = -2.04$$

14. **The correct answer is C.** Start with identifying the unknown variables and creating an equation with the information given:

- Let x = pounds of cocaine confiscated
- Let y = the total pounds of narcotics confiscated

If there are 15 pounds of marijuana, then the total amount of both narcotics can be expressed as follows:

$$x + 15 = y$$

Next, we need to include the value per pound into our equation. This can be expressed as:

$$5x + 15(2) = 3.50y$$

Use substitution to solve for x.

$$5x + 15(2) = 3.50(x + 15)$$
$$5x + 30 = 3.50x + 52.5$$
$$5x - 3.50x + 30 = 52.5$$
$$1.5x + 30 = 52.5$$
$$1.5x = 52.5 - 30$$
$$1.5x = 22.5$$
$$x = 15$$

So the ICE agents confiscated 15 pounds of cocaine. Now we can solve for y as follows:

$$y = x + 15$$
$$y = 15 + 15$$
$$y = 30$$

Check the solution:

$$5(15) + 15(2) = 3.50(30)$$
$$75 + 30 = 105$$
$$105 = 105$$

The solution holds true, so the agents confiscated a total of 30 pounds of narcotics.

15. **The correct answer is B.** Divide the number of hack attempts (1,000) by the number of hack attempts per hour of monitoring (250) to find out how long cyber investigators have to monitor cyberspace in order to track 1,000 hack attempts.

$$\frac{1,000}{250} = 4 \text{ hours}$$

16. **The correct answer is A.** Divide the number of blinks (1,000) by the number of blinks per minute (20).

$$\frac{1,000}{20} = 50 \text{ minutes}$$

17. **The correct answer is E.** Add the test grades and divide the sum by the number of tests.

$$(60 + 68 + 91) \div 3 = 73$$

18. **The correct answer is B.** Use a proportion comparing females to males in the Florida ICE office to solve.

$$\frac{4}{6} = \frac{50}{x}$$
$$(6)(50) = 4x$$
$$300 = 4x$$
$$x = 75$$

Answers | Practice Test 2

19. **The correct answer is C.** Remember that an arithmetic mean is an average. To solve, you will need to add the four test scores (assigning x for the fourth unknown score) and divide by 4. The result must equal the arithmetic mean of 90.

$$\frac{83 + 90 + 95 + x}{4} = 90$$
$$83 + 90 + 95 + x = 90(4)$$
$$268 + x = 360$$
$$x = 92$$

Doug will need to earn a score of 92 on his next test to achieve an arithmetic mean of 90.

20. **The correct answer is B.** To solve, multiply the capacity of the coffee pot by how full it is.

$$\frac{240}{1} \times \frac{3}{4} = 180$$

Part C—Writing Skills Assessment

1. A	5. E	9. C	13. A	17. E
2. C	6. C	10. D	14. D	18. A
3. A	7. C	11. C	15. A	19. E
4. B	8. D	12. E	16. D	20. A

1. **The correct answer is A.** The sentence talks about access and clear entry to the investigation site. The proper colored vest and name tag provide identification.

2. **The correct answer is C.** The word *loud-speaker* indicates that an audible sound had to be made. The correct word choice is *announcements*.

3. **The correct answer is A.** *Certified* means to be officially qualified to provide a particular service.

4. **The correct answer is B.** The sentence uses the word *violent* to describe the tone of the conflict between groups of people. *Hostile* agrees in tone with *violent*.

5. **The correct answer is E.** *Abroad* indicates "away from the mainland or stateside."

6. **The correct answer is C.** The plural of *family* is *families*. An *s* cannot be added to a word ending in a consonant-*y* pattern. The *y* must be changed to an *i* before adding -*es* to make it plural. The sentence should read: During World War II, many Jewish families struggled to stay safe.

7. **The correct answer is C.** In this context, the correct word choice is *boroughs*, which is defined as one of the five constituent political divisions of New York City. A *burrow* is a hole or tunnel dug by a small animal. New York is a proper noun, and both words in the city title (but not the word city itself) must be capitalized. Northeastern is descriptive of a region not a proper name, so it does not need to be capitalized.

8. **The correct answer is D.** *Know* and *no* are homophones, which are words that sound the same but are spelled differently and have different meanings. To *know* is to have an understanding of and is the wrong word choice in this case. *White lies* is not a proper noun, so it need not be capitalized. *Protecting* is in the correct tense. The subject and the verb need to be in agreement. In this case, since there is more than one person, the plural verb *are* is correct.

9. **The correct answer is C.** Two independent clauses can either be separated by a period or connected with a semicolon. The first sentence is a statement not an exclamation or a question. Colons are used for lists inside a sentence.

10. **The correct answer is D.** Beginning and ending quotation marks are used to set apart a phrase that someone said. A comma is placed inside the ending quotation mark.

11. **The correct answer is C.** Apostrophes are used to indicate possession. In this case, the clothing was children's clothing.

12. **The correct answer is E.** The correct spelling is *guarantee*.

13. **The correct answer is A.** The correct spelling is *foundational*.

14. **The correct answer is D.** The correct spelling is *effect*. Although *affect* is spelled correctly, it is a verb and does not fit in this sentence.

15. **The correct answer is A.** Proper nouns, such as titles and names of organizations, should be capitalized in their entirety. In this case, Operation Stolen Promise (a title) and Eat Our Profits (the name of an organization) should be capitalized.

16. **The correct answer is D.** Official titles such as Agent Rhodes must be entirely capitalized. In addition, Immigration and Customs Enforcement must be capitalized since it is the name of the agency and a proper noun phrase.

17. **The correct answer is E.** Sentence 1 is a topic sentence. Sentence 2 explains Sentence 1. Sentence 3 provides additional information. Sentence 4 wraps up the ideas in the paragraph, which indicates it is a concluding sentence. No correction is necessary.

18. **The correct answer is A.** Sentence 1 is a topic sentence. Sentence 2 further states the problem. Sentence 4 provides a potential solution to the problem raised in Sentence 2. The phrase "In conclusion" in Sentence 3 indicates that this sentence is a closing sentence.

19. **The correct answer is E.** No corrections are necessary. Paragraph 1 opens with "At first glance." Paragraphs 2 and 3 support the last statement in Paragraph 1, "it is clear cruising is a very economical way to vacation." Paragraph 4 begins and ends with finalizing statements, "It is clear" and "Cruising is an economical way to vacation," thus restating the original thesis statement in the first paragraph.

20. **The correct answer is A.** All the paragraphs contain time clues as to their order placement. Paragraph 1 sets the stage with "Last August." Paragraph 3 provides the next time clue with the phrase "After one week." The phrase "By the end of the second week" in Paragraph 4 continues the timeline progression. And Paragraph 2 is placed last with the phrase "After three weeks."

PRACTICE TEST 3: FBI PHASE I SPECIAL AGENT EXAM

The following is a sample practice test that contains the types of questions found on Phase I of the FBI Special Agent Exam: Logic-Based Reasoning, Figural Reasoning, Personality Assessment, Preferences and Interest, and Situational Judgment.

If you decide to time yourself, you have 75 minutes to complete this practice test. Use this time limit to gauge your comfort level under time constraints and your level of mastery of the types of questions found in the exam. The actual test session is approximately three hours long. No calculators or electronic devices are permitted.

After you have completed this practice test, check your answers for Questions 1–24 against the answer key and explanations that follow the test. Remember, only the Logic-Based Reasoning and Figural Reasoning questions will have one correct answer and be scored on the actual exam. The other parts of the exam are character and personality assessments.

PRACTICE TEST 3: FBI PHASE I SPECIAL AGENT EXAM ANSWER SHEET

1. Ⓐ Ⓑ Ⓒ Ⓓ Ⓔ
2. Ⓐ Ⓑ Ⓒ Ⓓ Ⓔ
3. Ⓐ Ⓑ Ⓒ Ⓓ Ⓔ
4. Ⓐ Ⓑ Ⓒ Ⓓ Ⓔ
5. Ⓐ Ⓑ Ⓒ Ⓓ Ⓔ
6. Ⓐ Ⓑ Ⓒ Ⓓ Ⓔ
7. Ⓐ Ⓑ Ⓒ Ⓓ Ⓔ
8. Ⓐ Ⓑ Ⓒ Ⓓ Ⓔ
9. Ⓐ Ⓑ Ⓒ Ⓓ Ⓔ
10. Ⓐ Ⓑ Ⓒ Ⓓ Ⓔ
11. Ⓐ Ⓑ Ⓒ Ⓓ Ⓔ
12. Ⓐ Ⓑ Ⓒ Ⓓ Ⓔ
13. Ⓐ Ⓑ Ⓒ Ⓓ Ⓔ
14. Ⓐ Ⓑ Ⓒ Ⓓ Ⓔ
15. Ⓐ Ⓑ Ⓒ Ⓓ Ⓔ

16. Ⓐ Ⓑ Ⓒ Ⓓ Ⓔ
17. Ⓐ Ⓑ Ⓒ Ⓓ Ⓔ
18. Ⓐ Ⓑ Ⓒ Ⓓ Ⓔ
19. Ⓐ Ⓑ Ⓒ Ⓓ Ⓔ
20. Ⓐ Ⓑ Ⓒ Ⓓ Ⓔ
21. Ⓐ Ⓑ Ⓒ Ⓓ Ⓔ
22. Ⓐ Ⓑ Ⓒ Ⓓ Ⓔ
23. Ⓐ Ⓑ Ⓒ Ⓓ Ⓔ
24. Ⓐ Ⓑ Ⓒ Ⓓ Ⓔ
25. Ⓐ Ⓑ Ⓒ Ⓓ
26. Ⓐ Ⓑ Ⓒ Ⓓ
27. Ⓐ Ⓑ Ⓒ Ⓓ
28. Ⓐ Ⓑ Ⓒ Ⓓ
29. Ⓐ Ⓑ Ⓒ Ⓓ
30. Ⓐ Ⓑ Ⓒ Ⓓ

31. Ⓐ Ⓑ Ⓒ Ⓓ
32. Ⓐ Ⓑ Ⓒ Ⓓ
33. Ⓐ Ⓑ Ⓒ Ⓓ
34. Ⓐ Ⓑ Ⓒ Ⓓ
35. Ⓐ Ⓑ Ⓒ Ⓓ
36. Ⓐ Ⓑ Ⓒ Ⓓ
37. Ⓐ Ⓑ Ⓒ Ⓓ Ⓔ
38. Ⓐ Ⓑ Ⓒ Ⓓ Ⓔ
39. Ⓐ Ⓑ Ⓒ Ⓓ Ⓔ
40. Ⓐ Ⓑ Ⓒ Ⓓ Ⓔ
41. Ⓐ Ⓑ Ⓒ Ⓓ Ⓔ
42. Ⓐ Ⓑ Ⓒ Ⓓ Ⓔ
43. Ⓐ Ⓑ Ⓒ Ⓓ Ⓔ
44. Ⓐ Ⓑ Ⓒ Ⓓ Ⓔ
45. Ⓐ Ⓑ Ⓒ Ⓓ Ⓔ

46. Ⓐ Ⓑ Ⓒ Ⓓ Ⓔ
47. Ⓐ Ⓑ Ⓒ Ⓓ Ⓔ
48. Ⓐ Ⓑ Ⓒ Ⓓ Ⓔ
49. Ⓐ Ⓑ Ⓒ Ⓓ Ⓔ
50. Ⓐ Ⓑ Ⓒ Ⓓ Ⓔ
51. Ⓐ Ⓑ Ⓒ Ⓓ Ⓔ
52. Ⓐ Ⓑ Ⓒ Ⓓ Ⓔ
53. Ⓐ Ⓑ Ⓒ Ⓓ Ⓔ
54. Ⓐ Ⓑ Ⓒ Ⓓ Ⓔ
55. Ⓐ Ⓑ Ⓒ Ⓓ Ⓔ
56. Ⓐ Ⓑ Ⓒ Ⓓ Ⓔ
57. Ⓐ Ⓑ Ⓒ Ⓓ Ⓔ
58. Ⓐ Ⓑ Ⓒ Ⓓ Ⓔ
59. Ⓐ Ⓑ Ⓒ Ⓓ Ⓔ
60. Ⓐ Ⓑ Ⓒ Ⓓ Ⓔ

PRACTICE TEST 3: FBI PHASE I SPECIAL AGENT EXAM

75 minutes—60 questions

DIRECTIONS: For Questions 1–12, a paragraph of information is presented. Using *only* the information provided in the paragraph, choose the response option that best answers the question.

---

1. All offenses committed via the internet are considered cybercrimes. Some offenses committed via the internet are not punished with jail time. Some of those found guilty of cybercrime are sentenced with up to 20 years of jail time. Not all persons sentenced with up to 20 years of jail time are guilty of cybercrimes.

   Based on the information above, which of these statements MUST be true?

   A. Not all offenses committed via the internet are considered cybercrimes.

   B. Cybercrime is never punishable with up to 20 years of jail time.

   C. Some cybercrimes are not punished with jail time.

   D. All cybercrimes are punishable with up to 20 years of jail time.

   E. All persons sentenced with up to 20 years of jail time are guilty of cybercrime.

2. All persons who harbor unauthorized aliens with the knowledge that such persons are aliens are committing an illegal offense. All noncitizen persons that have entered into the country without authorization are considered aliens. Not all persons who harbor unauthorized aliens with the knowledge that such persons are unauthorized aliens are sentenced to 10 years in prison.

   Based on the information above, which of these statements MUST be true?

   A. Some persons who harbor unauthorized aliens are not sentenced to 10 years in prison.

   B. All persons who harbor unauthorized aliens are sentenced to 10 years in prison.

   C. No person sentenced to 10 years in prison is an unauthorized alien.

   D. Some noncitizen persons that have entered into the country without authorization are not considered aliens.

   E. Not all aliens are sentenced to 10 years in prison.

3. All things that are considered mail fraud are intended to defraud. Some things considered mail fraud are not fraudulent documents sent through the mail. All theft of a person's social security number is intended to defraud. Not all things that are intended to defraud are considered mail fraud.

   Based on the information above, what MUST be true?

   A. Some things considered mail fraud are theft of a person's social security number.

   B. Nothing intended to defraud is considered mail fraud.

   C. Not all things considered mail fraud are intended to defraud.

   D. All things considered mail fraud are theft of a person's social security number.

   E. Some things intended to defraud are not fraudulent documents sent through the mail.

4. Only seniors students are given lead roles in musicals. Some people cast in the musical are not given lead roles in the musical. All people cast in the musical are students at the school. Some people cast in the musical are dancers.

   Based on the information above, what MUST be true?

   A. Not all seniors are given lead roles in the musical.

   B. Some people cast in the musical are not dancers.

   C. All students at the school are cast in the musical.

   D. Some students at the school are dancers.

   E. All seniors cast in the musical are dancers.

5. A waffle shop only sells four types of waffles. All waffles have two toppings on them. If the following guidelines are followed, which of the response options MUST be true?

   Two strawberries are sold on every waffle.

   The peanut butter waffle is always sold with chocolate chips.

   The blueberry waffle is never sold with chocolate chips.

   Two waffles are always sold with whipped cream.

   A. The blueberry waffle is always sold with whipped cream.

   B. The peanut butter waffle is always sold with chocolate chips and strawberries.

   C. Two waffles are never sold with chocolate chips.

   D. The peanut butter waffle is always sold with whipped cream.

   E. One waffle is sometimes sold with chocolate chips.

6. No cases of voter fraud are given to Agent B. Only Agent B is given cases that include campaign finance. Some cases that include bribery are given to Agent A. Some cases of voter fraud include bribery.

   Based on the information above, which of these statements MUST be true?

   A. Some cases of voter fraud are given to Agent A.

   B. Not all cases of bribery are given to Agent A.

   C. Some cases that include bribery are not given to Agent B.

   D. Some cases that include campaign finance are not given to Agent B.

   E. Not all cases of voter fraud are given to Agent B.

7. Not all candles have scents. All candles sold by a particular store have scents. Some candles with scents are not sold by a particular store. Not all candles made of beeswax are sold by a particular store.

What MUST be true?

A. Some candles are not sold by a particular store.

B. No candles made of beeswax have scents.

C. No candles made of beeswax are sold by a particular store.

D. All candles with scents are sold by a particular store.

E. Some candles are not made of beeswax.

8. All cats that are kept as domestic pets hate water. Not all cats are kept as domestic pets. Some dogs are kept as domestic pets. All animals that are kept as domestic pets are descended from wild ancestors. Some dogs hate water.

Based on the information above, what MUST be true?

A. Some cats are descended from wild ancestors.

B. No cats that are kept as domestic pets hate water.

C. All animals that hate water are descended from wild ancestors.

D. No animals that are descended from wild ancestors hate water.

E. Some dogs are descended from wild ancestors.

9. Some roasted marshmallows are burnt. Not all marshmallows are roasted over an open fire. Some things roasted over an open fire are not marshmallows. No thing that is considered a s'more is not made with marshmallows. Some things that are considered s'mores are made with caramel.

What MUST be true?

A. Some things that are made with marshmallows are also made with caramel.

B. No things that are considered s'mores are made with caramel.

C. All things roasted over an open fire are not included in s'mores.

D. Only things that are considered s'mores are made with marshmallows.

E. Some things that are made with marshmallows are not burnt.

10. All instances where a person uses authority given to him/her by a local, state, or federal government agency to deprive a person of their rights protected under the US Constitution is a Color of Law violation. Some Color of Law violations occur in instances where sexual assault was perpetrated. No instance where sexual assault is perpetrated is punished with less than 1 year in prison.

Based on the information above, what MUST be true?

A. All instances where sexual assault is perpetrated are punished with more than 1 year in prison.

B. Some instances where persons use authority given to them by a local, state, or federal government agency to deprive a person of their rights protected under the US Constitution are not Color of Law violations.

C. Some Color of Law violations are not punished with less than 1 year in prison.

D. Not all things punished with less than 1 year in prison are instances where sexual assault was perpetrated.

E. All instances where Color of Law violations were perpetrated are punished with more than 1 year in prison.

11. All instances where a person is responsible for smuggling contraband into state and local prisons are instances where a person is guilty of prison corruption. No instances where a person is guilty of prison corruption occur outside of prisons. Not all instances of prison corruption are instances where prison gangs are involved. Jones is involved in a prison gang.

What MUST be true?

A. All instances of prison corruption involve prison gangs.

B. No instances where a person is responsible for smuggling contraband into state and local prisons occur outside of prisons.

C. Jones must be responsible for prison corruption.

D. Jones is involved in some instances of prison corruption where prison gangs are involved.

E. No instances of prison corruption are instances where prison gangs are involved.

12. All instances of border corruption occur across or at points of entry into the United States. Not all things that occur across or at points of entry into the United States happen in relation to drug smuggling. All things that occur across or at points of entry into the United States are under the jurisdiction of the United States. All drug smuggling is illegal. All instances of border corruption are illegal.

Based on the information above, what MUST be true?

A. No instances of border corruption occur at points of entry.

B. All instances of border corruption are instances of drug smuggling.

C. Some things under the jurisdiction of the United States are not in relation to drug smuggling.

D. No things that occur across or at points of entry into the United States are illegal.

E. Some drug smuggling is under the jurisdiction of the United States.

DIRECTIONS: For Questions 13–24, review the sequenced images and patterns. Focus on the arrangement and how each sequence connects to each other. Select the logical missing piece in the last sequence using the information provided in the overall nine-part sequence.

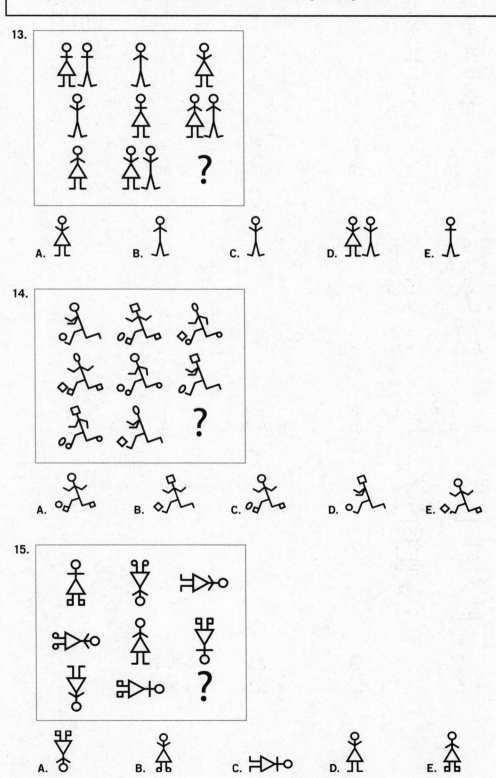

13.

14.

15.

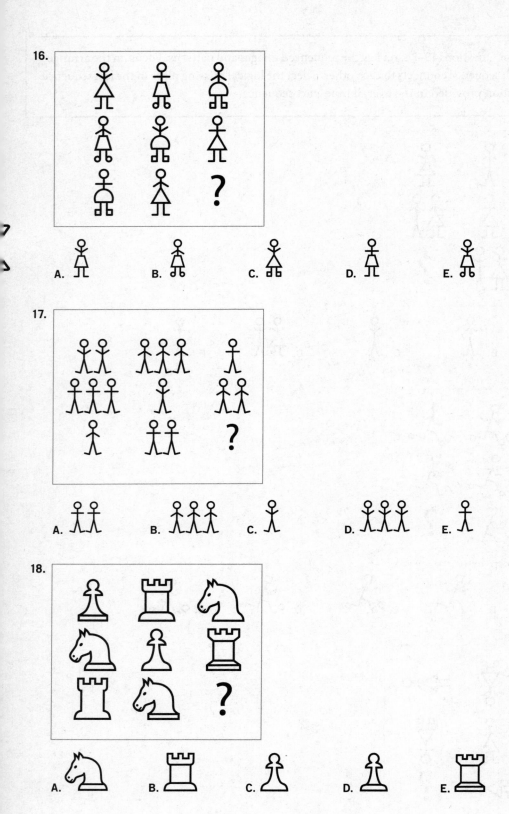

16.

A.   B.   C.   D.   E.

17.

A.   B.   C.   D.   E.

18.

A.   B.   C.   D.   E.

19.

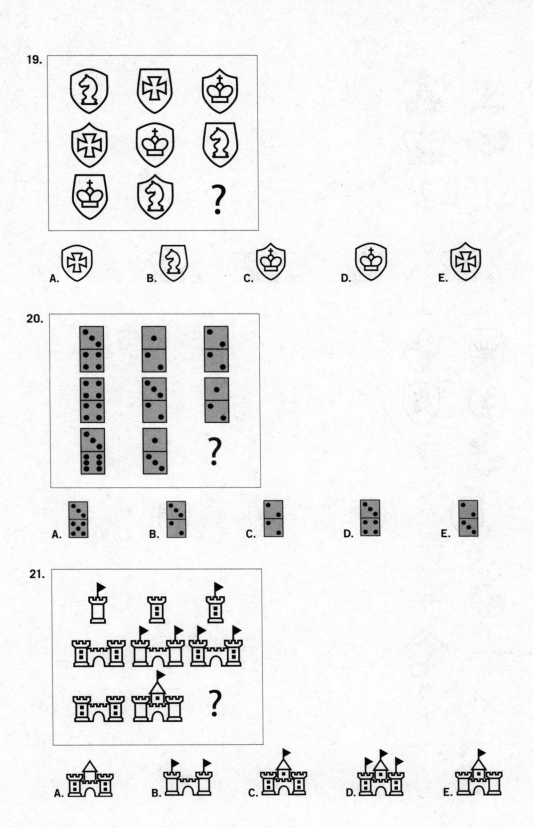

A.　B.　C.　D.　E.

20.

A.　B.　C.　D.　E.

21.

A.　B.　C.　D.　E.

22.

A.   B.   C.   D.   E.

23.

A.   B.   C.   D.   E.

24.

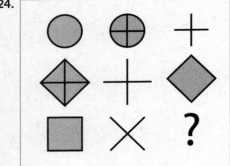

A.   B.   C.   D.   E.

Part IV

Practice Test 3

DIRECTIONS: For Questions 25–36, you will be presented with a pair of statements. Read each statement carefully and mark the corresponding letter that best fits your answer. At times, it may be difficult to choose which one you relate to more as the statements may present topics that you connect with on both sides. This is normal and expected. There are no right or wrong answers since the answers are based on your personal characteristics.

25.

Statement A: I appreciate organized instructions from my supervisor.	**Statement B:** I efficiently address personal grievances with coworkers when necessary.

A. I Agree with Statement A.

B. I Slightly Agree with Statement A.

C. I Slightly Agree with Statement B.

D. I Agree with Statement B.

26.

Statement A: I enjoy individual tasks.	**Statement B:** When solving a complex problem, I devise a strategy before moving forward.

A. I Agree with Statement A.

B. I Slightly Agree with Statement A.

C. I Slightly Agree with Statement B.

D. I Agree with Statement B.

27.

Statement A: If someone is struggling, I encourage them to move forward.	**Statement B:** If the leadership of my organization has made a wrong decision, I will do what I know is best.

A. I Agree with Statement A.

B. I Slightly Agree with Statement A.

C. I Slightly Agree with Statement B.

D. I Agree with Statement B.

Practice Test 3

28.

Statement A: I enjoy the ability to be flexible with my schedule.	Statement B: I am unwavering in my beliefs.

A. I Agree with Statement A.

B. I Slightly Agree with Statement A.

C. I Slightly Agree with Statement B.

D. I Agree with Statement B.

29.

Statement A: I enjoy putting the details of a problem together to produce a clear answer.	Statement B: I can adopt an opposing viewpoint if there are logical arguments to support the claims.

A. I Agree with Statement A.

B. I Slightly Agree with Statement A.

C. I Slightly Agree with Statement B.

D. I Agree with Statement B.

30.

Statement A: I am able to maintain confidentiality with my coworkers when they are not following standard protocols.	Statement B: I try to get my point across without compromising my opponent's integrity.

A. I Agree with Statement A.

B. I Slightly Agree with Statement A.

C. I Slightly Agree with Statement B.

D. I Agree with Statement B.

31.

Statement A: I work best with little to no oversight from my direct supervisor.	Statement B: I am willing to do whatever it takes to meet an urgent deadline.

A. I Agree with Statement A.

B. I Slightly Agree with Statement A.

C. I Slightly Agree with Statement B.

D. I Agree with Statement B.

32.

Statement A: If my supervisor suggests a different method of executing my work, I follow the given instructions.	**Statement B:** I do not pressure my leadership to give me extra responsibilities; instead, I focus on doing what I have been given.

A. I Agree with Statement A.

B. I Slightly Agree with Statement A.

C. I Slightly Agree with Statement B.

D. I Agree with Statement B.

33.

Statement A: If there is drama at work, I will admit my faults in the situation.	**Statement B:** At times, I will do what needs to be done even if it goes outside of standard protocol.

A. I Agree with Statement A.

B. I Slightly Agree with Statement A.

C. I Slightly Agree with Statement B.

D. I Agree with Statement B.

34.

Statement A: I don't waste time trying to solve the problems of my other team members.	**Statement B:** When confronted with a problem, I will find a solution that is in the best interests of the people around me.

A. I Agree with Statement A.

B. I Slightly Agree with Statement A.

C. I Slightly Agree with Statement B.

D. I Agree with Statement B.

35.

Statement A: I will straightforwardly discuss problems in my life without exaggeration.	**Statement B:** When someone comes to me with a problem, I tend to quickly develop an action plan to help solve the problem.

A. I Agree with Statement A.

B. I Slightly Agree with Statement A.

C. I Slightly Agree with Statement B.

D. I Agree with Statement B.

36.

Statement A: I defer to upper management to delineate tasks.	**Statement B:** When two friends are having an argument, I try to make both sides come to an agreement.

A. I Agree with Statement A.

B. I Slightly Agree with Statement A.

C. I Slightly Agree with Statement B.

D. I Agree with Statement B.

DIRECTIONS: For Questions 37–48, read each statement carefully. Respond with how strongly you agree or disagree with the statement provided. Choose the statement that most accurately describes you. Try not to dwell too long on each question and do not attempt to "read into" the statement. There are no right or wrong answers since the answers are based on your personal characteristics.

---

37. It is preferable to be busy and work with a full schedule rather than focus on a few tasks at a time.

A. Strongly Agree

B. Agree

C. Neither Agree nor Disagree

D. Disagree

E. Strongly Disagree

38. It can be easy to lose interest in attempting to solve complex problems after a certain amount of time.

A. Strongly Agree

B. Agree

C. Neither Agree nor Disagree

D. Disagree

E. Strongly Disagree

39. It is always important to be able to work alone without the help of a team.

A. Strongly Agree

B. Agree

C. Neither Agree nor Disagree

D. Disagree

E. Strongly Disagree

40. If a party of nine were to book a hotel room that only allows six people, it is not necessary to tell the hotel staff how many people are staying in the room.

A. Strongly Agree

B. Agree

C. Neither Agree nor Disagree

D. Disagree

E. Strongly Disagree

41. I tend to spend a great deal of time weighing pros and cons when making a difficult decision.

   A. Strongly Agree

   B. Agree

   C. Neither Agree nor Disagree

   D. Disagree

   E. Strongly Disagree

42. When I am given a task, I avoid doing the task right away if I have ample time to complete it.

   A. Strongly Agree

   B. Agree

   C. Neither Agree nor Disagree

   D. Disagree

   E. Strongly Disagree

43. It is preferable to lead conversations with others as opposed to remaining quiet.

   A. Strongly Agree

   B. Agree

   C. Neither Agree nor Disagree

   D. Disagree

   E. Strongly Disagree

44. When faced with difficult decisions, I am more likely to follow the will of a group than to make my own individual choice.

   A. Strongly Agree

   B. Agree

   C. Neither Agree nor Disagree

   D. Disagree

   E. Strongly Disagree

45. If my coworkers were to be found breaking rules in a way that benefited me, I would turn them in to the proper superior authorities.

   A. Strongly Agree

   B. Agree

   C. Neither Agree nor Disagree

   D. Disagree

   E. Strongly Disagree

46. I need time to absorb, contemplate, and solve problems in an orderly fashion or else I become easily overwhelmed.

   A. Strongly Agree

   B. Agree

   C. Neither Agree nor Disagree

   D. Disagree

   E. Strongly Disagree

47. It can be difficult to work with people who hold different beliefs than my own.

   A. Strongly Agree

   B. Agree

   C. Neither Agree nor Disagree

   D. Disagree

   E. Strongly Disagree

48. Only success can build confidence in an individual, and success comes from proving one's abilities and accumulating achievements.

   A. Strongly Agree

   B. Agree

   C. Neither Agree nor Disagree

   D. Disagree

   E. Strongly Disagree

Practice Test 3

DIRECTIONS: For Questions 49–60, you will be presented with various scenarios, each of which will have five response options to choose from. The scenarios describe situations and problems that you are likely to encounter in a typical work environment. Each response option will propose a different way of responding to the scenario. Choose the response option that is most consistent with how you would actually respond. Try not to dwell too long on each question and do not attempt to "read into" the response. There are no right or wrong choices, just what is best for you.

49. During an out-of-town mission, you are sharing a room with another agent of the same gender. You have worked with them for some time and really respect their work ethic and their passion for getting ahead. After a long night in the field, the two of you stop for takeout and come back to the hotel room to eat dinner. They invite you to sit on their bed to eat and watch a movie to relax. You feel uncomfortable by this gesture. What would you MOST likely do?

    A. Say nothing and eat dinner together but request a new partner after the trip.

    B. Kindly decline and decide to eat outside so you don't feel uncomfortable.

    C. Kindly decline and change the subject as you remain on your own bed to eat dinner.

    D. Eat dinner on their bed but make a mental note not to eat in the hotel room anymore.

    E. Call HR and file a sexual harassment complaint.

50. As you are organizing the evidence room, you discover a loose $100 bill that does not appear to be connected to any evidence bags. You recheck every bag, but none present have money in them. None of the cases your team has worked on in the past six months has involved any confiscated money. What would you MOST likely do?

    A. Keep the money as it is clearly not connected to any case.

    B. Explain to your supervisor that you found a $100 bill that is unconnected to any case and ask if you can keep it.

    C. Discuss your findings with a trusted coworker and ask for their input on how to proceed.

    D. Report the money directly to your supervisor and request direction on how to proceed.

    E. Call HR and report your findings, requesting direction as to how to proceed.

51. An informant that has worked three large money laundering cases over the past year has just been arrested on conspiracy charges. The District Attorney wants to charge the informant with the highest crime possible based on his criminal background. You are concerned that the DA is not considering all the help the informant has provided the FBI over the past year and decide to speak up. What would you MOST likely do?

    A. Inform your supervisor of your concerns and let them handle it.

    B. Request a personal meeting with the DA to discuss the matter.

    C. Call the Assistant District Attorney and inform them of your concerns.

    D. Send a formal letter outlining the assistance the informant has provided over the past year and mail it to the DA's office.

    E. Confront the DA outside of the courtroom so you can catch the DA off guard before he has a chance to formulate a canned response.

52. You and Agents Ramirez, Pulaski, and Tran have worked undercover together on a case for the past three months. Because the focus of the case is illegal gambling, a great deal of time must be spent at the casino. You, Agent Ramirez, and Agent Pulaski notice that Agent Tran is becoming more and more engrossed in the actual games and less engaged in the investigation at hand. You suspect that Agent Tran may have a gambling problem. What would you MOST likely do next?

   A. Plan an intervention that includes a mutual supervisor to ensure that Agent Tran gets necessary help for his gambling addiction.

   B. Discuss your concerns directly with Agent Tran and provide resources for a gambling addiction.

   C. Report your concerns to a mutual supervisor and let the supervisor address it.

   D. Report to HR that Agent Tran has a gambling problem and needs help.

   E. Rework the assignment so Agent Tran is no longer the lead agent on the gambling floor, thus reducing his temptation to gamble.

53. You receive your paycheck and notice an added bonus of $1,500. There is no specific line item on your paystub to explain the bonus other than the word "bonus." You and your partner just success-fully apprehended one of the Top Ten most wanted criminals in New York City, and you suspect the bonus may be tied to that. You casually ask your partner if they also received a bonus, and they report that they did not. What do you MOST likely do next?

   A. Say nothing as the bonus was labeled "bonus" and is a financial reward for a job well done.

   B. Ask your partner what they would do in your situation.

   C. Call HR and report the discrepancy.

   D. Report the discrepancy to your supervisor and ask for guidance.

   E. Return the money and ask for an audit of the payroll department based on possible money mismanagement.

54. A company vehicle is allowed to be used to go back and forth from home when an agent is on assignment. However, any use outside of this is explicitly prohibited. You receive an emergency call from your daughter's school stating that she has fallen during recess and appears to have sprained her ankle. She needs to be picked up from school for a medical examination of her foot as soon as possible. You are currently in the company vehicle and are approximately 20 minutes away from home where your personal car is located. Which of the following would you MOST likely do?

   A. Immediately proceed to the school and explain the prohibited vehicle use later since it is an emergency.

   B. Immediately proceed to the school and then take her to the hospital, omitting the vehicle use from your vehicle log since the school is only one mile from your current location.

   C. Go home and trade out vehicles before going to the school since the injury is not life-threatening.

   D. Call your spouse to see if they can go to the school since you will have to waste 40 minutes trading out vehicles.

   E. Call your supervisor for guidance on using the company vehicle in this situation.

55. Agent Marks is working on a 15-page report and developing photos from a crime scene investigation. His partner, Agent Rose, is compiling evidence found at the crime scene and organizing all the data. They will submit the comprehensive data to their supervisor by the end of the week for an upcoming trial. The agent's supervisor is going to present this information to the prosecutor and the Assistant District Attorney on Monday morning. On Thursday night, Agent Marks accidentally sends incorrect photos to Agent Rose, and, in turn, Agent Rose's 20-slide presentation is incorrect. Since this is a high-profile case, the supervisor is looking for a strong and concise presentation to be ready by Friday morning. What is the MOST appropriate response?

   A. The agents should explain to the supervisor that Agent Marks made a mistake gathering the data that will probably cause a delay in the presentation. Agent Marks should make the corrections, as it is his initial error.

   B. The agents should tell their supervisor that they both made a mistake building the presentation from the data. The agents then both amend the presentation.

   C. The agents should not tell their supervisor about the mistake and hand in an additional informational sheet listing the corrections.

   D. The agents should not involve their supervisor and work through the night to make the corrections.

   E. Agent Rose should take ownership of the mistake, make the corrections, and talk to Agent Marks privately.

56. A shopper comes to your customer service counter complaining about a new employee that started several weeks ago. This is the third complaint since the beginning of their employment. Your supervisor is not available but will be back from lunch in 10 minutes. Which approach is the LEAST desirable?

   A. Advise the shopper that your manager will be back in a few minutes to handle their concern.

   B. Work with the customer to de-escalate the situation.

   C. Take notes as the shopper files their complaint so you will not forget.

   D. Pull the customer to the side so you can talk in private.

   E. Attempt to work through the problem in an effort to find a solution.

57. An agent comes into the storage room to retrieve three pieces of clothing found at the scene of a crime that were processed as evidence. He becomes increasingly frustrated when the clothing cannot be found and is disgruntled with the way the evidence room is maintained. After assisting the evidence room clerk in searching for the items, the clerk tells the agent that the clothing is considered "lost." If you were the clerk, which of the following would you MOST likely do?

   A. Apologize that the clothing is unavailable and search for the items in another department.

   B. Offer to scour the evidence room and call the agent when you find the clothing.

   C. Go on your scheduled lunch break and allow the agent to search for the items himself.

   D. Suggest to the agent that he go back to the crime scene to make sure the items were indeed collected.

   E. Involve your supervisor and other evidence room clerks in the search for the missing items and be prepared to change the procedures so it does not happen again.

Part IV

58. At an agency meeting with your field supervisor and the assistant director, you find yourself in the middle of a disagreement between them. You are aware that they do not get along professionally and that they are in a constant dispute. They are now arguing about tactics for a new program and are asking you to pick a side. Which one of the following options would you MOST likely do?

   A. Agree with the tactics of the assistant director because she is high-ranking and has more influence on your status in the agency.

   B. Agree with the tactics of your supervisor because he is your immediate boss and has more influence on your day-to-day operations in the agency.

   C. Evaluate the pros and cons of each side and make an informed decision but do not become involved in the personal disputes.

   D. Choose to not pick sides because you believe both approaches are equally effective and deem that getting involved in this dispute would be a disadvantage to you as both sides are senior in position to you.

   E. Recognize that there will be consequences regardless of the decision made so you go with the program that is best based on your evaluation.

59. You have worked in the same field office for the past four years and have worked your way up to supervisor. You have started to look for better opportunities with other agencies because you have maximized your potential in the current field office. You are now in the process of negotiating for a different position. Gossip that you are leaving soon has spread throughout the current office. Which one of the following options would you MOST likely do?

   A. Since the rumor is circulating, you update all your field colleagues that you are in the process of negotiating for a new position.

   B. Because nothing has been decided and it is still a rumor, you do not say anything.

   C. Since you know the rumor is out, you focus less on your current job's responsibilities and more on getting the new position.

   D. Although the rumor is out, but the position is not secured, you decide to inform your manager of your intent to leave and continue with your job as usual.

   E. You downplay it and do not give the rumor any credence so that you do not ruin your chances of getting the job.

60. You and your boss have a friendly working relationship, but, at the last few staff meetings, your boss has been oversharing personal details about his marital problems. Since your office is in another building and you do not have to be around your boss daily, you just deal with the dramatic stories. The agency has just released plans to reorganize the directors and place them with their appropriate department personnel. Which of the following would you MOST likely do next?

   A. Wait and see if your boss continues to overshare after the move and address it then.

   B. Go out to lunch with your boss and ask him to refrain from oversharing during meetings as it is awkward for the staff.

   C. Encourage your boss to seek help for his marital problems.

   D. Contact HR to discuss a solution since you are worried about repercussions if you do not speak up.

   E. Ask coworkers if they also feel uncomfortable and create a plan with them to discuss this with their boss when it comes up again.

Answers

Practice Test 3

ANSWER KEY AND EXPLANATIONS

1. C	7. A	13. E	19. A
2. A	8. E	14. A	20. E
3. E	9. A	15. B	21. C
4. D	10. C	16. E	22. E
5. B	11. B	17. D	23. B
6. C	12. C	18. D	24. A

1. **The correct answer is C.** According to the information given in the first two statements, cybercrimes are defined as all offenses committed via the internet, and some offenses via the internet are not punished with jail time. Therefore, some cybercrimes are not punished with jail time. Statement 1 invalidates the conclusion reached in choice A. Statement 3 invalidates the conclusions stated in choices B and D. The last statement invalidates the statement in choice E.

2. **The correct answer is A.** According to the information given in the last statement, not all persons who harbor unauthorized aliens are sentenced to 10 years in prison. A "not all" statement implies that "some are not." Therefore, some persons who harbor unauthorized aliens are not sentenced to 10 years in prison. This eliminates choice B. Choice C cannot be verified because the passage does not discuss prison sentences given to unauthorized aliens, just those who knowingly harbor them. Choice D is false based on the information given in the second statement. Choice E is not a valid conclusion that can be reached given that the information is primarily focused upon persons who harbor unauthorized aliens.

3. **The correct answer is E.** According to the information provided in the first statement, all things that are considered mail fraud are intended to defraud. However, according to the second statement, some things that are considered mail fraud are not fraudulent documents sent through the mail. Therefore, some things that are intended to defraud are not fraudulent documents sent through the mail.

4. **The correct answer is D.** Based on the information provided in the final two statements, we know that all people cast in the musical are students at the school and that some of those people cast are dancers. If only students are allowed to be cast in the school musical, then those dancers must be students at the school, and at least some of the students at the school must be dancers.

5. **The correct answer is B.** Based on the information given, we know that all waffles sold have two toppings on them. If strawberries are sold on every waffle, and the peanut butter waffle is known to always be sold with chocolate chips, then it must be true that the peanut butter waffle is always sold with strawberries and chocolate chips.

6. **The correct answer is C.** Given the information in the first and last statements, we know that no cases of voter fraud are given to Agent B. Some cases of voter fraud that are never given to Agent B include bribery. Therefore, the set of cases not given to Agent B includes cases of bribery.

7. **The correct answer is A.** Given the information in the first and second statements, we know that there are some candles without scents and that only candles with scents are sold at a particular store. If this is true, then it must be true that there are some candles that are not sold at a particular store.

8. **The correct answer is E.** Given the information in the second statement, it must be true that some cats are *not* kept as domestic pets. However, we don't know that some cats *are* kept as domestic pets. We only know that some dogs are kept as domestic pets and that all animals kept as domestic pets are descended from wild ancestors. If that statement is true, then it must be true that some dogs are descended from wild ancestors.

9. **The correct answer is A.** Given the information in the final two statements, it must be true that all things considered s'mores are made with marshmallows. It must also be true that some things considered s'mores are also made with caramel. Therefore, it must be true that some things made with marshmallows (i.e., s'mores) are also made with caramel.

10. **The correct answer is C.** Going off the third statement, it must be true that no instance where sexual assault is perpetrated is punished with less than 1 year in prison. Some Color of Law violations occur in instances where sexual assault is perpetrated, which means that some Color of Law violations are not punished with less than 1 year in prison.

11. **The correct answer is B.** Given that no instances where a person is guilty of prison corruption occur outside of prisons and that all instances where a person is responsible for smuggling contraband into state and local prisons is considered prison corruption, then it must be true that no instances where a person is responsible for smuggling contraband into state and local prisons occur outside of prisons.

12. **The correct answer is C.** Given that the information provided in the passage is true, it must hold true that all things that occur across or at points of entry into the United States are under the jurisdiction of the United States. It must also be true that some things that occur across or at points of entry

into the United States do not happen in relation to drug smuggling. In that case, it must be true that some things that are under the jurisdiction of the United States are not in relation to drug smuggling.

13. **The correct answer is E.**

There are two parts to this sequence: (1) female/male grouping and (2) arm placement. In every sequence of three, there must be the following:

- 1 male alone, 1 female alone, and 1 female/male pair
- 1 set of arms going up, 1 set of arms going down, and 1 set of arms straight across

Upon analysis of the missing sequence, there is no male alone, and there are no arms straight across. The image shown in choice E completes the sequence.

14. **The correct answer is A.**

There are four parts to this sequence: (1) head shape, (2) arm placement, (3) ball shape, and (4) foot shape.

In every sequence of three there must be the following:

- 1 square head, 1 oval head, and 1 circle head
- 1 set of arms going up, 1 set of arms going down, and 1 set of arms straight across
- 1 circle ball, 1 oval ball, and 1 square ball
- 1 circle foot, 1 square foot, and 1 line foot

Based on this information, the third row sequence is missing a circle head, arms straight across, a circle ball, and a square foot. The image shown in choice A contains the correct image that completes the sequence.

15. The correct answer is B.

There are three parts to this figure sequence: (1) foot shape, (2) body position, and (3) arm position. In every sequence of three, there must be the following:

- 1 square foot, 1 circle foot, and 1 line foot
- 1 upright figure, 1 upside down figure, and 1 laying down figure
- 1 set of arms going up, 1 set of arms going down, and 1 set of arms straight across

Based on this information, the third sequence is missing a circle foot, an upright figure, and arms going up. The image shown in choice B completes the sequence.

16. The correct answer is E.

There are three parts to this figure sequence: (1) foot shape, (2) body shape, and (3) arm position. In every sequence of three, there must be the following:

- 1 square foot, 1 circle foot, and 1 line foot
- 1 triangle-shaped body, 1 bell-shaped body, and 1 domed-shaped body
- 1 set of arms going up, 1 set of arms going down, and 1 set of arms straight across

Upon analysis of the missing sequence, there is no circle foot, no bell-shaped body, and no arms going up. The image shown in choice E completes the sequence.

17. The correct answer is D.

There are two parts to this pattern. The first part is that there is one person, two people, and three people in each row. The second part of the pattern follows arm placement. In every sequence, there must be 1 set of arms going up, 1 set of arms going down, and 1 set of arms straight across. Therefore, the bottom sequence is 1-2-3 people, and the next part is the arm position going up. The missing piece to complete the last sequence is the grouping of 3 with the arm positions going up.

18. The correct answer is D.

There are two parts to this chess piece sequence: (1) chess piece type and (2) base shape. In every sequence of three, there must be the following:

- 1 knight, 1 pawn, and 1 rook
- 1 flat base, 1 round base, and 1 rectangular base

The third row sequence is missing a pawn and a round base. The image shown in choice D contains these missing elements.

19. **The correct answer is A.**

There are two parts to this sequence (1) shield shape and (2) emblem design. Each sequence must contain the following:

- 1 arched shield, 1 pointed shield, and 1 flat shield
- 1 cross emblem, 1 knight emblem, and 1 crown emblem

Based on this information, the third row sequence is missing an arched shield and a cross emblem. The image shown in choice A contains these missing elements.

20. **The correct answer is E.**

There are two parts to this sequence: (1) a basic subtraction problem subtracting the total number of dots on the second domino from the total number of dots on the first domino to get the total number of dots on the third domino, and (2) a subtraction problem in which each section of the domino is dealt with separately.

In the first sequence, subtracting the total number of dots on the second domino from the total number of dots on the first domino creates the equation 7 - 3 = 4. The top halves of the dominoes create the subtraction problem 3 − 1 = 2. The bottom half creates the problem 4 - 2 = 2.

The domino that will complete the pattern in the third row would need to solve

the problem of 3 - 1 for the top half of the dominoes, 6 - 3 for the bottom half of the dominoes, and 9 - 4 for the total number of dots on the dominoes.

The domino shown in choice E with two dots on its top half and three dots on the bottom half, giving it a total count of 5 dots, completes the pattern correctly.

21. **The correct answer is C.**

In this sequence, two images are combined—or laid over each other—to create a new image. In each row, the first two castle images are laid over each other, from left to right, to create the third new castle image. The image shown in choice C is a combination of the first two images on the third row.

22. **The correct answer is E.**

In this sequence, two images are combined—or laid over each other—to create a new image. In addition, shading is eliminated to showcase the jewels on the crown. In each row, the first two crown images are laid over each other, from left to right, to create the third new crown image with the shading eliminated to showcase the jewels on the crown. Based on this information, the image shown in choice E shows the correct overlay combination to complete the third row.

Answers | Practice Test 3

23. The correct answer is B.

There are two parts to this sequence:
(1) shield emblem and (2) shield design.
Each sequence must contain the following:

- 1 checkered emblem, 1 knight emblem, and 1 crown emblem
- 1 arched shield, 1 pointed shield, and 1 flat shield

Based on the sequence information provided, the third row is missing a knight emblem and a flat shield. The image shown in choice B contains these missing elements.

24. The correct answer is A.

In this sequence, two images are combined—or laid over each other—to create a new image. Specifically, each line image is laid over a geometric shape. Based on this sequence information, the image shown in choice A contains the correct overlay.

PART V

APPENDIX

Appendix A: Federal Law Enforcement
Training Center

Federal Law Enforcement Training Center

OVERVIEW

No law enforcement agency will send a new recruit into the field without appropriate training. All law enforcement agents are trained in self-defense, use of weapons, rules and regulations of the department, and, of course, the specific duties of the job.

Most federal criminal investigators and uniformed police officers complete introductory basic and in-service training at the Federal Law Enforcement Training Center (FLETC) in Glynco, Georgia. Likewise, many federal law enforcement technicians, inspectors, specialists, general compliance investigators, and other support staff complete courses of study at FLETC.

A few agencies, including the FBI, DEA, Postal Inspection Service, and Air Force Office of Special Investigations operate independent academies specifically for the training of their own personnel. These agencies operate programs to meet their own training requirements as well as to offer specialized courses related to their own particular areas of expertise.

FLETC serves as an interagency law enforcement training organization for a wide range of federal agencies. FLETC also provides services to state, local, and international law enforcement agencies. Although the training center is headquartered in Glynco, Georgia, FLETC also operates two other residential training sites in Artesia, New Mexico, and Charleston, South Carolina. FLETC also operates an in-service requalification training facility in Cheltenham, Maryland, for use by agencies with large concentrations of personnel in the Washington, D.C., area.

Partner organizations have input regarding training issues and functional aspects of FLETC. Agencies take part in curriculum review and development conferences and help develop policies and directives. This relationship is characteristic of a "true partnership," responsive to the training mission.

Consolidation of law enforcement training permits the federal government to emphasize training excellence and cost effectiveness. Professional instruction and practical application provide students with the skills and knowledge to meet the demanding challenges of a federal law enforcement career. They learn not only the responsibilities of a law enforcement officer, but, through interaction with students from many other agencies, they also become acquainted with the missions and duties of their colleagues.

This interaction provides the foundation for a more cooperative federal law enforcement effort. FLETC's parent agency, the Department of Homeland Security (DHS), supervises its administrative and financial activities. FLETC's director serves under the authority of the Under Secretary for Border and Transportation Security. The director is assisted with operational oversight and execution in the management of FLETC by an executive team with breadth and depth of experience in training and administration. Also, as an interagency training organization, the FLETC has assembled professionals from diverse backgrounds to serve on its faculty and staff. Approximately one third of the staff are permanent FLETC employees. The rest are federal officers and investigators on short-term assignment from their parent organizations or recently retired from the field. This mix of staff members provides a balance of experience and fresh insight from the field.

CRIMINAL INVESTIGATOR TRAINING PROGRAM

The Criminal Investigator Training Program (CITP) is a part of the Center Basic Programs Branch. It provides basic and fundamental training in the techniques, concepts, and methodologies of conducting criminal investigations. The CITP underwent a full Curriculum Review Conference in 2017. This continuous review process ensures that trainees have the best and most current training consistent with developing the knowledge, skills, and abilities necessary to perform as a criminal investigator or special agent.

The length of training is 59 days in this program. Throughout this training period, trainees are mentored by Continuing Case Investigation Coordinators. Subjects in the training include interviewing, surveillance, computer-based case management, legal training, physical techniques and conditioning, tactical training, firearms precision shooting, emergency response driving, and other courses that provide the essential knowledge, skills, and abilities needed by a new federal criminal investigator.

Lectures, laboratories, practical exercises, and tests are used to ensure that each trainee acquires all of the critical knowledge, skills, and abilities required of new criminal investigators. Each trainee must participate as a member of a small task force team in a continuing case investigation. The investigation is sequentially structured, allowing each trainee to utilize new skills immediately. Interviewing of witnesses, surveillance, and undercover operations enable trainees to develop a case, write and execute search and arrest warrants, arrest a suspect, write a criminal complaint, obtain an indictment, and testify in a courtroom hearing.

Program Prerequisites

The training program is designed for full-time criminal investigators, GS-1811 series, from the partner organizations. However, a partner organization may request that a non-1811 law enforcement employee be permitted to attend the program if the agency believes that investigative training is essential for the employee.

The program manager will review the request and determine whether the prospective student will be allowed to attend the training. All attendees must meet the employing agency's recruitment standards and the FLETC's Practical Exercise Performance Requirements for the CITP prior to arriving for the training program.

Nonpartner federal agencies may send students on a space-available basis, and state and local law enforcement officers may attend if sponsored by a federal partner organization. Applications for attendance to all basic training programs must be submitted through supervisory channels to each agency's FLETC liaison/training officer.

Student Evaluation

The CITP cognitive testing system consists of five examinations: three legal examinations and two comprehensive examinations. In addition, students are expected to satisfactorily complete a series of practical exercises and/or homework assignments. Satisfactory completion of all examinations, practical exercises, and assignments is required for graduation.

Written Examinations

Students are required to achieve a score of at least 70 percent on each of the five written examinations. Students have a total of 1 hour, 45 minutes to complete each examination. Immediately following each examination, a 15-minute examination review is conducted, allowing students to assess their performance. Official results are posted as soon as possible after the completion of the examination. Students' grades are maintained in confidentiality as far as fellow classmates are concerned. Student examination scores are available to the students' agencies through official channels.

In the event that a student fails to achieve a score of at least 70 percent on any written examination, he or she will be placed on probation. During this period, additional assistance will be made available, upon request, in the form of counseling, out-of-class study assignments, and personal instructional sessions. The student will then take a remedial examination covering the same subjects as the original failed examination. The student must successfully pass this remedial examination to remain eligible for graduation.

A student may be placed on probation for failing a regularly scheduled examination only two times. In the event that a student fails a third regularly scheduled examination (or fails to achieve a passing score on any remedial examination), he or she will not be eligible for graduation from the Criminal Investigator Training Program.

Practical Exercises

The second component of the CITP evaluation system is the measurement of physical skills acquired during training. Students must satisfactorily complete all phases of the practical exercises to successfully complete the training program. The practical exercises are designed to provide students with as much individual attention and instruction as possible. This area involves the development of psychomotor skills and the basic knowledge needed to perform at least minimally in the occupational role. Each student is given a reasonable number of opportunities to meet the minimum standards of performance established by the learning objectives. Evaluation of student performance is made during various practical exercises. Performance will be judged by the student's actual ability to satisfactorily complete the required tasks.

FLETC encourages students to repeat the practical exercise portions of their training until mastery is achieved. Accordingly, students who do not achieve mastery in any of these tasks are not placed on probation. However, if a student cannot demonstrate the ability to satisfactorily perform the tasks prior to the completion of the program, a certificate will not be awarded.

In addition to practical exercises in many specific areas, students are required to successfully complete a final "single thread" practical exercise that lasts for three training days. Each student, assigned to an investigative team, will be assigned a particular problem in which the tasks learned in prior training will be tested. Once assigned the problem, each student will employ techniques acquired in interviewing, surveillance, execution of search and arrest warrants, crime scene investigation, and testifying at trial. Grades will be based on each student's performance. In addition, each team member must contribute to a written case report documenting each individual's actions as well as the actions of the team in acquiring evidence during the exercise. The case report will be used as the basis for the mock trial and related court hearings pursuant to the trial.

Firearms Training

Marksmanship is evaluated on a point system. Each student must qualify with a minimum of 70 percent on the Practical Pistol Course. A student who does not achieve a satisfactory level of proficiency on the Practical Pistol Course (210 points out of 300 possible = 70 percent) will be offered the opportunity to participate in remedial training to correct the deficiency. The total amount of scheduled firearms remedial training offered to students will not exceed eight hours and two retests. Failure to qualify on this course will preclude students from successful completion of the training program.

ADDITIONAL INFORMATION

In addition to CITP, each agency has additional training opportunities. For more information, go online to FLETC's website and search their training catalog (**www.fletc.gov/training-catalog**).

notes

notes

notes

notes

notes

notes

notes

notes

notes

notes

notes

notes

notes

notes

notes

notes

notes

notes

notes